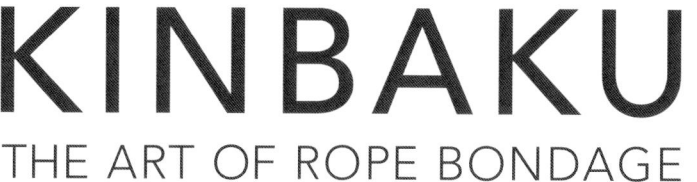

KINBAKU
THE ART OF ROPE BONDAGE

KINBAKU
THE ART OF ROPE BONDAGE

Kahboom

First published in the United Kingdom in 2013

By Kahboom Media

94 High Street

Linton

Cambridge CB21 4JT

www.kahboom.com

©Kahboom Media

ISBN : 978-0-9576275-0-5

Printed in China

Contents

Forward by Nawashi Murakawa

Kinbaku: The punishment and the beauty of Japanese rope bondage

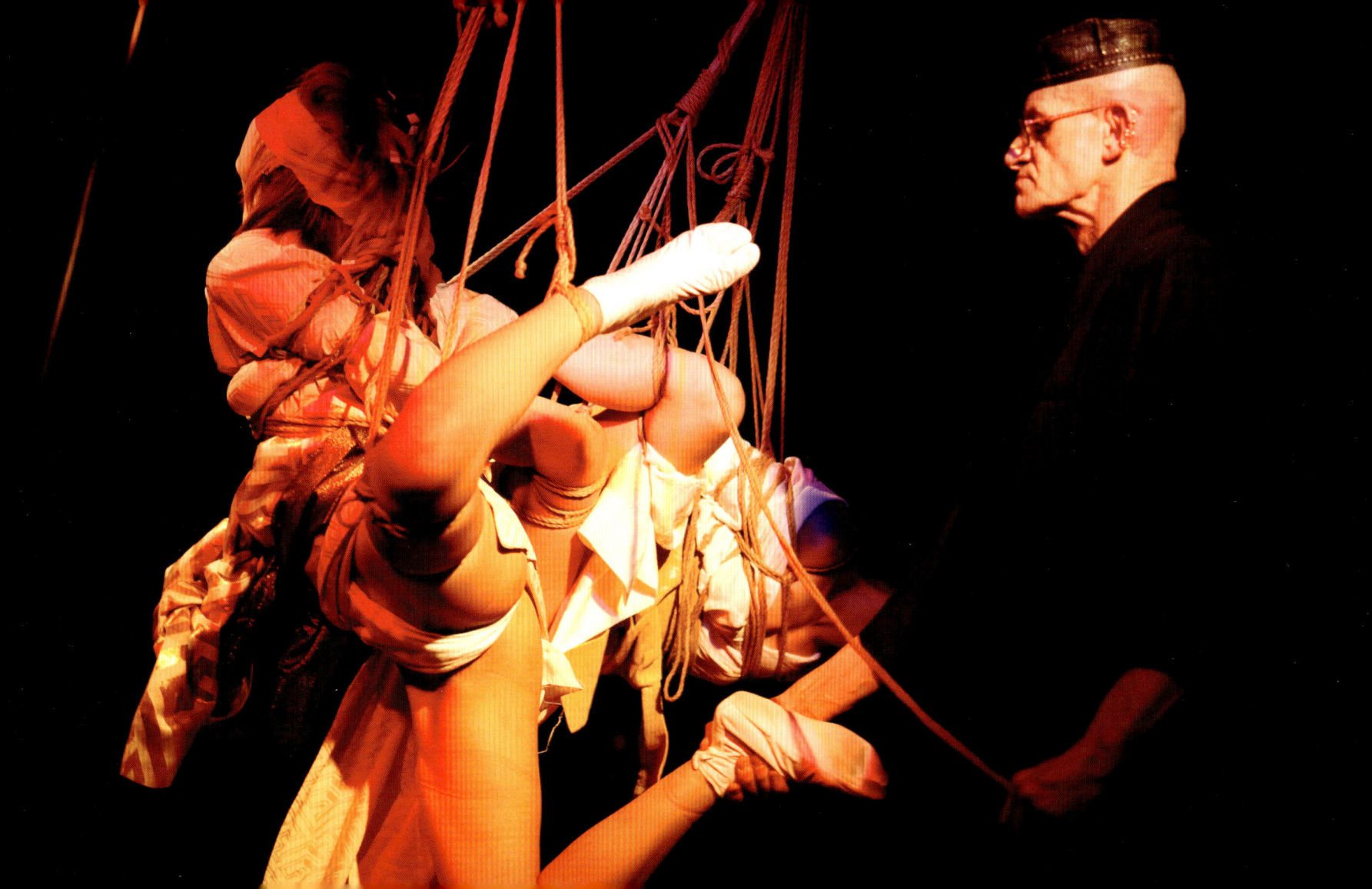

Japanese history is a rich hunting ground, within which the complex mystery of how, when and where rope bondage (*Kinbaku*) developed, is further cloaked by myth, legend, philosophy and ethnic religions, which to the outsider (*Gaijin*) initially represent an almost impenetrable barrier.

The dawn of Kinbaku lies buried somewhere far, far away in the Jomon Period of Japan, starting some 12,000 years ago, 10,000 years long and ending around 300 BC, where numerous examples of pottery bear the use of special markings made by the pressure of rope (*Nawa*) into a complex and mysterious language of decoration.

More links lie in Japan's past, and thus there is something curiously significant that connects the Japanese mind to Nawa, and all its possibilities, both practical, aesthetic and spiritual. In Japan's ethnic religion, *Shinto*, there is a 'holy rope', called *Shimenawa*, which you must walk under as you pass through the entrance gateway, called a *Torii*, to proceed along the central avenue into the sacred grounds of the main shrine (*Honden*) beyond. The Shimenawa is strung and suspended between the two pillars of the Torii, and is a strong symbol of the special significance of Nawa to mark the transition from the ordinary world into that of the Gods. (*Kami*)

This religion, based on the ancient animism of the nature Gods, and partially infused with Buddhism, uses Nawa to deify all things deemed holy, especially such things as a beautiful rock, or a very old pine tree considered to possess a spirit. There are many such Shimenawa, even in the middle of a busy street in a town centre, indicating there is more to this than just decoration.

During late medieval Japan, the Tokugawa government which was established in 1742, seized their chance to lay out co-ordinated and well organized plans for the establishment of a proper system of public law and order.

Upon sentence, punishment was handed down to miscreants, utilizing one, or a mixture of seven different types of physical retribution which mostly consisted of the usual variations of incarceration, exile, forced labour or death and to which it was also likely that four strict forms of torture by use of rope bondage could be added.

These additional four Kinbaku tortures were generally described as heavy whipping and flagellation (*Mutchiuchi*) of restrained prisoners, use of heavy stones used to press down upon parts of the body (*Ishidaki*), especially the legs of tied prisoners, bent by rope, tied in a very uncomfortable posture, and around a horizontal beam (*Ebizeme*) and, finally, hung by rope, positioned by vertical suspension so as to be accessible for further tortures (*Tsurizeme*).

Many of these punishments were carried out in public; a deliberate intention to add shame and disgrace and with the frequent addition of public beatings to further remind the prisoner of the error of their ways. These same four forms of Kinbaku are now regarded as the direct predecessors of the bondage that is generally in use in modern Japan today. The essence and the spirit remain very much unchanged: the work must be inspired, aesthetic and balanced, but also highly restrictive and likely with diabolical intention.

The contemporary Japanese terminology for Kinbaku is the simple term SM, and it has been accepted as the sex industry term for rope bondage. However, this must not be confused with the use of the very same definition in the West where SM (sado masochism) is more likely to be defined as something done between consenting partners, involving what is described as either the submissive/masochist or dominant/sadist. This stance is seen fundamental to the role playing games of sexuality, or even denial, that is often fetishised by the use of restrictive costumes, hoods, corsets and boots made of such materials as rubber or leather, including the use of special implements to give pain, and often with dungeon equipment used to restrain the submissive for their punishment.

In the first half of the Twentieth Century, the history of Kinbaku has become associated with the name of **Sei Ito** (1905-1969) He was a respected Japanese writer, poet, literary critic and translator, who is probably best remembered for his translation of the notorious English novel *Lady Chatterley's Lover*, by D H Lawrence, into Japanese. This was done at the same time as the famous obscenity trial in London, to ban the book, and very much in support of the publishers, Penguin, to show his belief in the freedom of expression for that same novel in Japan. It was also well known that he bondaged women, and was fascinated by the darkness, and artistic possibility of Kinbaku, shame and torture.

Consequently, Ito was considered more than just a writer, his

mind and spirit being steeped in the world of old Japan. The art and expression of Kabuki and Noh theatre, the beauty of ritual suicide (*Seppuku*) and the traditional values of chivalry and The Way of the Warrior (*Bushido*) were all things that drove him to tie women as a further expression of his creativity within that of his nations cultural identity.

His rationale can be seen as both educated, connective and philosophical and carried out within a full and well rounded artistic spirit, by an almost academic hand. As such his contribution brought grace and dignity and helped to reignite Kinbaku during his lifetime and afterwards.

Despite Ito's input, pre World War Two Kinbaku in Japan had largely become moribund, with little organization, outlet, or way to express itself in any media or printed form. It survived, much in isolation, without direction, and without the general public knowing much about it. It was only kept alive by the dedicated and hidden enthusiast. Indeed, and to this day such aficionados are referred to as Kinbaku Maniacs.

At this juncture it is perhaps ironic that a new impetus from an almost unexpected quarter, and from a very different modern civilization, was about to provoke a change, and provide inspiration, not by design, but more by circumstance.

The Americans were finally victorious over Japan in World War II in mid 1945 and with them, and their occupation, came the new blood and ideas which were soon to fuel the regeneration of Japanese Kinbaku. The American influence was further extended by the onset of the Korean War in 1950. It was into this strange and mysterious land of Japan, where the ancient and unchanging traditional values survived, and with many of the populace still wearing simple kimono, came the arrival of thousands of members of the US armed forces. The servicemen in Japan duly brought with them examples of American popular culture to remind them of home. Besides newspapers, they harvested the best of mass printed magazines, including not only the comics showing super heroes, but the numerous and cheap, yet rather racy publications that contained cheesecake, girly pin-ups, pulp horror, and gaudy detective tales with full colour semi naked and abused women on their covers. This included individual private collections of porn imagery and also the more edgy and risqué publications that featured the subject of fetish.

However, without doubt the most significant publication of all, and one which was to influence Kinbaku in Japan, was *Bizarre Magazine*. Founded in 1946, this underground black and white magazine was edited, illustrated, written and photographed by the extraordinary underground fetishist, artist and writer, **John Willie**.

The magazine regularly featured rope bondage in photographs and drawings, but usually with a kind of glossy American almost Hollywood inspired fetishist bent of style not normally understood in Japan. At the time, this new visual language of Willie, aided from time to time by another important US contributor, **Eric Stanton**, provided depictions of women hobbled by corseted skirts and complete rubber enclosures of the human form. These were extremely potent symbols, to the point that even

today they still have the power to fascinate us, seeming as fresh and challenging as ever, and not merely something done for a fashionable effect.

Via this material, the darker side of sexuality is both made vulnerable and is forever stimulated. We are persistently drawn back into the world it depicts: extremes of deprivation, torture, humiliation and punishment. It is here that the fetishization of the human mind, and body, are put to the test in all kinds of surprising and ingenious mechanical ways. In fact, it might be said that these ideas are not that different to those employed within the Japanese mind and within the act of making Kinbaku, where there is a use of artistic expression and understanding of a very high order but with a Japanese twist as pure as ancient Japan itself.

After initial gestation, Japanese Kinbaku enthusiasts became very aware and completely spellbound by the contents of Bizarre. As it was so visual and clear, they did not have to worry that they could not read the wording and captions properly. John Willie's own bondage artworks then began to be printed, with permission, in the fledgling issues of the new Japanese publication, *Kitan Club Magazine*, which first appeared in Tokyo during the early 1950's. The aims of this unique new Japanese bondage magazine were probably inspired by the boldness of its American counterpart, and may also have happened because post war Japan was now wanting to move on towards the new industrialism that would eventually become the Japanese economic miracle.

John Willie's bondage masterwork, which he illustrated, and also wrote, was his comic strip depiction of *The Adventures of*

Sweet Gwendoline. Without doubt it is the most iconic item that ever graced its pages. With Gwendoline's sexual punishments explored before them, readers could allow themselves to move on from the almost sadistic, yet rugged politeness and crazy humour of the early silent films, *The Perils of Pauline*. These featured Pearl White as the eternal damsel in distress.

Alhough Pearl was often seen tied to the railway track at the end of an episode, Gwendoline always got into far deeper trouble, especially at the hands of her dastardly and villainous arch tormentor, Sir d'Arcy d'Arcy. These stories never failed to whet the sadistic appetite of ardent Kinbaku maniacs, both Japanese and American alike, as she... innocent, helpless and winsome ended up tied hard, humiliated, sexually exposed and tortured. In truth, her very struggles against the rope, and her futile attempts to escape were to delight and further feed the perverse (*Hentai*) mindset of the Japanese.

The progress of the magazine, the *Kitan Club Magazine*, spawned more like minded publications. These in turn created more events and a wider audience for the artistry of Kinbaku. The most important contributor to this process was without doubt **Chimuo Nureki**, who is generally acknowledged as Japan's greatest modern interpreter of the art of Kinbaku. His outstanding bondage work and energy in the development of the field, has done much to define the modern Japanese Kinbaku scene.

Nureki was born in 1930 in the lively downtown (*Shitamatchi*) District of Asakusa in central Tokyo surrounded by the stimulus of old fashioned bars, night life, fake Geisha, popular dance, light opera and the traditional Kabuki theatre. This childhood background never left him and later played a direct role in the inspiration of his chosen career.

His earliest thoughts of Kinbaku are said to have come from a picture that he saw while he was a ten year old schoolboy in the year 1940. The image showed a boy with his arms tied behind his back, and from this small seed, his thoughts and consideration about rope bondage began to develop. At that time, he was also influenced by ideas about theatre, the stage, and like Ito an attraction to the drama of ancient ritual suicide/ Seppuku.

By 1945 he met and befriended Sei Ito, for whom he had a deep admiration. Nureki's passionate interest in theatre, performance and stage craft led him to join a local Kabuki company as an apprentice actor, a path that he followed for the next few years. He also worked as a speaking film extra at the famous *Toho Film Studios* in Tokyo whose output included many famous titles, such as *The Seventh Samurai*, by the director **Akira Kurasawa**.

In 1953 Chimuo Nureki discovered *Kitan Club Magazine*. He became one of it's most important and major contributors, helping it to grow and create new ideas. Over the years he provided the magazine with an enormous amount of influential material which included exquisite photographs taken at his Kinbaku sessions, bondage stories he had written, scripts and instructional essays and critiques of the Japanese rope bondage scene. He also became involved with other important Kinbaku magazines such as *URA Mado*.

As his rope skill, confidence and fame increased, he created and developed better and more powerful work. His studio and workshop business soon became the home of the very best of bondage performance and a mecca for the eager student.

Although he was, and is, the major player in Japanese Kinbaku for several decades, his prolific output has led him to want to write more, including scripts for stage, screen and drama. This background work then became the substance of the countless legions of SM videos that he wrote, performed in and also directed. By the mid 80's, his pre-eminence in the field led him to take up a pivotal role as one of the co-founders of a special new event called *Kinbi-ken*.

The Japanese bondage photographer **Akio Fuji** was Nureki's associate in the development of Kinbi-ken. Together, they realized the needs of indigenous masochistic women who found bondage to be their way of achieving an inner spiritual stability, with devotion and a deferred sexual harmony. They found that these females were only too glad to stand and wait in line to suffer in the refined restriction of Chimou Nureki's rope, and also to be viewed by his many devotees.

The fetishistic act liberated by rope restraint, then becomes all the more powerful because of denial. The models heightened sense of masochism moves up a notch as does her sense of shame. This is released as the audience observe her body,

watch her breathing and her facial expression. She might be seen to tremble, but that only shows her pleasure in the ordeal.

Kinbi-ken quickly became important as a regular event, debating society and when established, the Kinbaku studio space (*Dojo*) bore witness to the best and the most celebrated work that was to come from the hands of Chimuo Nureki. Akio Fuji's black and white pictures, taken at many of his Kinbi-ken performances, have since been widely published, and are still very much admired. They probably inspired the bondage photographs of **Nobuyoshi Araki** who's work has introduced a wider audience to the subject, but cleverly without adding anything to the art. Nureki's undoubted devotion to Kinbi-ken was to remain solid and constant for over twenty years, and in this time he was known to have organized well over 170 meetings and workshops there.

Now in his 80's, he is still at work, writing, performing and producing a variety of theatrical events (*Gekijho*), stage reviews, and even a Puppet Show, all of which connect directly back to the spiritual values and background of his powerful and exquisitely artistic Kinbaku performances. His experience as an apprentice actor contributed to his theatrical style of Kinbaku, whilst in the background, his performances are emotive and tell a story. In essence Chimuo Nureki, throughout his fifty year career, has always demonstrated that the purely technical approach of perfect, but sterile Kinbaku, is simply an empty exercise.

The ethos that drove the creation of Kinbi-ken will no doubt raise some questions, as the average Westerner will perhaps be confused, scared or possibly outraged by the idea behind the dedication to the celebration of the Japanese masochistic woman. To clarify matters a little, this dilemma is partially due to the fact that in the West, sadism and masochism, and their attendant fetishes, are mainly defined within the rules of 'sub and dom'. This terminology has almost no relevance to the ideals and values of the typical female Japanese Kinbaku model (*Mj-yo*).

Because of Japanese shame culture and its complex social control mechanisms, the masochistic female can express her total joy and freedom whilst tied, tortured, humiliated and driven to the limit of physical and mental pain. Within a Kinbaku performance there is no direct sexual exchange between the artist and his model. Such rope sessions, and their scenario, are bound up and secured by the deferment of the usual outer expressions of human interaction.

Western values, even within the strict act of SM role play, are often far more simplistic and usually linked to direct physical gratification. One must consider that Japan, despite the widespread practice of Kinbaku, has one of the lowest sex crime rates in the World. We may contrast that with the Western idea and use of rope bondage as an instrument of danger, rape, violence and murder and certainly something that is not considered to have any artistic merit.

It is to their advantage and enrichment that Japanese women have good skin, being supple and thick; their hair is strong and capable of taking their body weight; their physique is small and light with shorter arms and legs for a low centre of gravity and therefore perfectly proportioned for Kinbaku. The purity of their

race, with its 12,000 year history, and the significance of Shinto and Buddhism in the spiritual and ritualistic refinement of Japan, coupled with the unique persistence of shame culture, all adds up to help us with the understanding of the joy to be found in suffering and pain as the gateway to the highest level of consciousness.

Nothing is really worthwhile, unless it is achieved by ordeal.

村川.

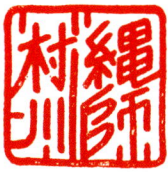

Introduction

Kinbaku: From Japan to the World

There are some people who like to be tied up; others who like to do the tying. Some outsiders will find this disturbing, but many may be intrigued and wish to understand what drives human beings to participate in this activity. Those that take part find it not only physically and emotionally challenging but also fulfilling, and it forms an important part of the relationship between the participants. To watch a performance of Kinbaku is to be allowed to witness the beauty, strength and vulnerability of human beings. It is the aim of this book to show glimpses of the beauty that arises from being bound with ropes. The images are fleeting since models are not in control of their pose and because they cannot remain bound in difficult postures for very long.

Kinbaku originated in Japan but has now spread throughout the world. In the west it is often known as Shibari. The classical form is found in Japan where there are clubs holding performances and also teaching both would-be kinbakushi (those who tie the ropes) and also models who wish to be tied. It takes years of practice to tie a model so that the interwoven rope looks beautiful and during this time the model and the kinbakushi must develop a trusting relationship.

The Eastern style of Kinbaku becomes modified when practised in other countries. In Japan there is a deep cultural basis for the activity but in other countries this historical tradition does not exist. Russian Shibari developed in isolation until the fall of communism and as a result the visual style is very different. In the USA the use of ropes in photo shoots reflects the freedom of expression that is accepted in that society.

In the UK, the increasing interest in Kinbaku owes a lot to Nawashi Murakawa who is featured in this book, and also to Esinem whose teaching and performances enabled many to become participants.

But why do people do it? What is it in the human psyche that resonates with being tied up? Maybe it is a 'womb experience.' In the womb we are constrained and even linked to another human with a cord. In this condition we are both secure due to the bondage, and yet insecure because we are totally at the mercy of another person. And so it is in rope bondage. There is a freedom in being tied up because you no longer have to make decisions of your own. In fact you are no longer responsible for what happens. There is also a deep trust between the two participants which is not often found in life. For some, the discomfort and pain itself brings a pleasure which leads to the world of SM.

This book seeks to show the artistic drama of Kinbaku as it is practised around the world. The photographs are not posed in the way of portraits. They are mostly taken while the model is first tied up, then often suspended and moved into different positions and then released. This forms a story. We hope you will sense the human drama that takes place in each of the short Kinbaku stories in this book.

Shibari in Canada

A Canadian Photographer, Tho4ns has been practising rope
bondage as well as bondage photography since early 2003.
His focus is on the more traditional Japanese aspects of
rope bondage and this is echoed in his style. His work aims
to inspire the emotion which a Shibari model experiences
within the binds of the tie.

In his own words:

"Much like an instrument, the forms created by rope can be
beautiful by themselves. But to truly appreciate the instrument,
one needs to hear the music. And like music, people play the
same notes, sometimes, very differently. It speaks to each of us
in a different voice. It is through this conversation that meaning
takes shape and comes to life."

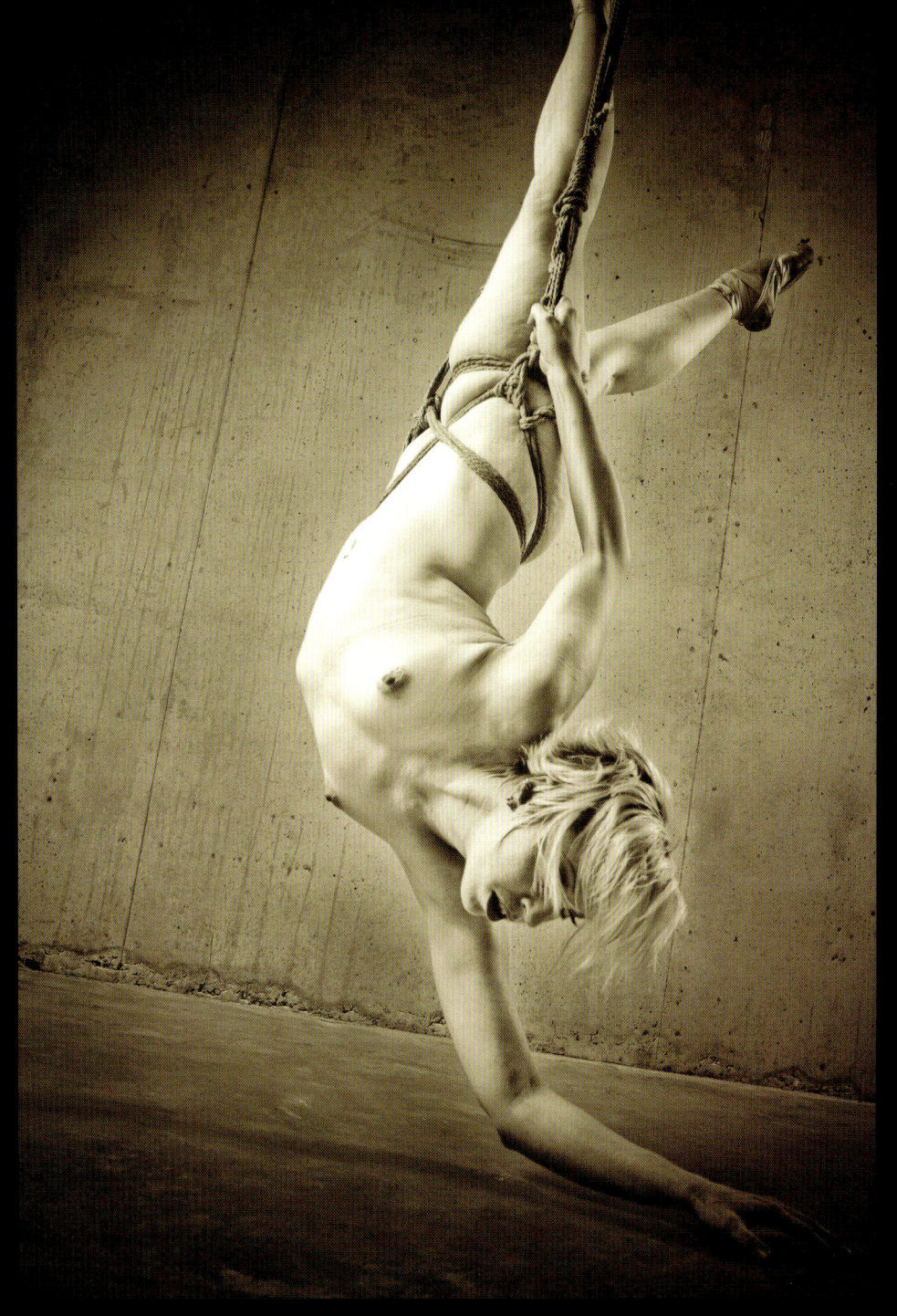

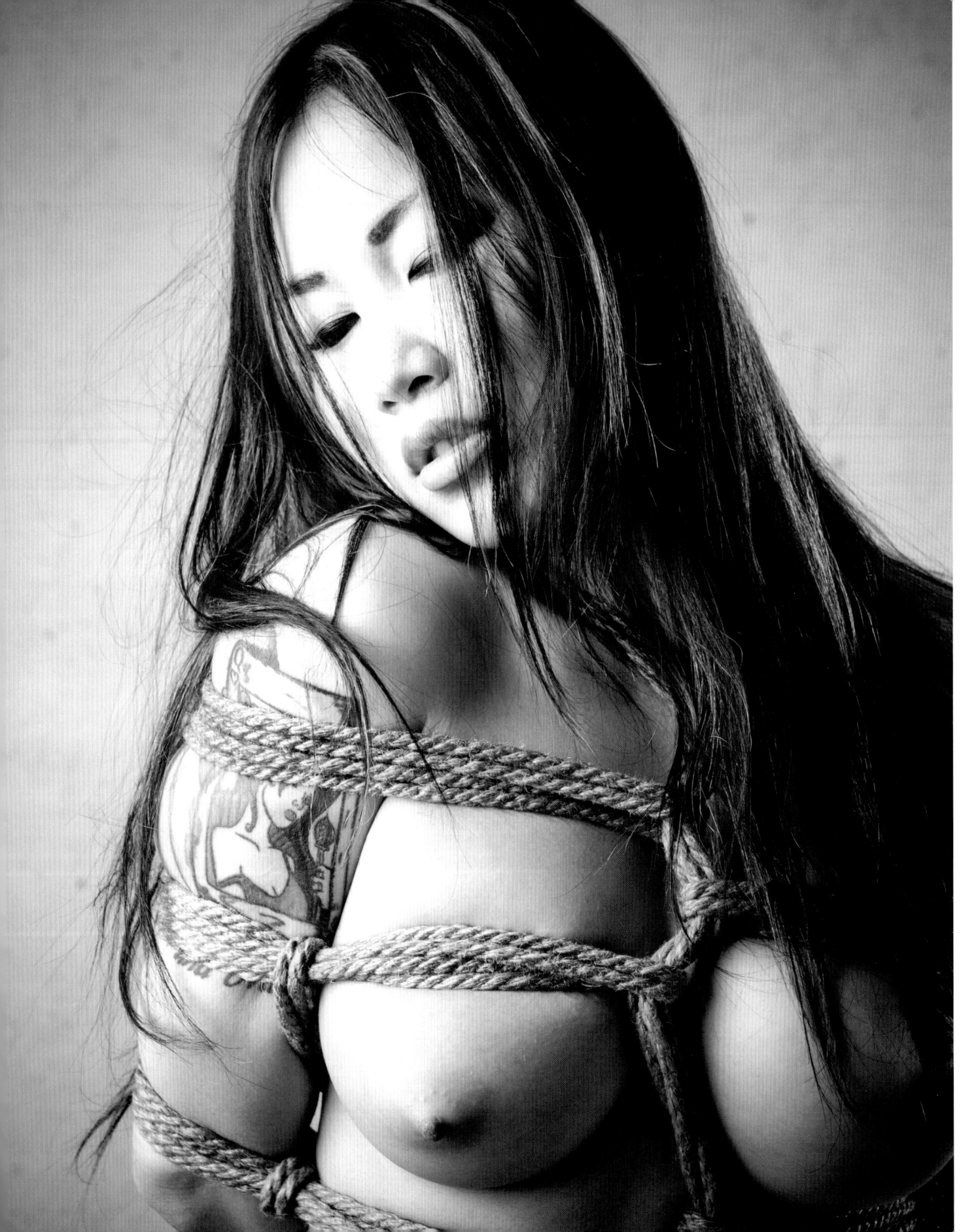

"Rope reveals a different character in people. Perhaps a window to a more true self; a sanctuary within the chaos."

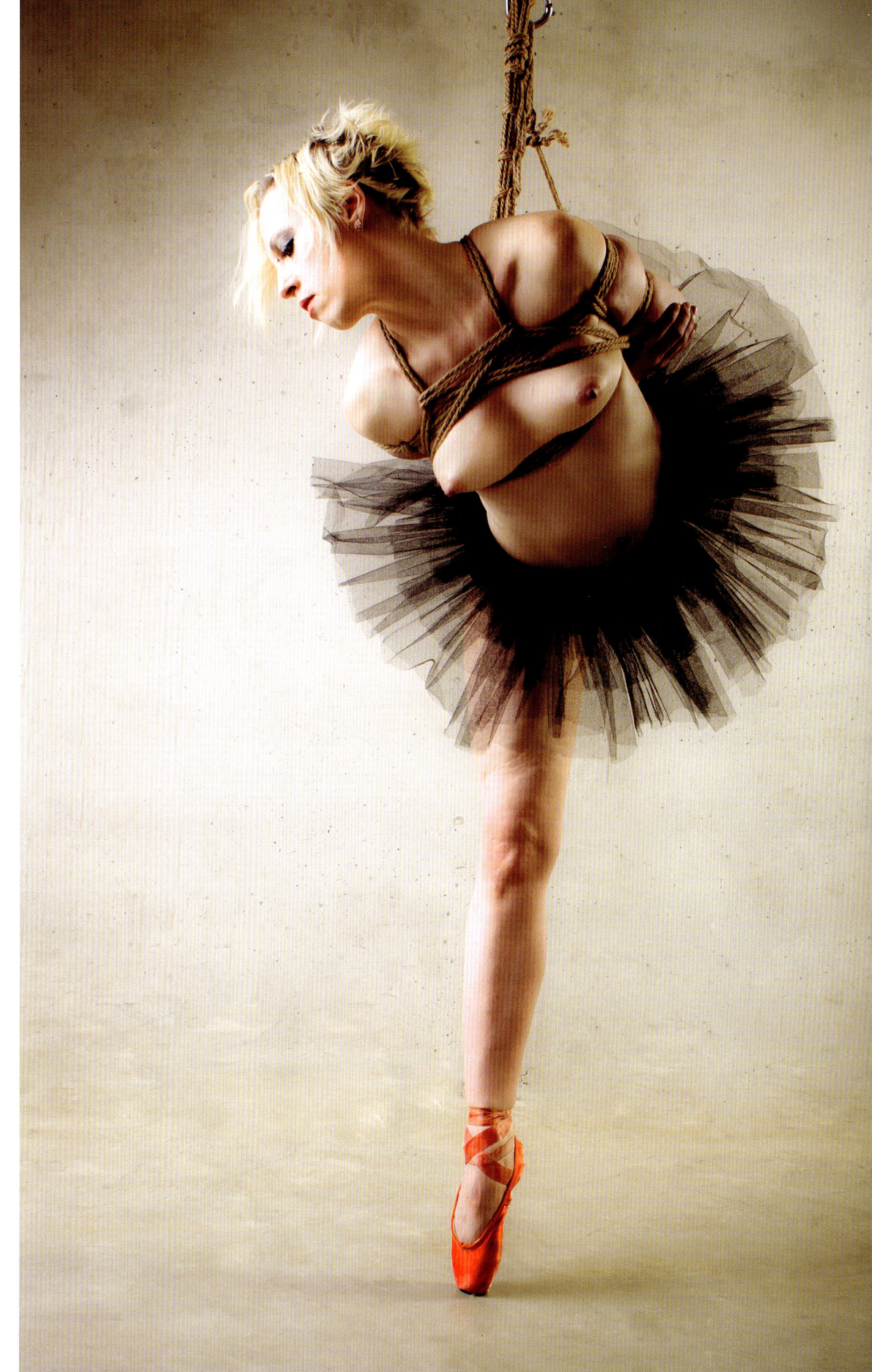

"There is something unique about rope bondage that captures one's imagination. For some it is the mystique and beauty of the ties or the idea of helplessness. For me it is the story that is brought to life through the process of tying and untying; to evoke a connection and the unscripted reaction."

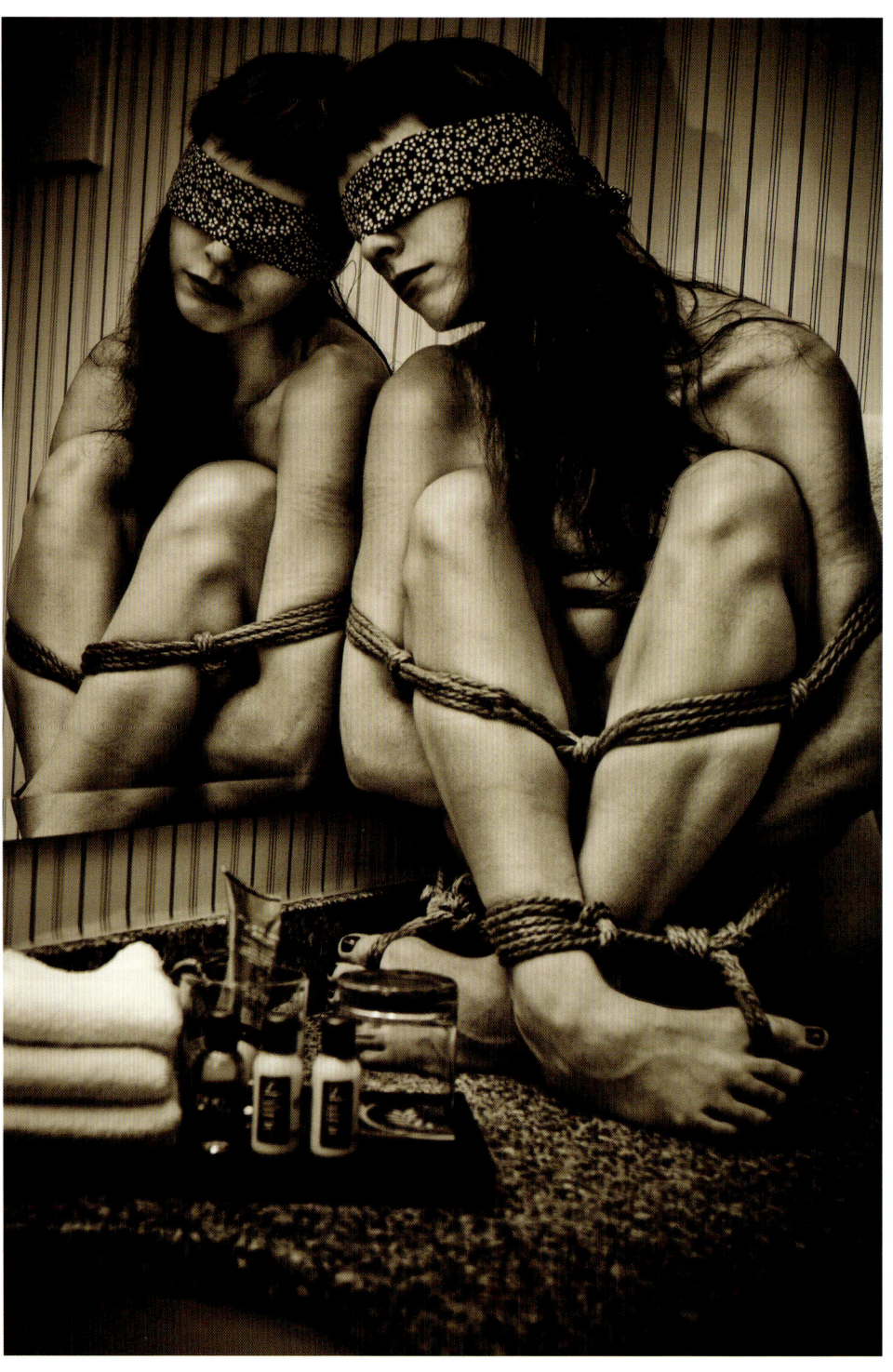

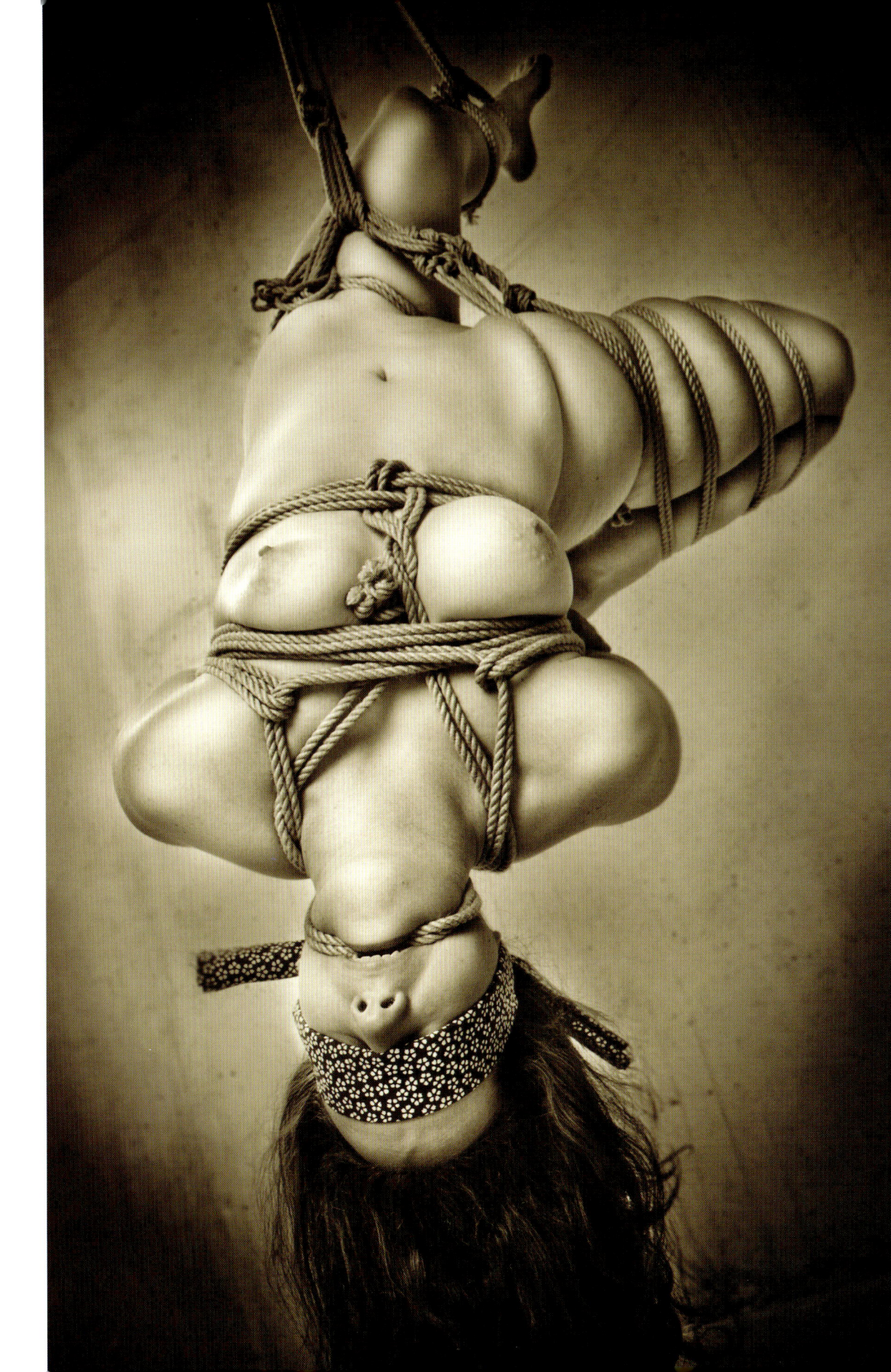

"I try to bring to light glimpses of these intimate moments through my photography. For this to be possible, the model too must have a story within her. In the confines of the ropes this story comes to the surface."

"To be clear, this is not a story of words, but rather of visuals, movements, emotions; a series of tiny moments strung together."

"Sometimes it's delicate, sometimes strong, it is always there though. Like a window, you can choose to look through it, or retreat back into yourself. It's up to you. Either is fine, there is no 'right'... just what is right for you in that moment."

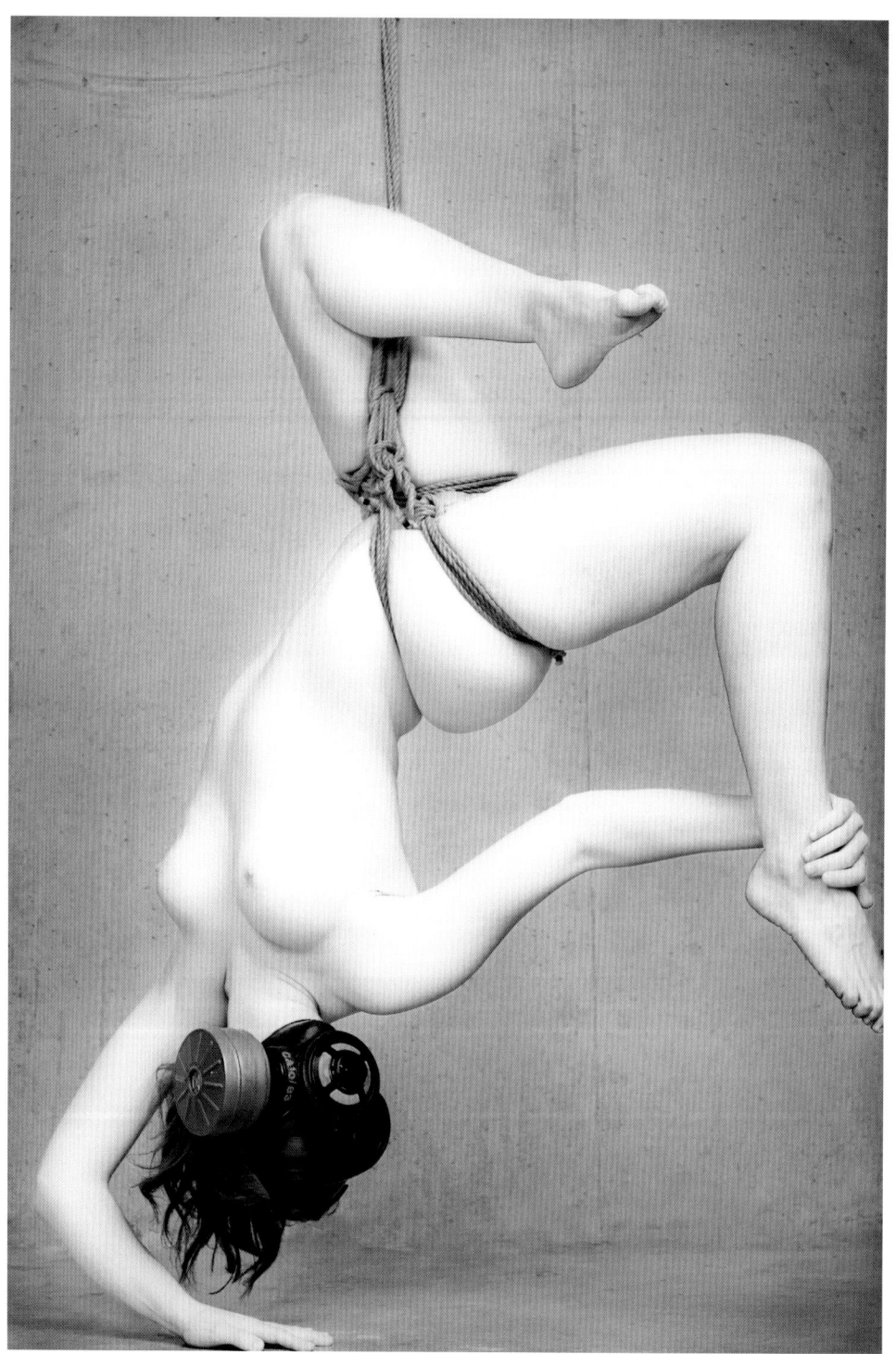

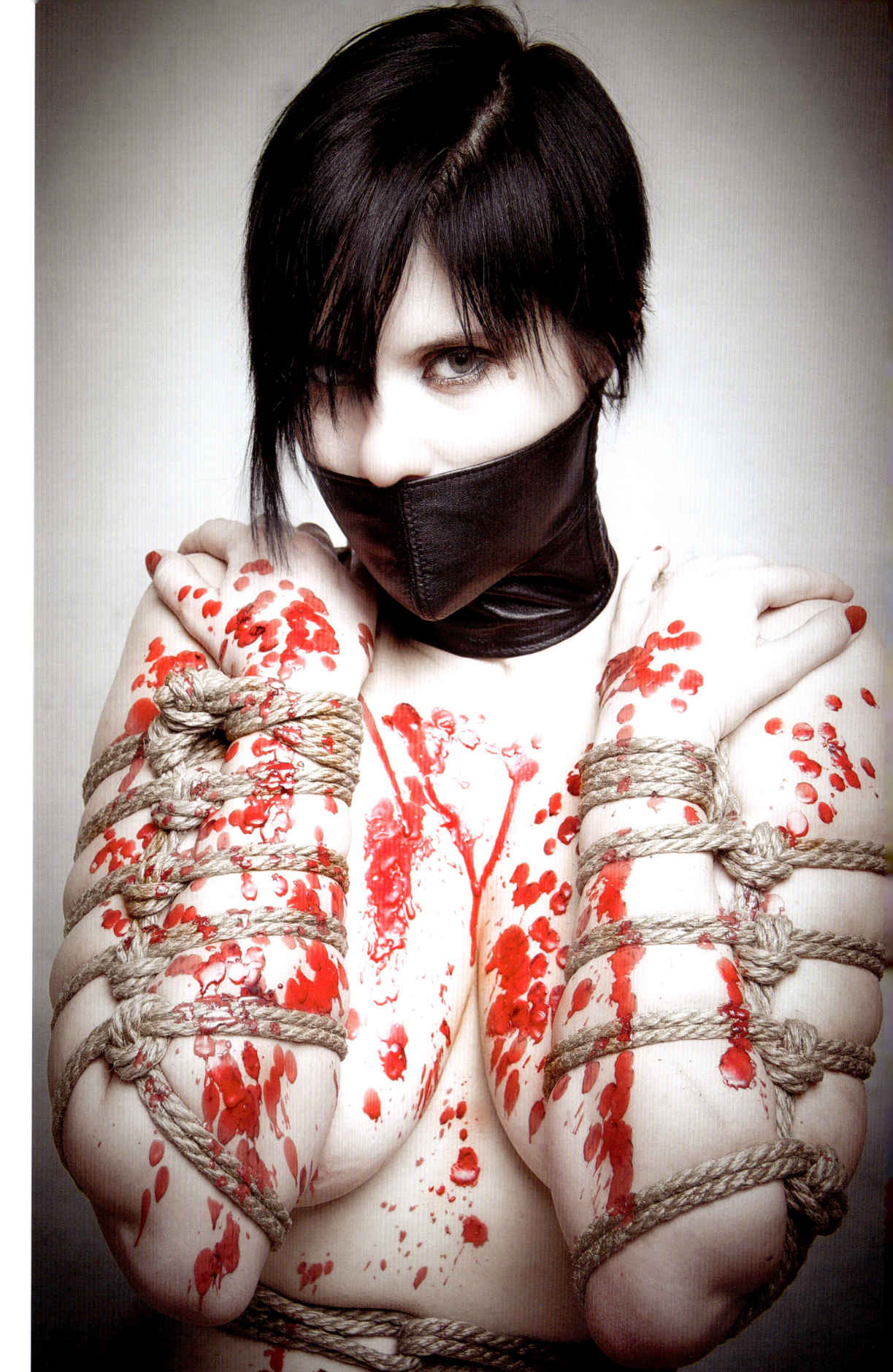

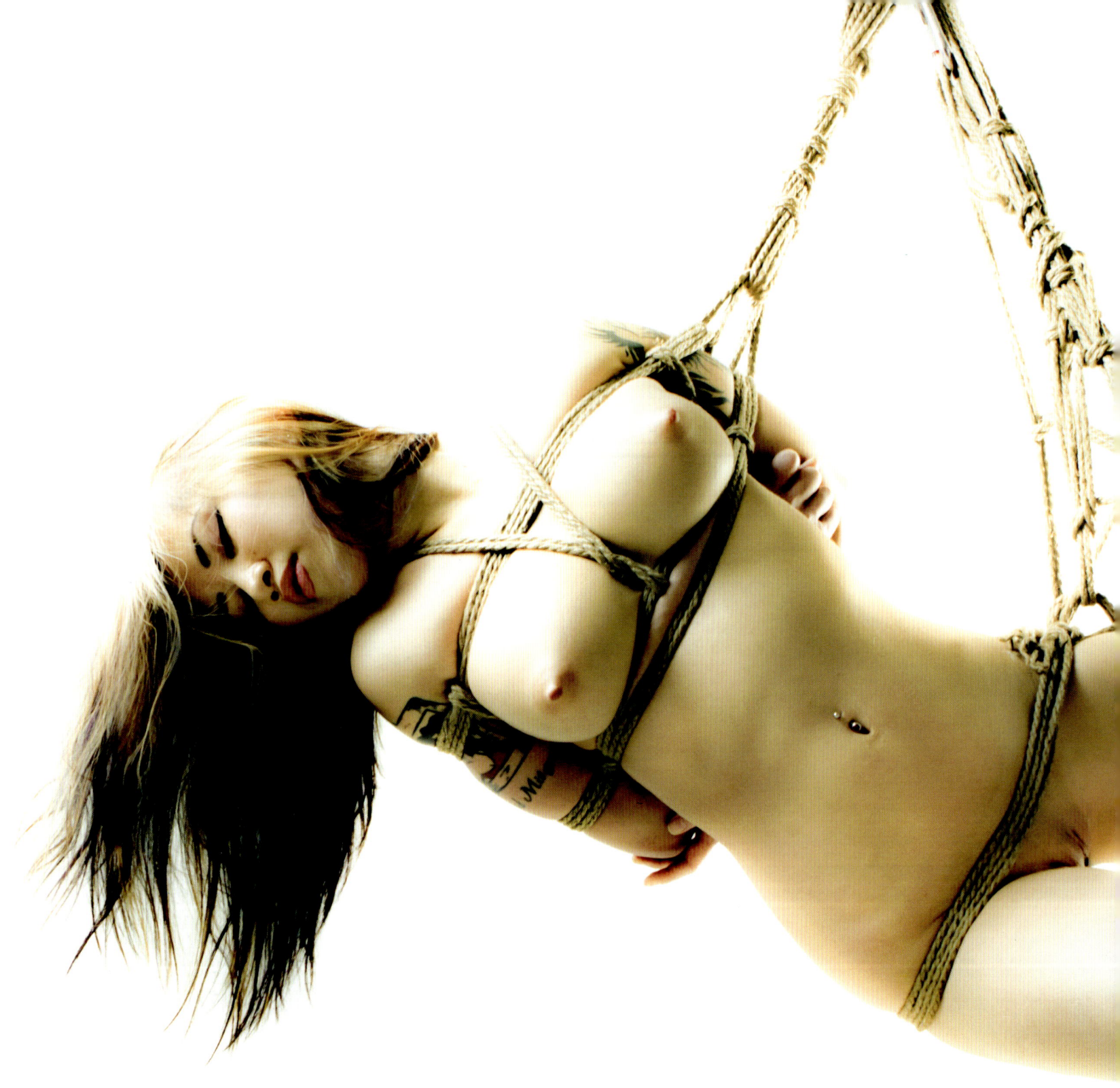

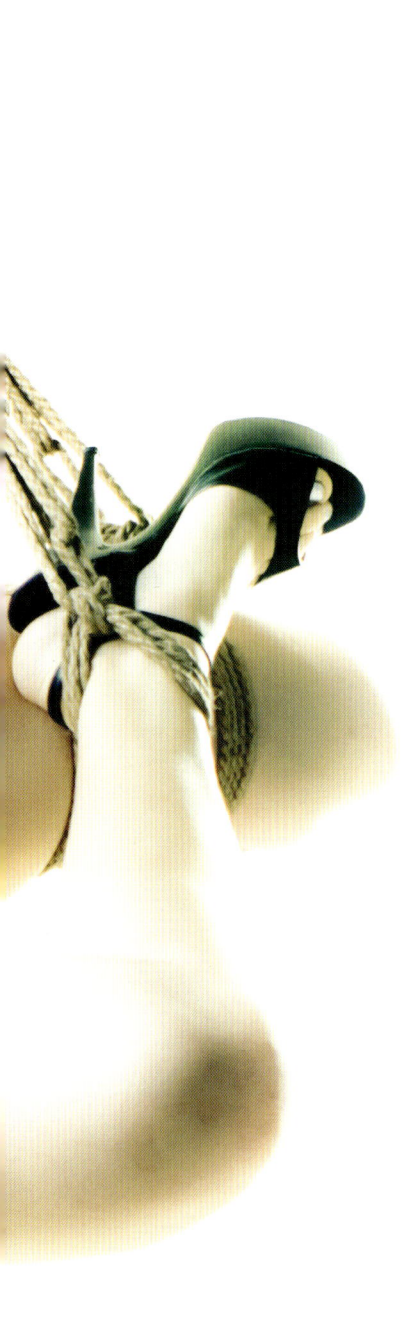

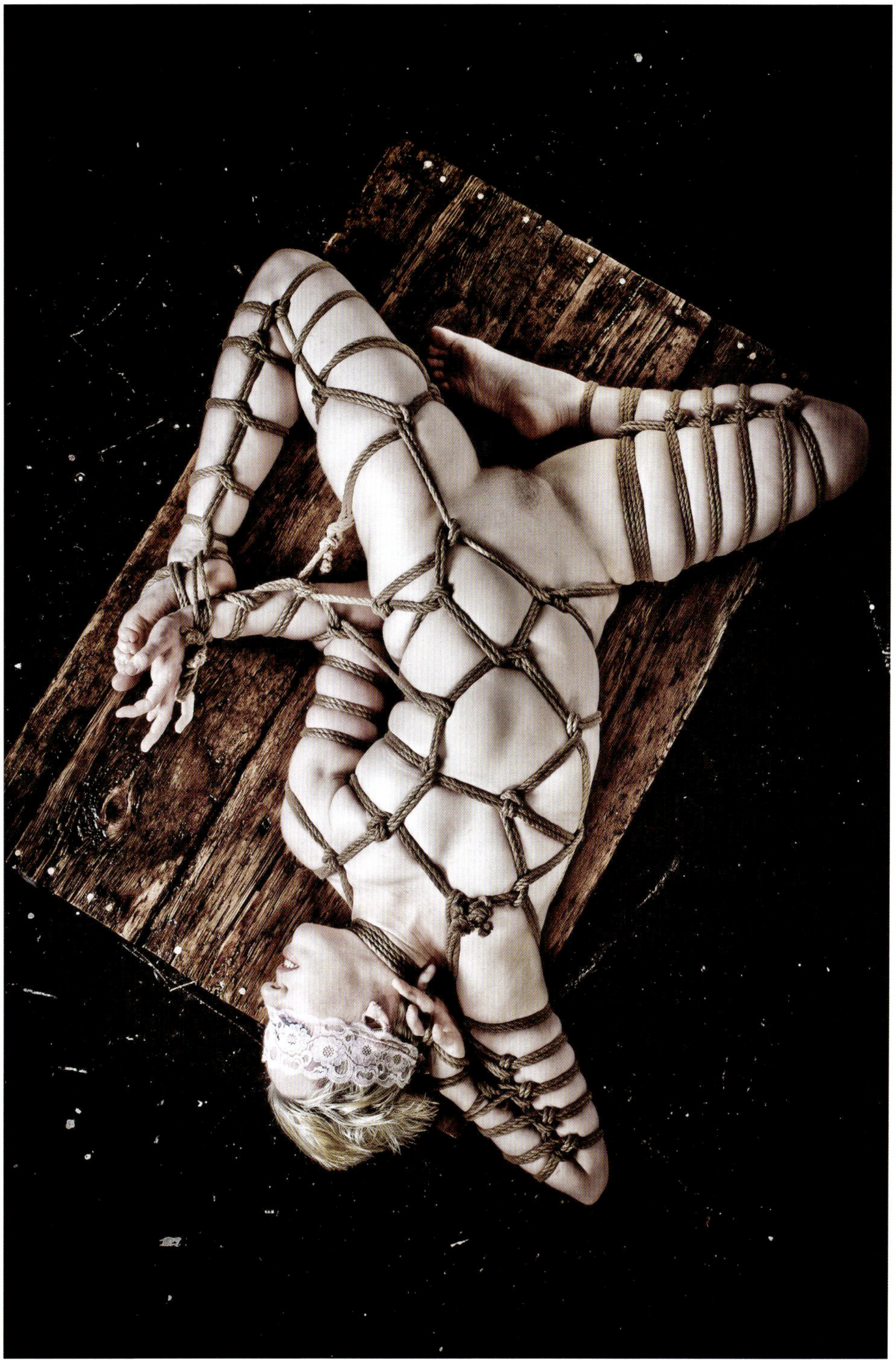

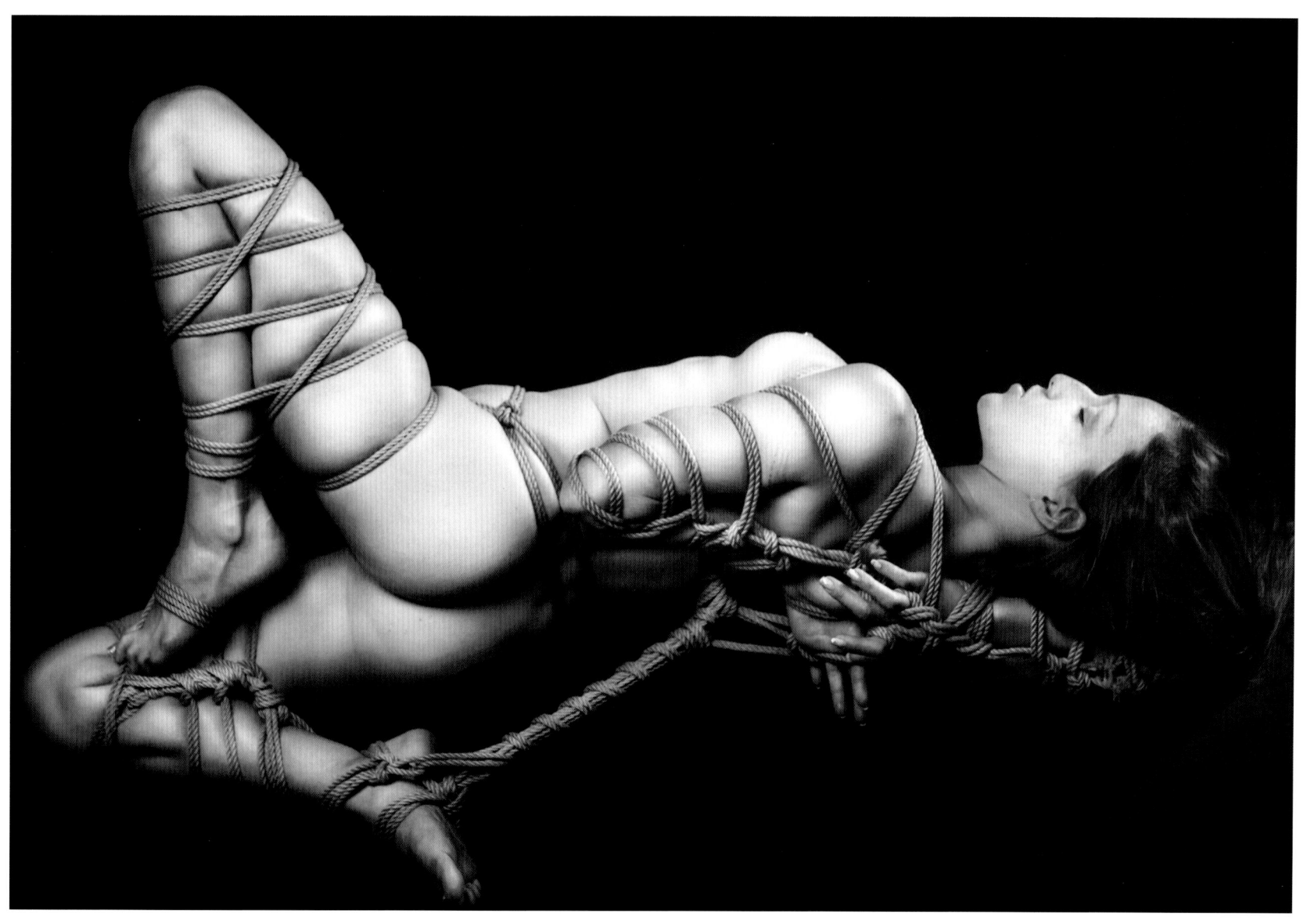

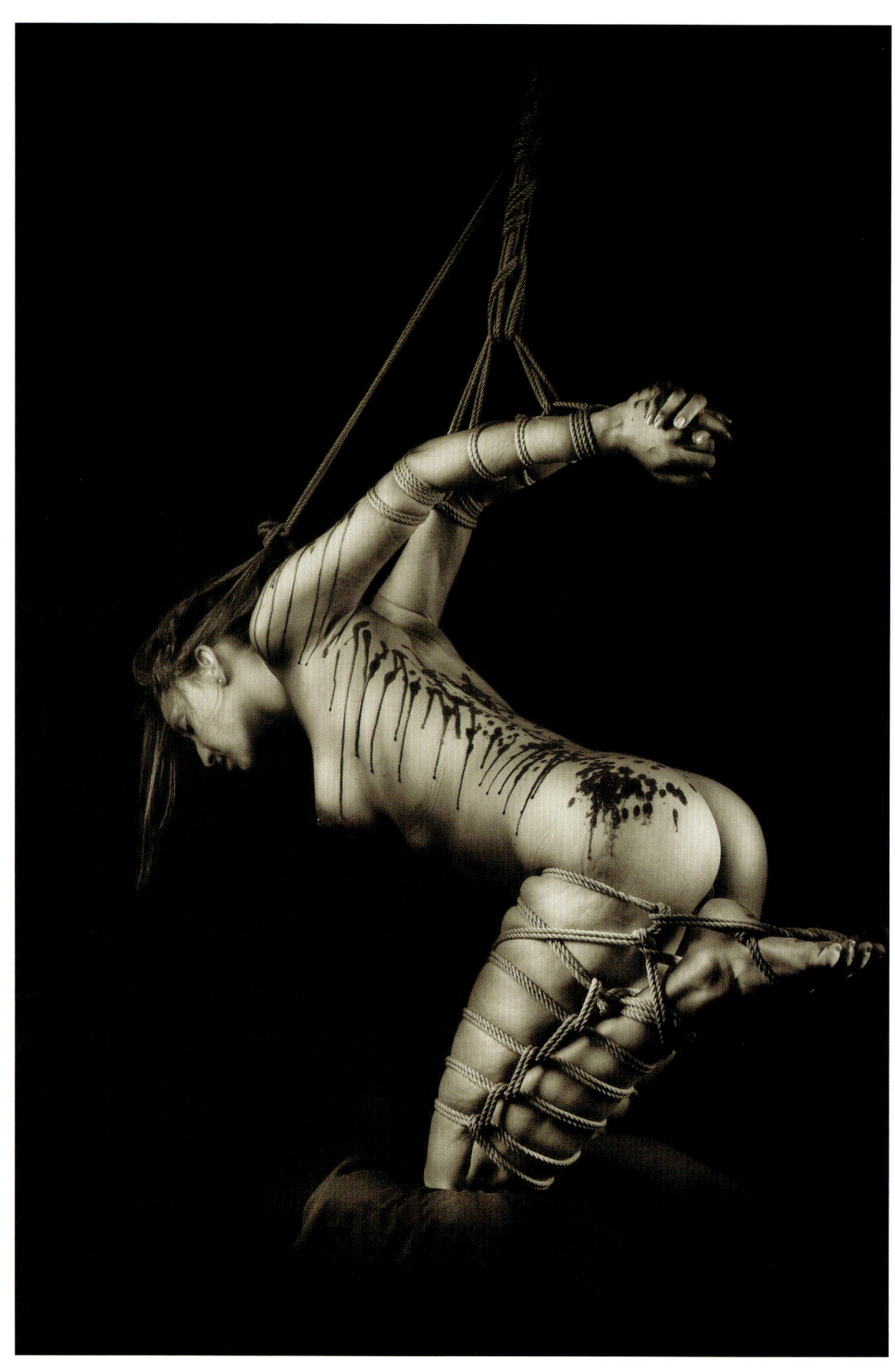

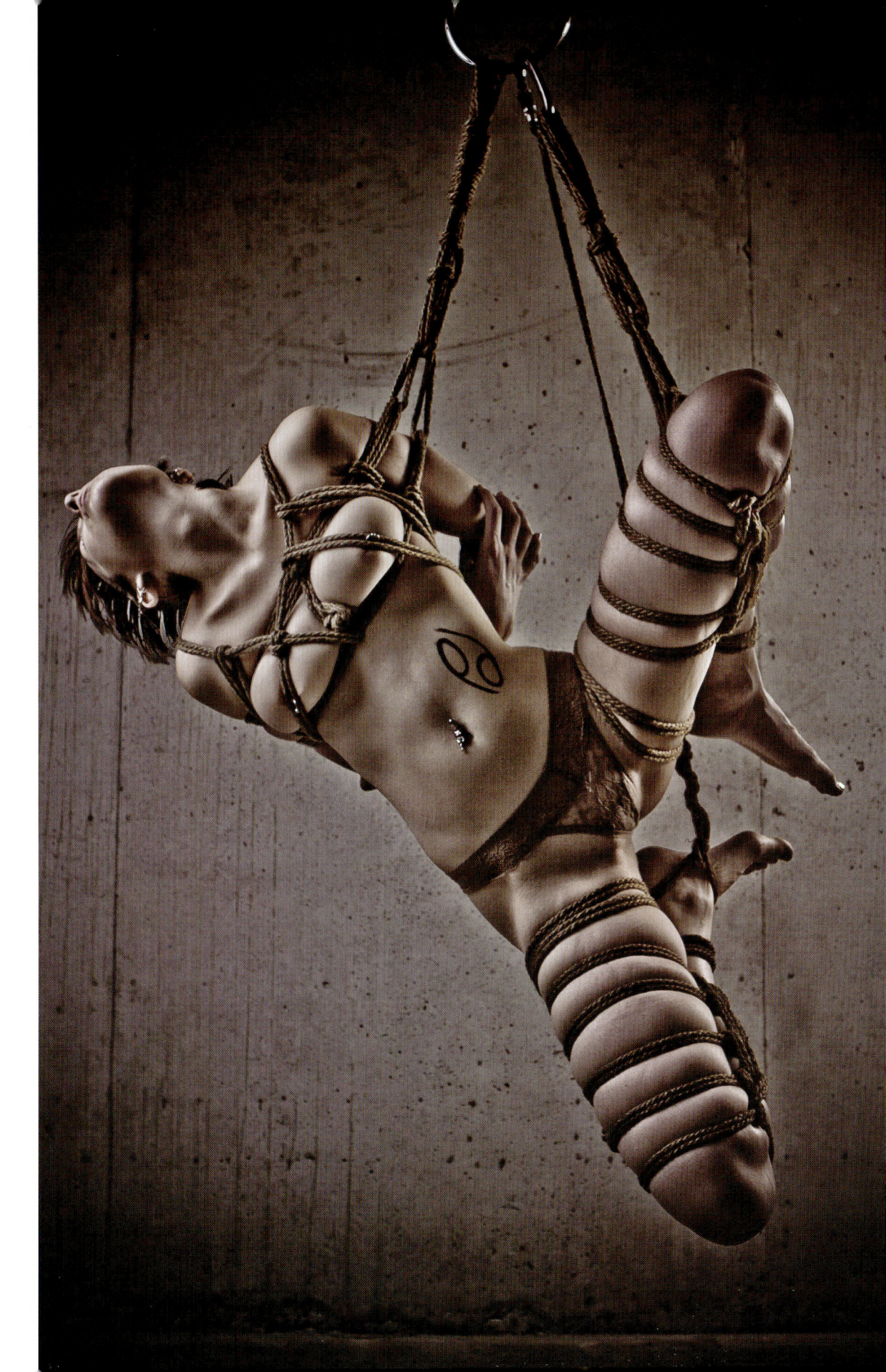

Chapter 2

Vlada and Falco

I am Vlada. It's my real name. I'm female rope artist from Moscow, Russia.

I got involved in bondage scene more then 5 years ago. I prefer torturous but brief bounds of a human body; in most cases I do variety of suspensions.

My learning approach is different - I deliberately avoid attendance of any master classes. I watch, absorb and try to work out the other Master's techniques; by doing so I am creating and developing my own style.

From all bondage diversity I only use ropes on the edge of the human ability. Quite recently I found a person, called Falco with extreme capabilities allowing us to make quite breathtaking bondage sessions. We have been practicing together for more than 1½ years by now. On rare occasions I do it with other people.

Both of us have a similar approach to the bondage: actions on borders of human capabilities - both sensual and extreme. Not that many people can enjoy these games physically and psychologically.

Photography: Vlada

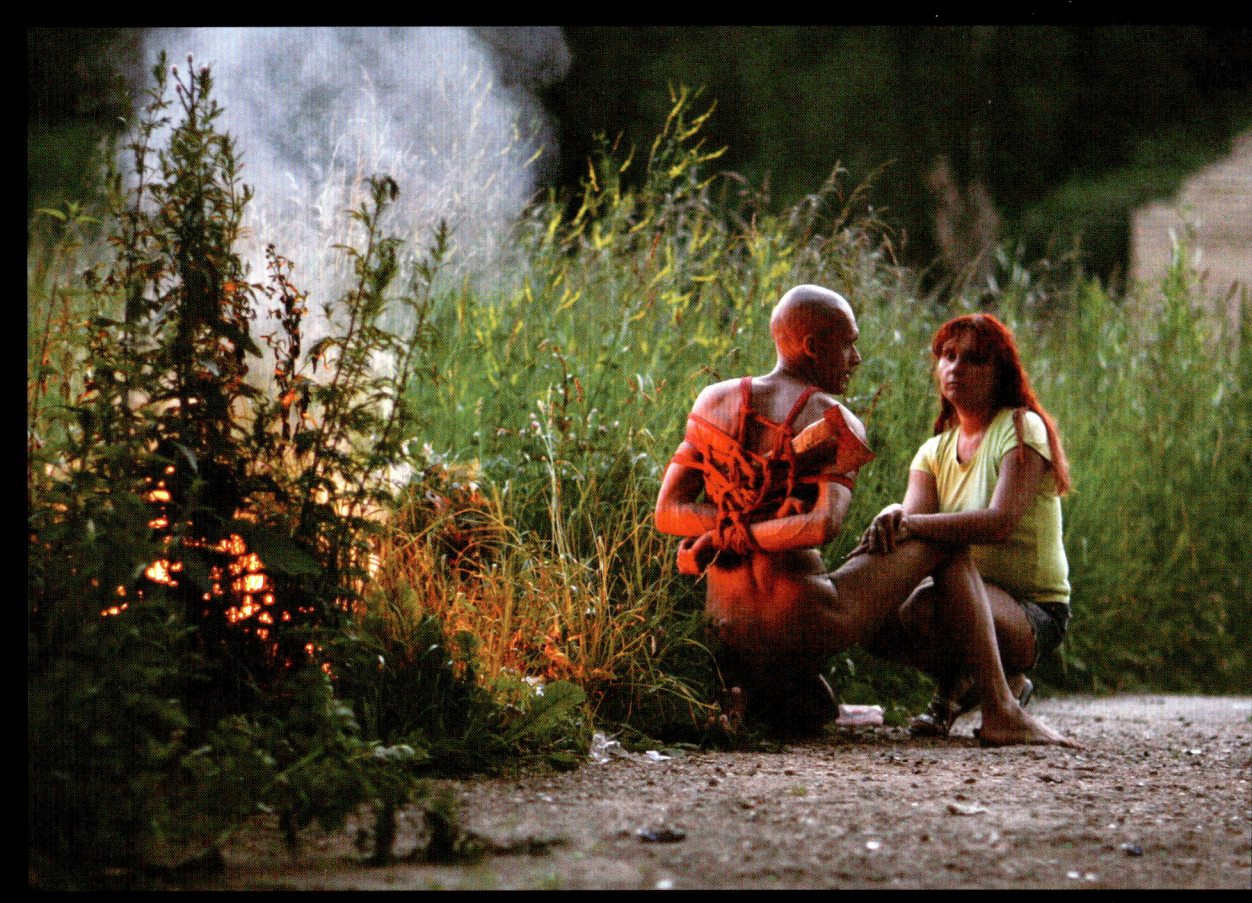

Bondage for me crosses over quite a few
traditional art forms: fine art, sculpture,
theatre, pantomime, music and dance,
sometime waltz or maybe tango
(depending on the mood).

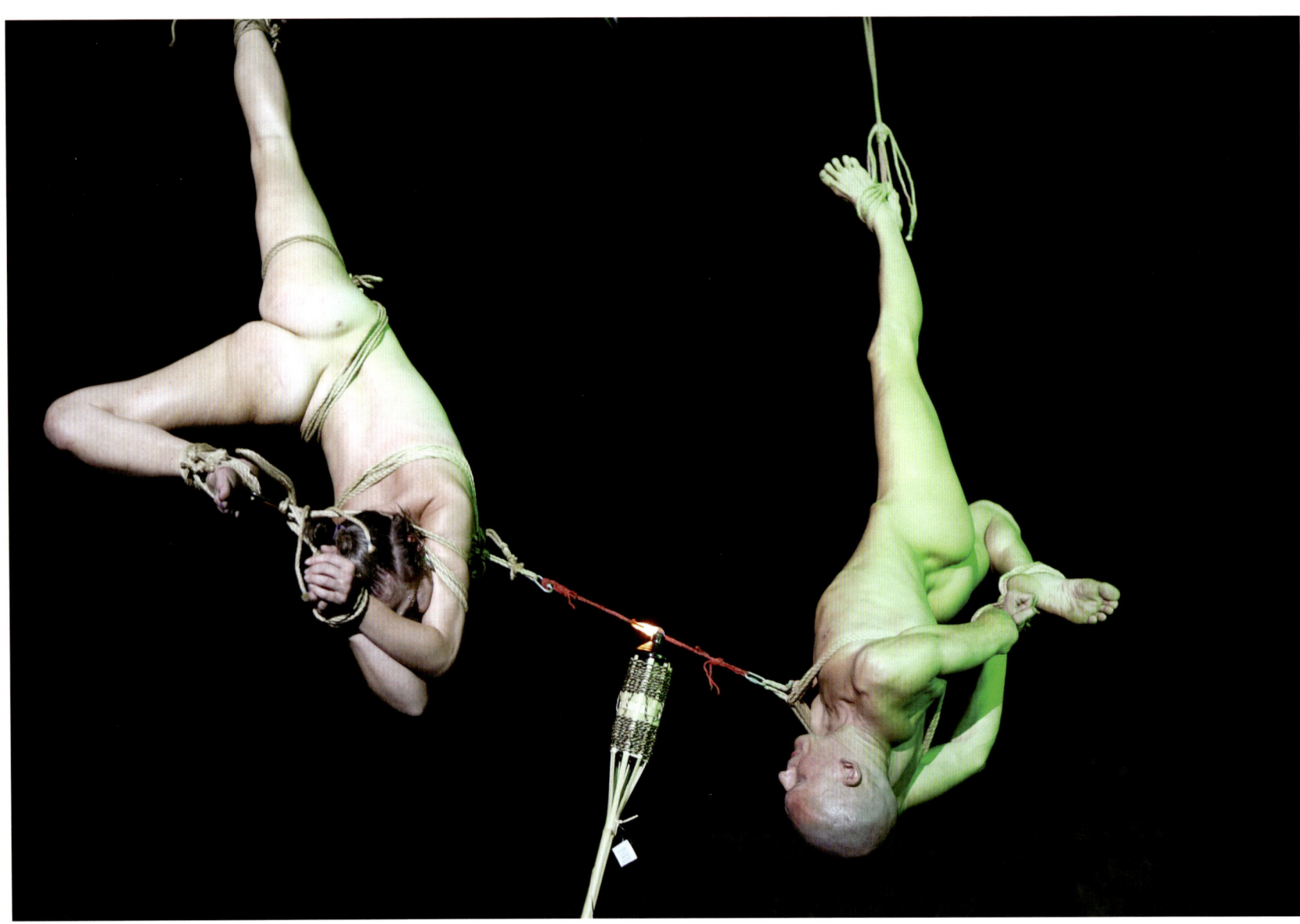

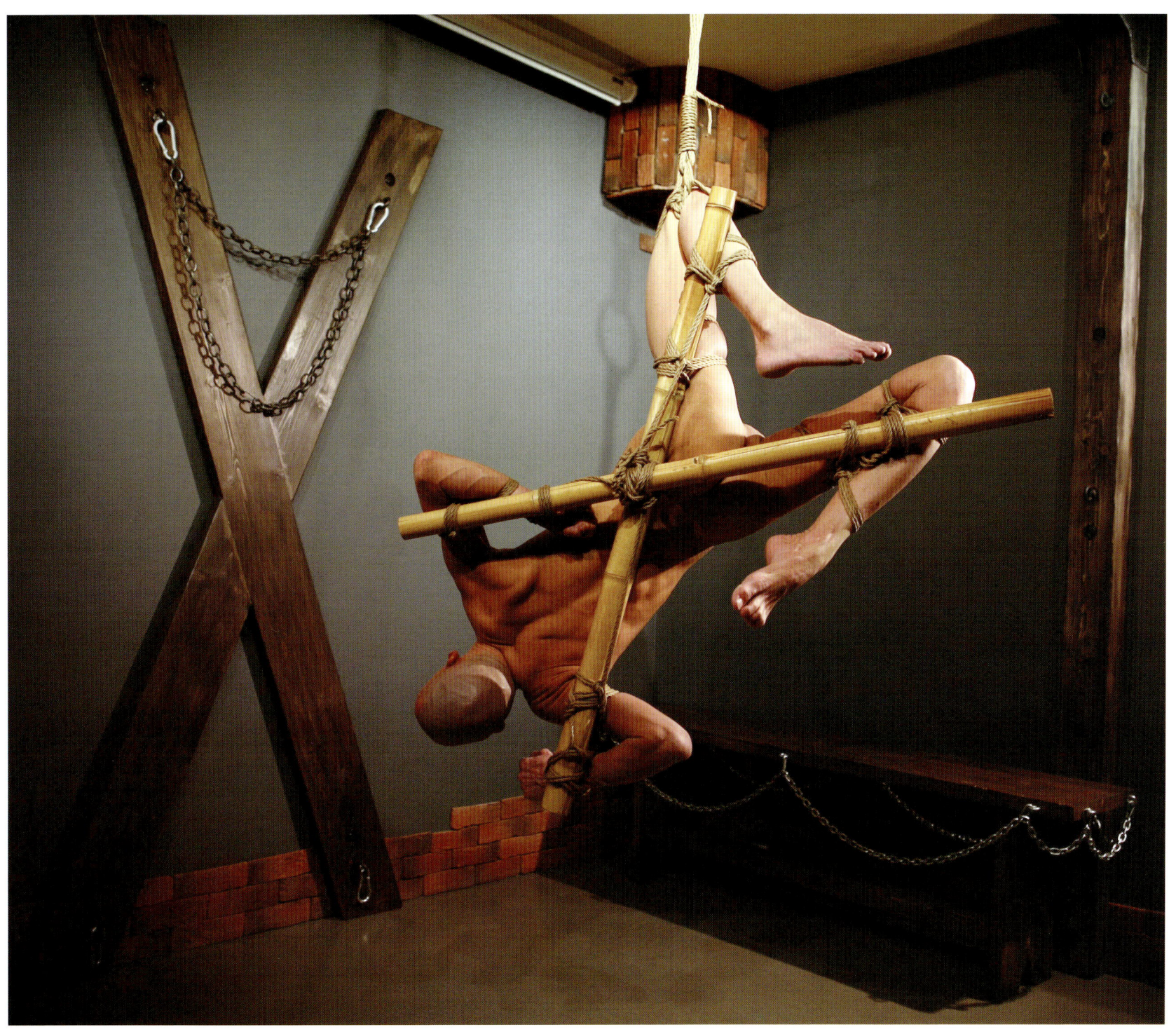

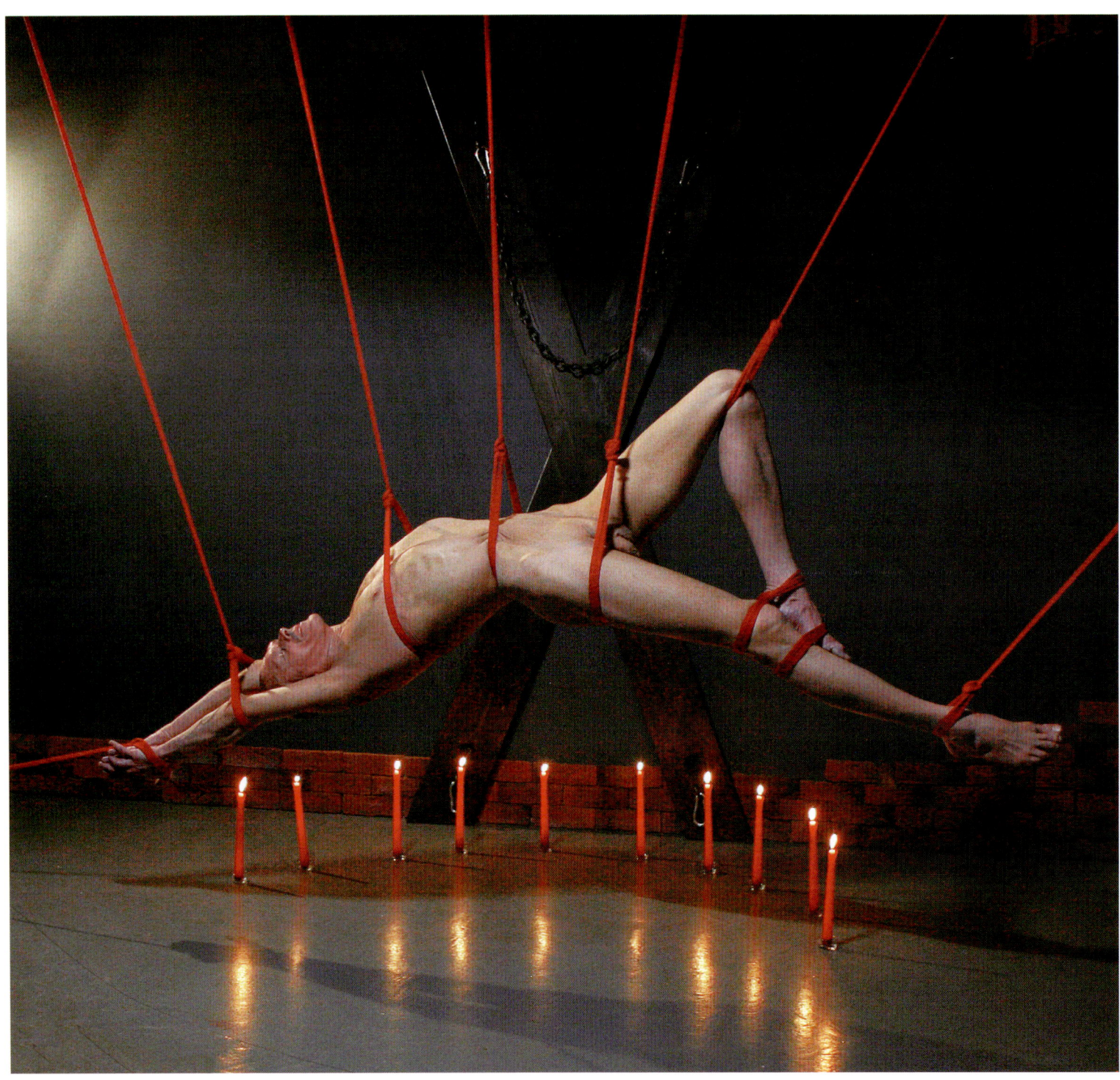

We've performed at variety of events from small BDSM parties to big festivals. Such as: "Ropefest" at St. Petersburg, major Moscow BDSM scene events: "Dead Moroz Show", "BDSM Castle", "BDSM Fishing", "London Festival of the Art of Japanese Rope Bondage" etc. We have also organised our own open air events called "Shabash".

Recently we took a tour around Europe with a view to make bondage performances next to the major sights of big cities as well as in quite remote corners of Europe. We went to England, France, Monaco, Germany and Spain. We had no Big Idea, we were just expressing ourselves that way and we have found it extremely exciting, a bit naughty and enormously satisfying. It felt like being a part of some sort of conspiracy. We would pick a location, check for CCTV cameras, wait till the place is almost clear of people, make a little dressed rehearsal, set up the lighting for the photo shoot etc.

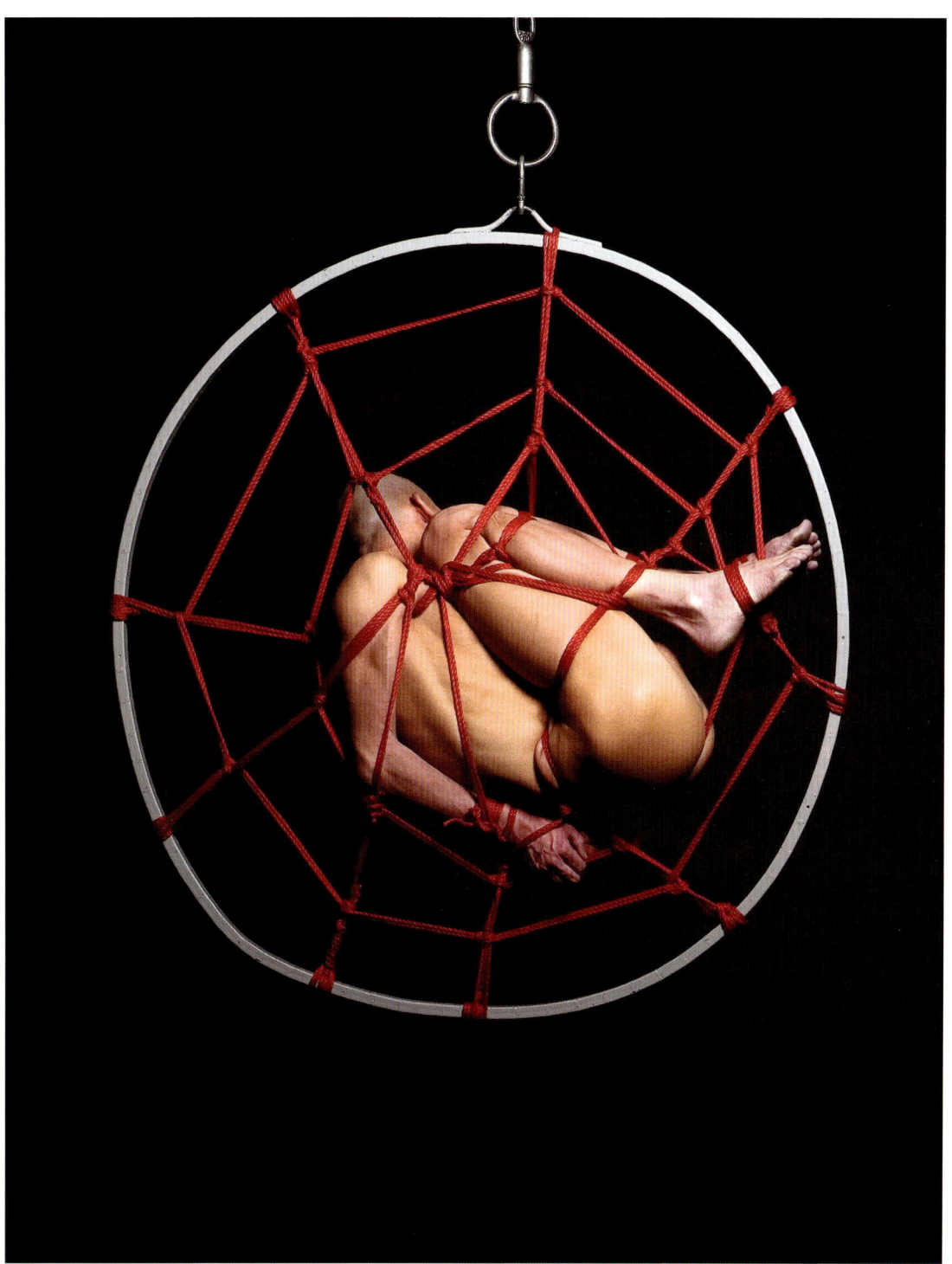

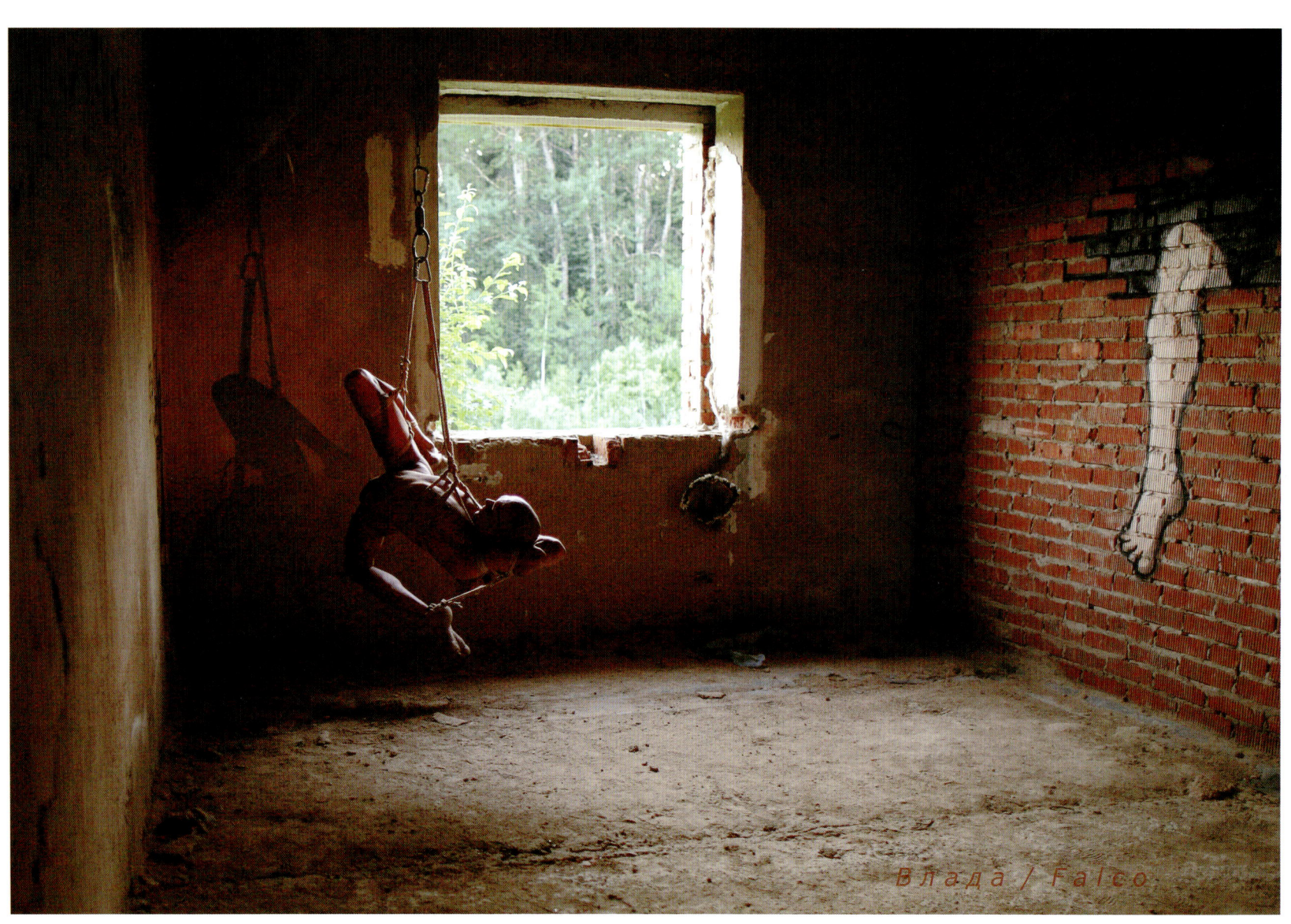

Влада / Falco

The most memorable and fun place to perform was London. We were lucky to have Jon Murakawa by our side. He kindly advised us on locations, organised a filming crew. Feeling more confident, we could concentrate on performance while Jon was answering the questions of the curious passers-by.

We were pleasantly surprised by the level of tolerance in London – people would step over the ropes and would apologize for disturbing us. I remember there was a cyclist who had to stop unable to move further; he gave us the biggest smile, moved his bicycle over Falco and carried on as if it was normal. In Russia we would have been in jail in minutes, sharing the cell with infamous Pussy Riots!

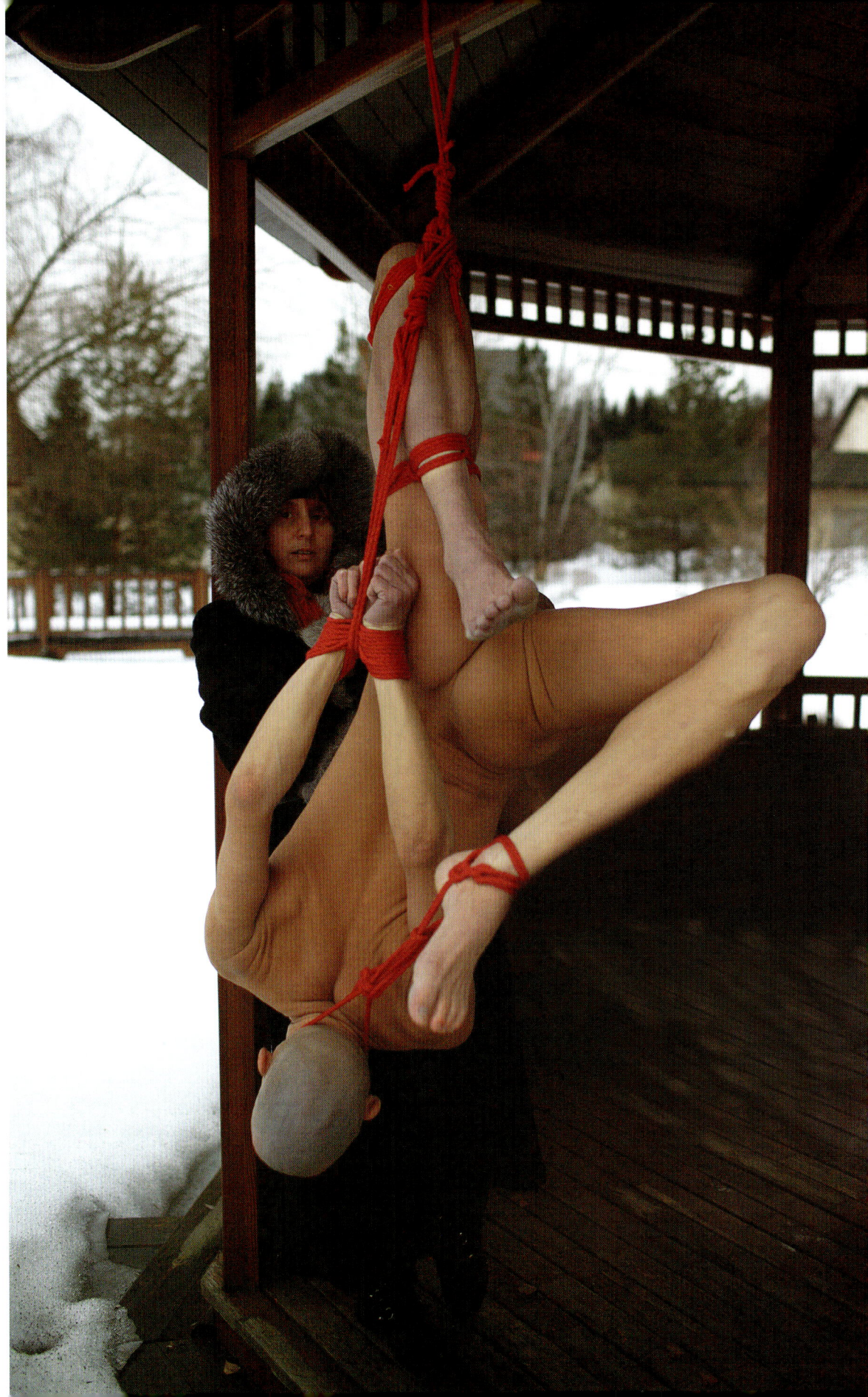

We have produced vast amounts of pictures
at the end but they were not the reason for
our performances.

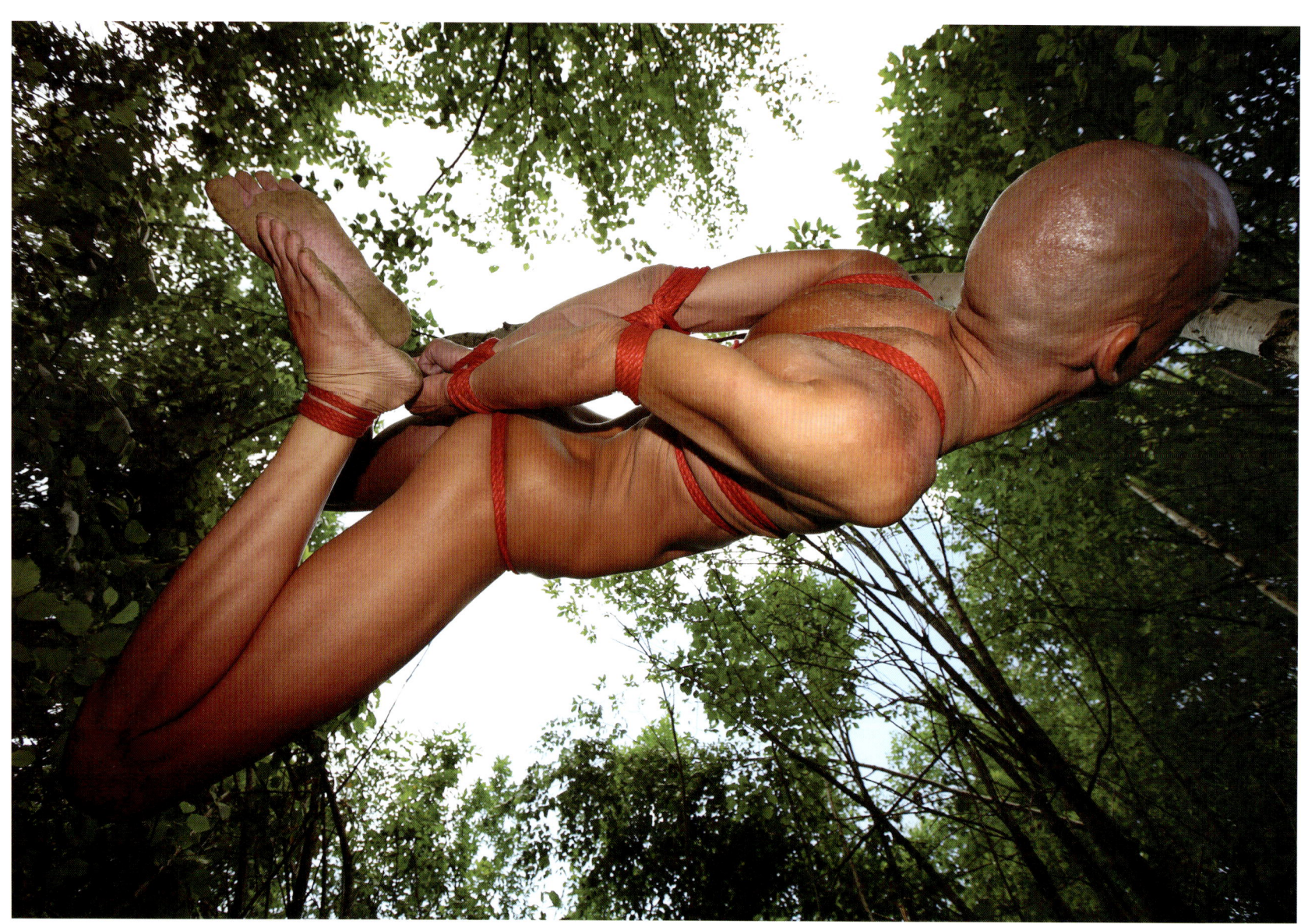

My interest lays in the process rather then in the result. Bondage for me is not a goal, neither a reason; it is a never ending process like growing a bonsai-tree. A person involved is a reflection of the complexity of the world; a metaphor for fluid's elusive flexibility. The flexible ones do not break down.

Bondage is also a metaphor for a constant search for a counteraction, the unity and struggle of the opposites. The world is also flexible – we can not bind it to our needs, no matter how hard we try.

The other reasons for our performances are desire to shock, the sense of power and a search for boundaries. The creativity is not significant, nether the momentum of the performance, nor the self-expression – these are all different sides, sparks of the fireworks. Fireworks are as exciting as the many fires they produce… They change , and so do we.

Tomorrow I will be different, my motives will be different but today I absorb the multiple diversity of the universe and share its provocative seductiveness with you.

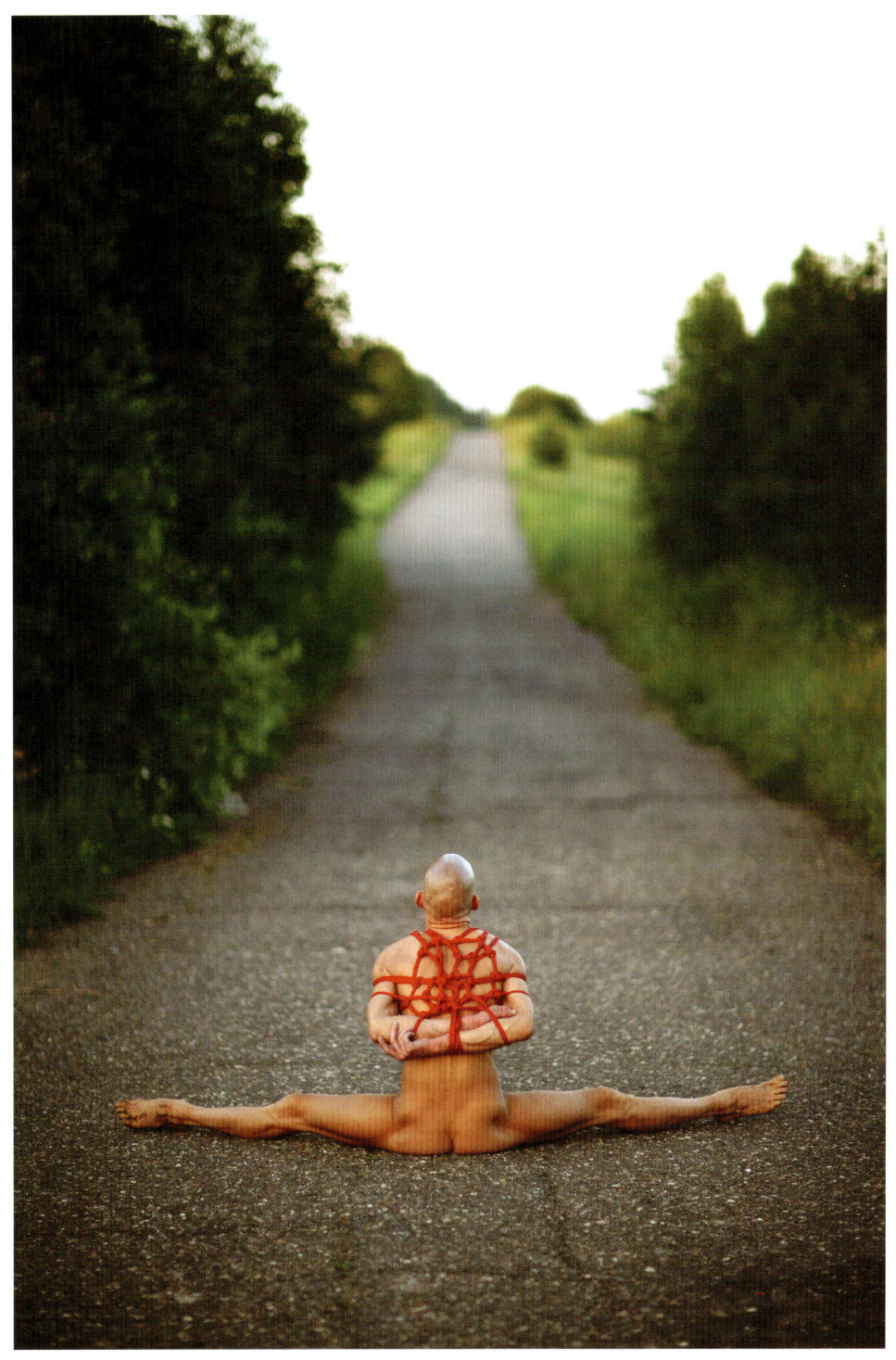

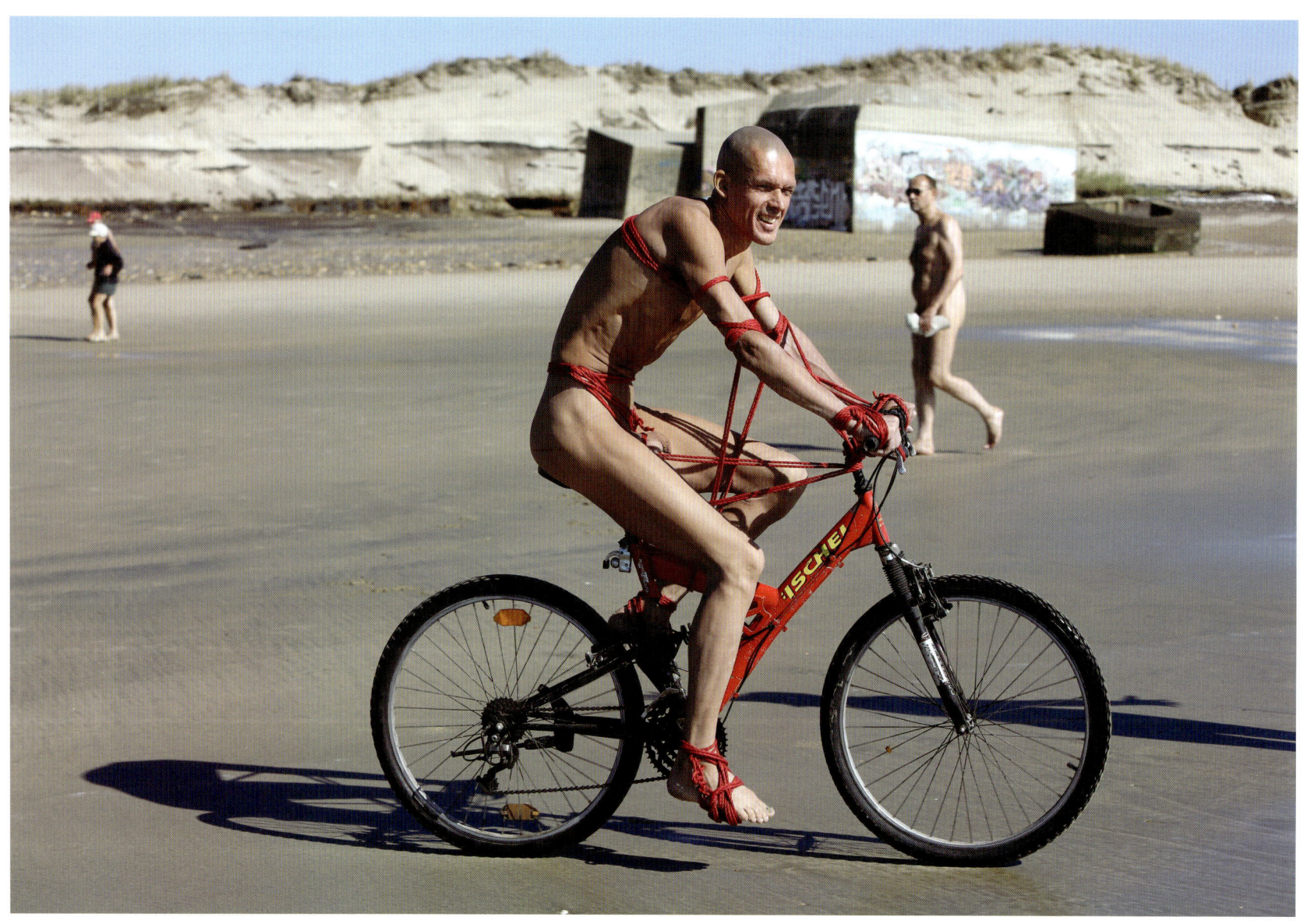

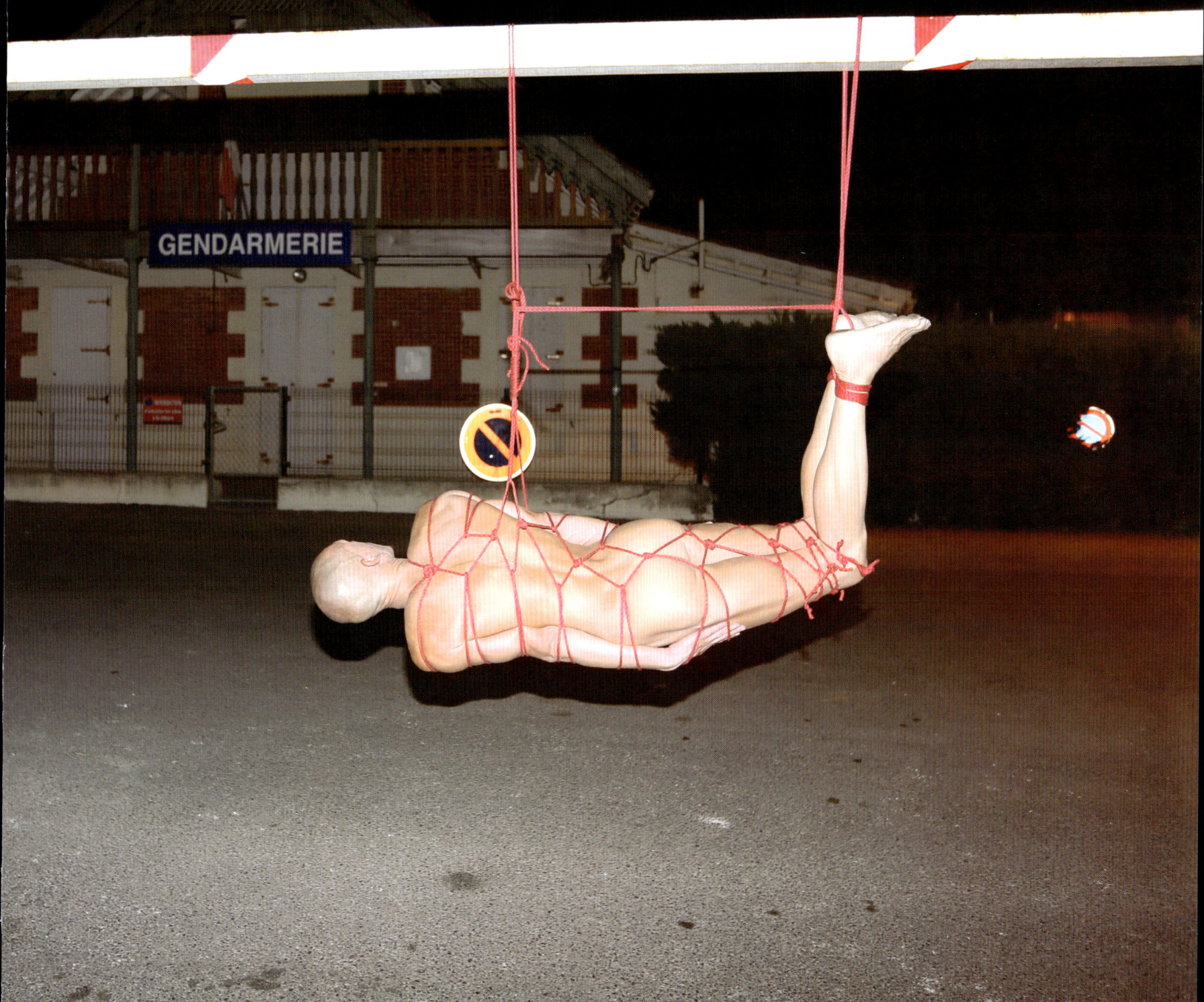

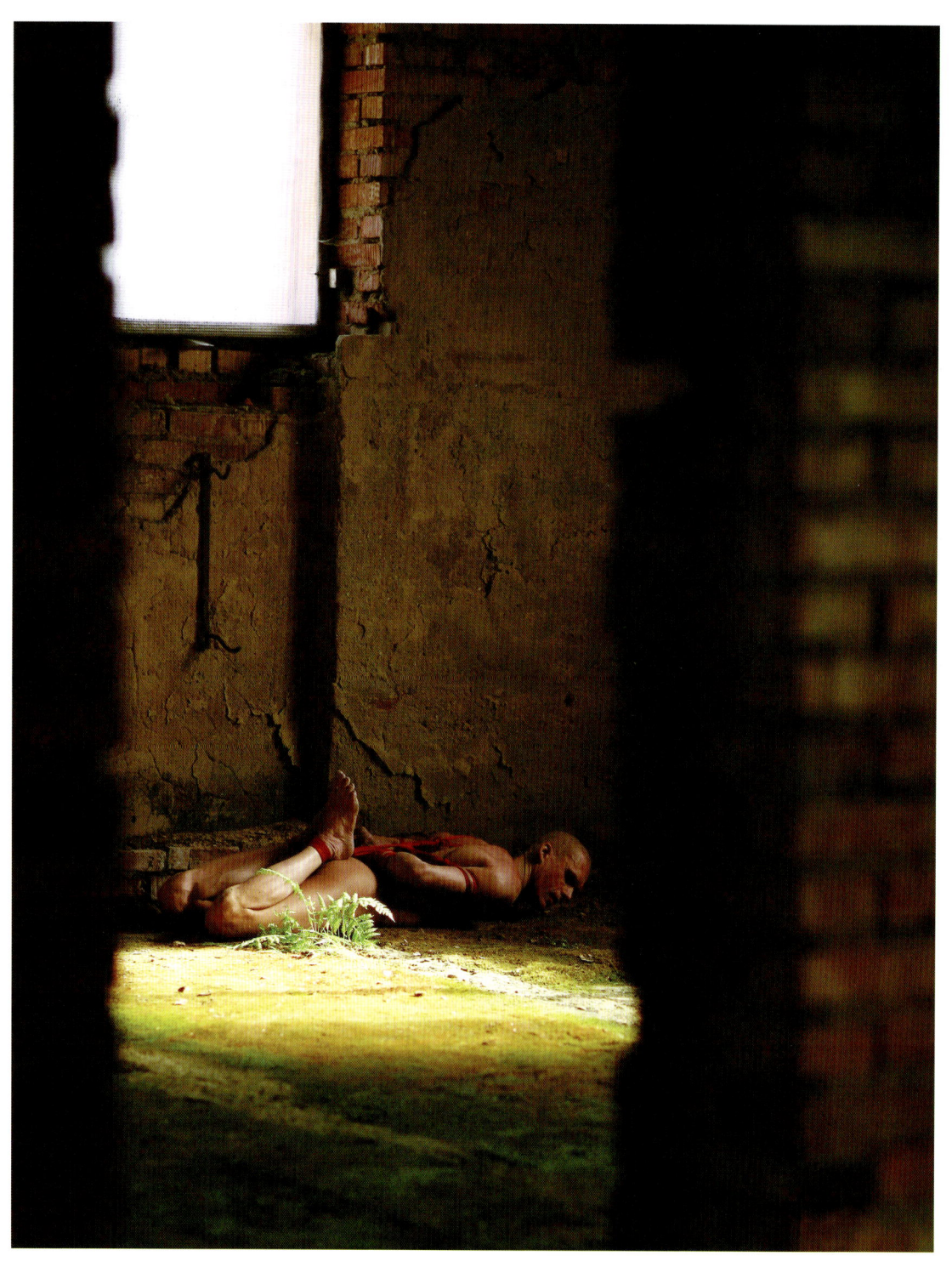

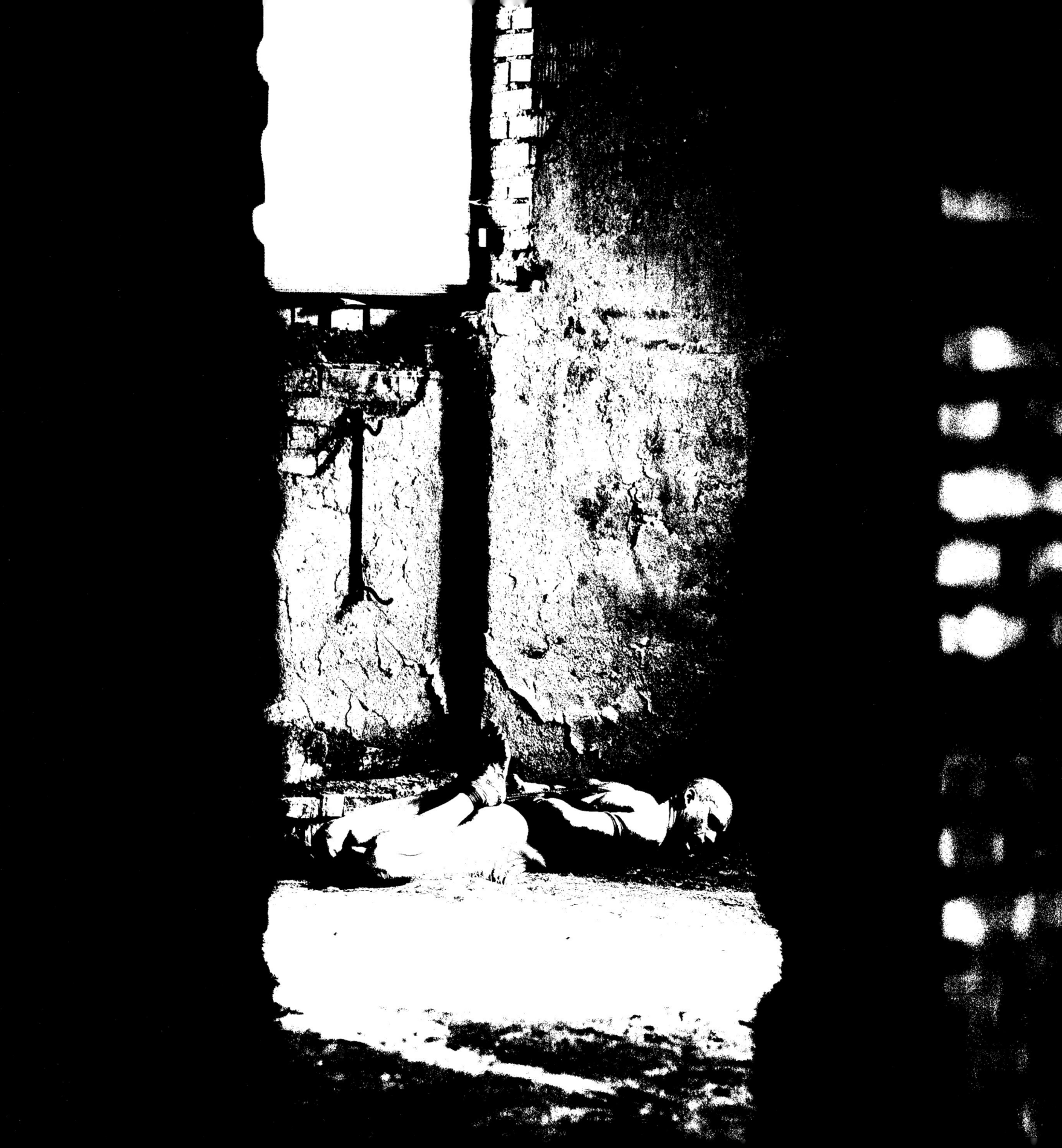

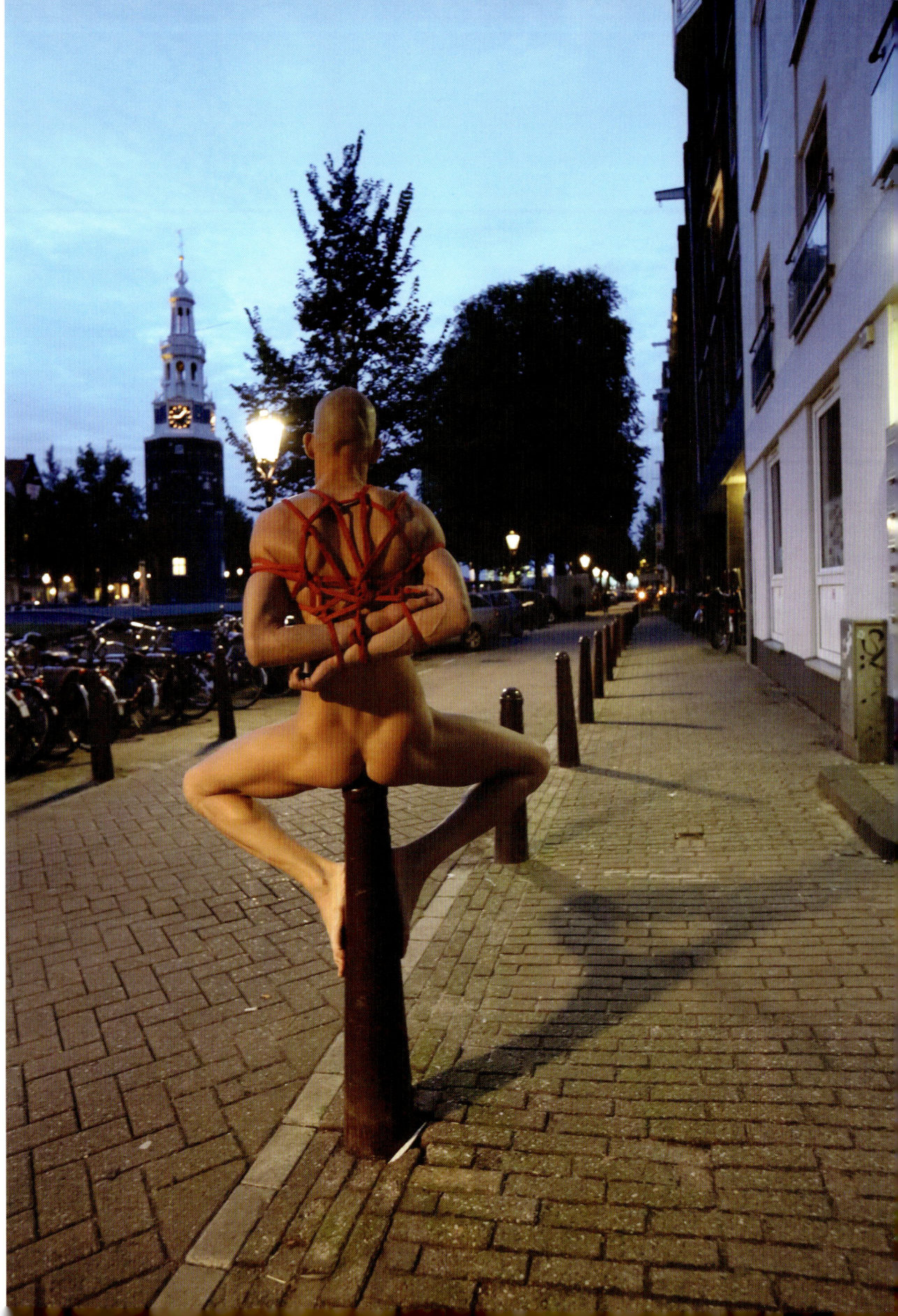

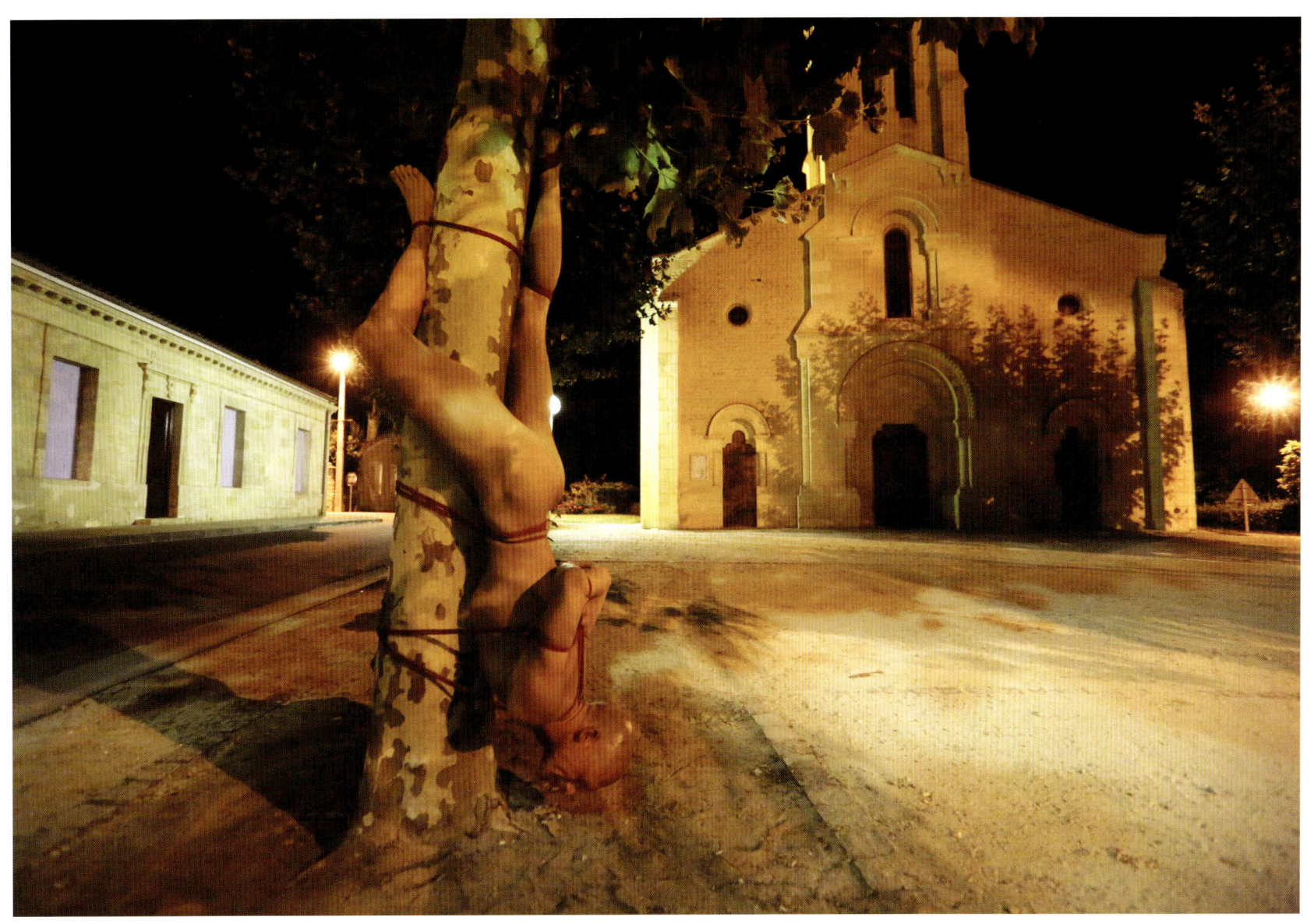

Chapter 3

Suspended sentence

Sam had contacted me occasionally for about a year to ask if I needed a model. It was, however, a year in which I had decided to concentrate on abstract art, so I declined her offers. But eventually I decided to get back to working with people and was beginning to think of a book featuring Shibari. When she next contacted me I invited her to meet up with me and told her that I did need a model but also told her that she would be tied up. At this point, I had no idea what her reaction would be, but her response was: "Have you got any ropes here, we can start now?" It became obvious during a practice session that she was not only a good model to work with, but also she enjoyed being bound and preferably unclothed.

The location we chose for the photographs shown here was a disused Magistrates Court. This is a court house in the UK where petty crimes are dealt with by a Judge known as a Magistrate. Since one of the punishments that the judge can give is a "suspended sentence," it seemed appropriate to try Sam in this location. A suspended sentence is a punishment which is withheld providing the guilty person commits no further crimes. But it can mean something else as you see …

Photography: Kahboom

Sam is an experienced model, but only had a couple of previous sessions of rope bondage before taking part in this scene.

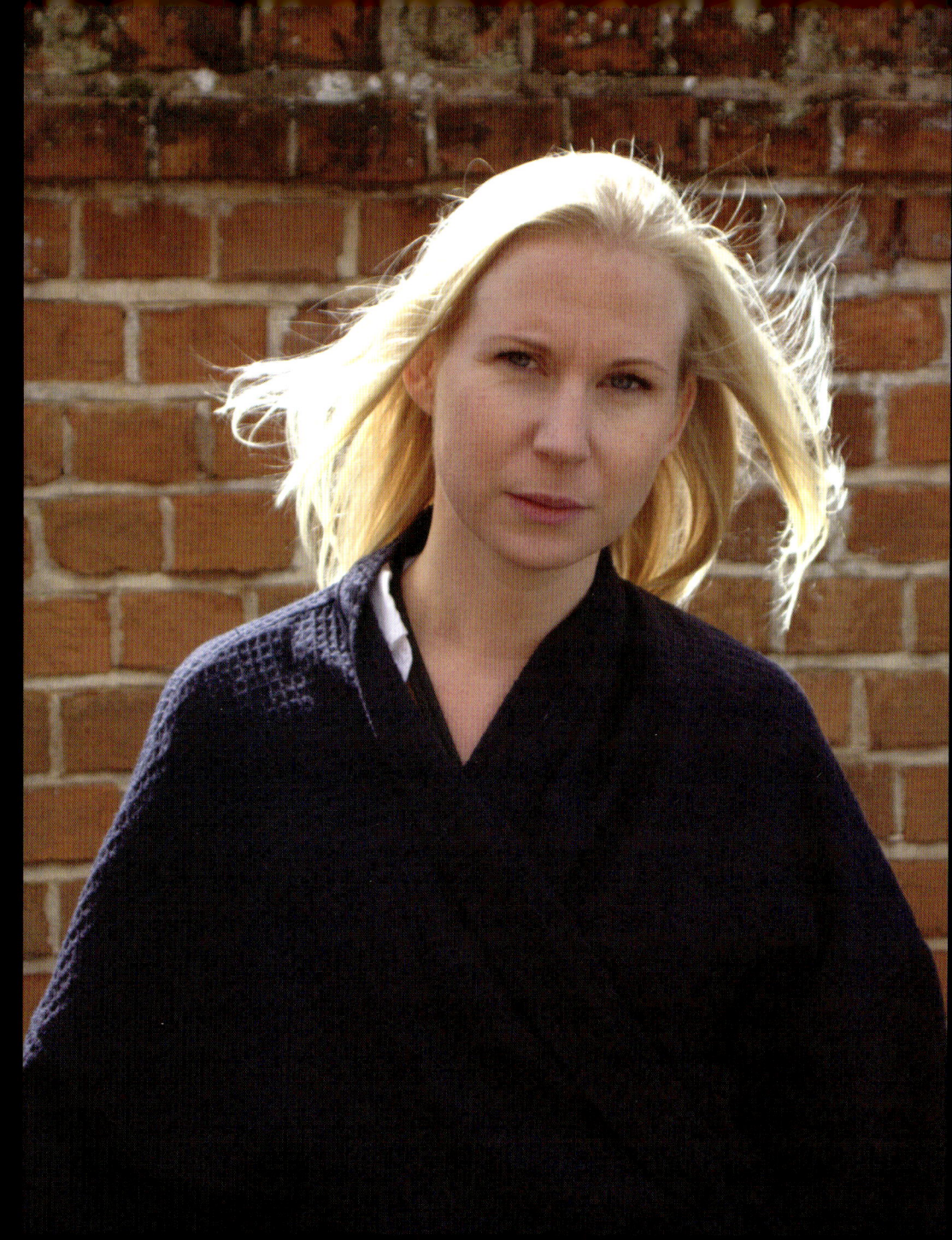

When she arrived she was clearly nervous
and I was concerned that she would be too
tense to go through with it.

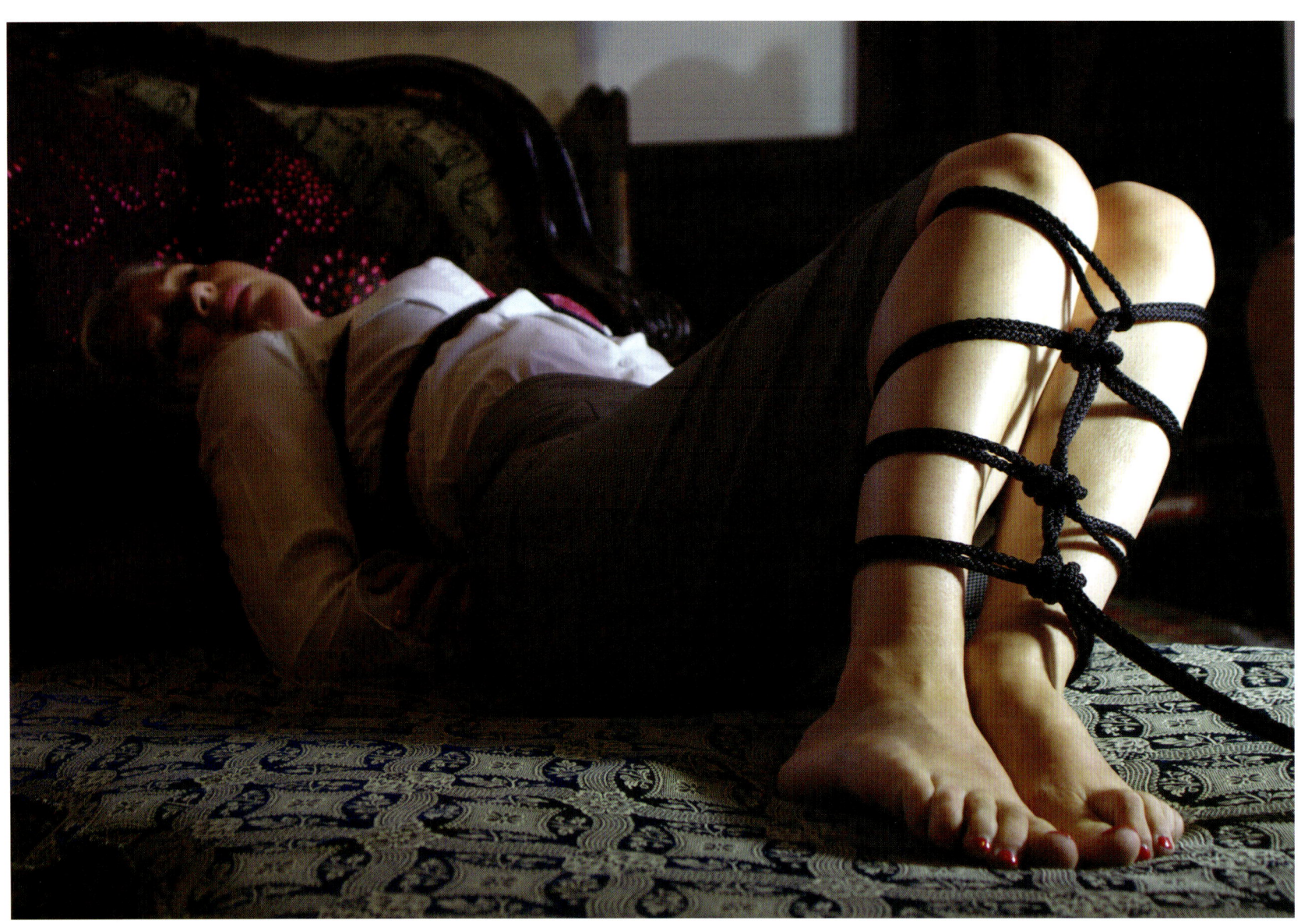

What followed was amazing to watch. As her clothes were gradually replaced by ropes, she became more and more confident.

A new, stronger Sam emerged even as she was more and more immobilised.

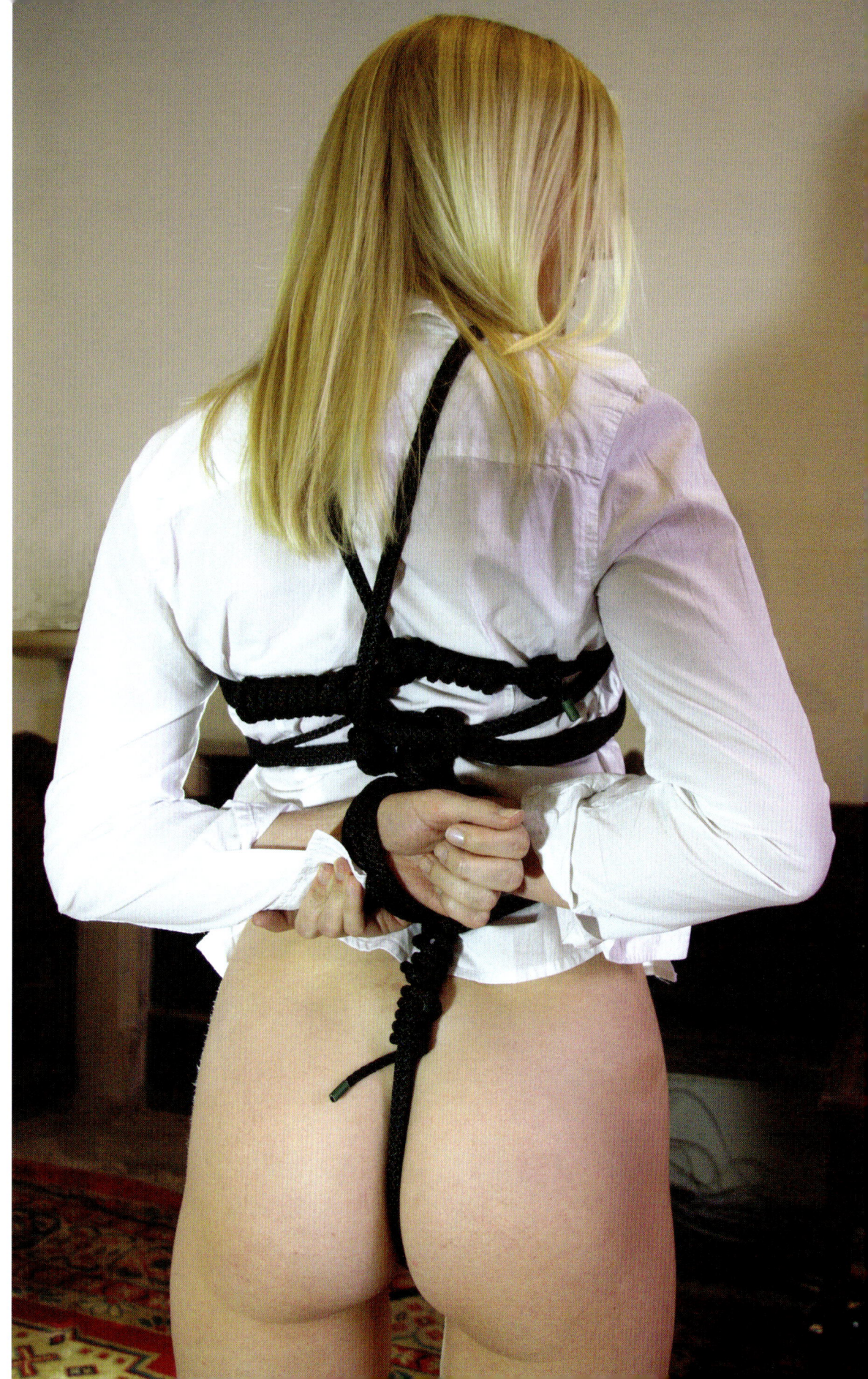

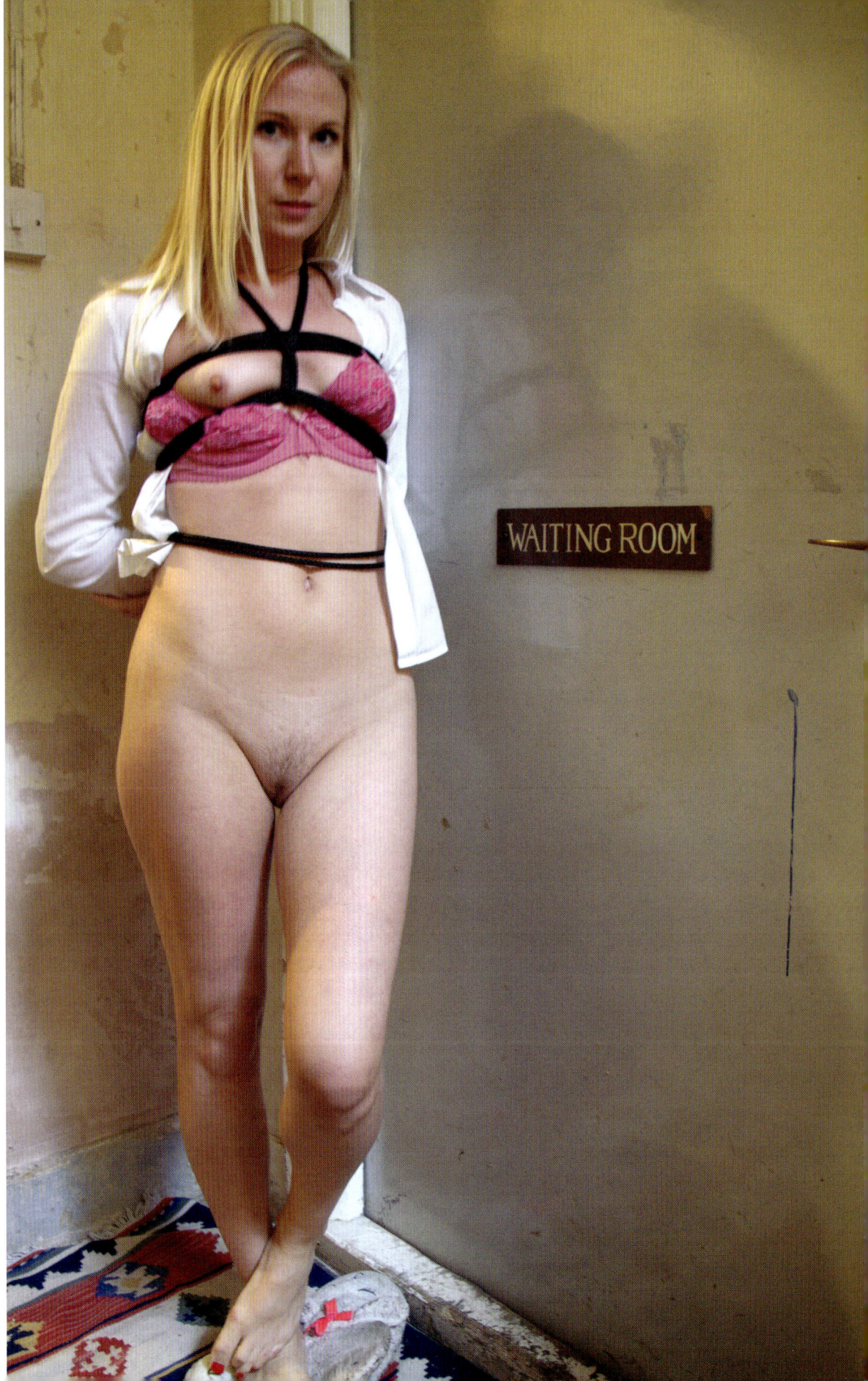

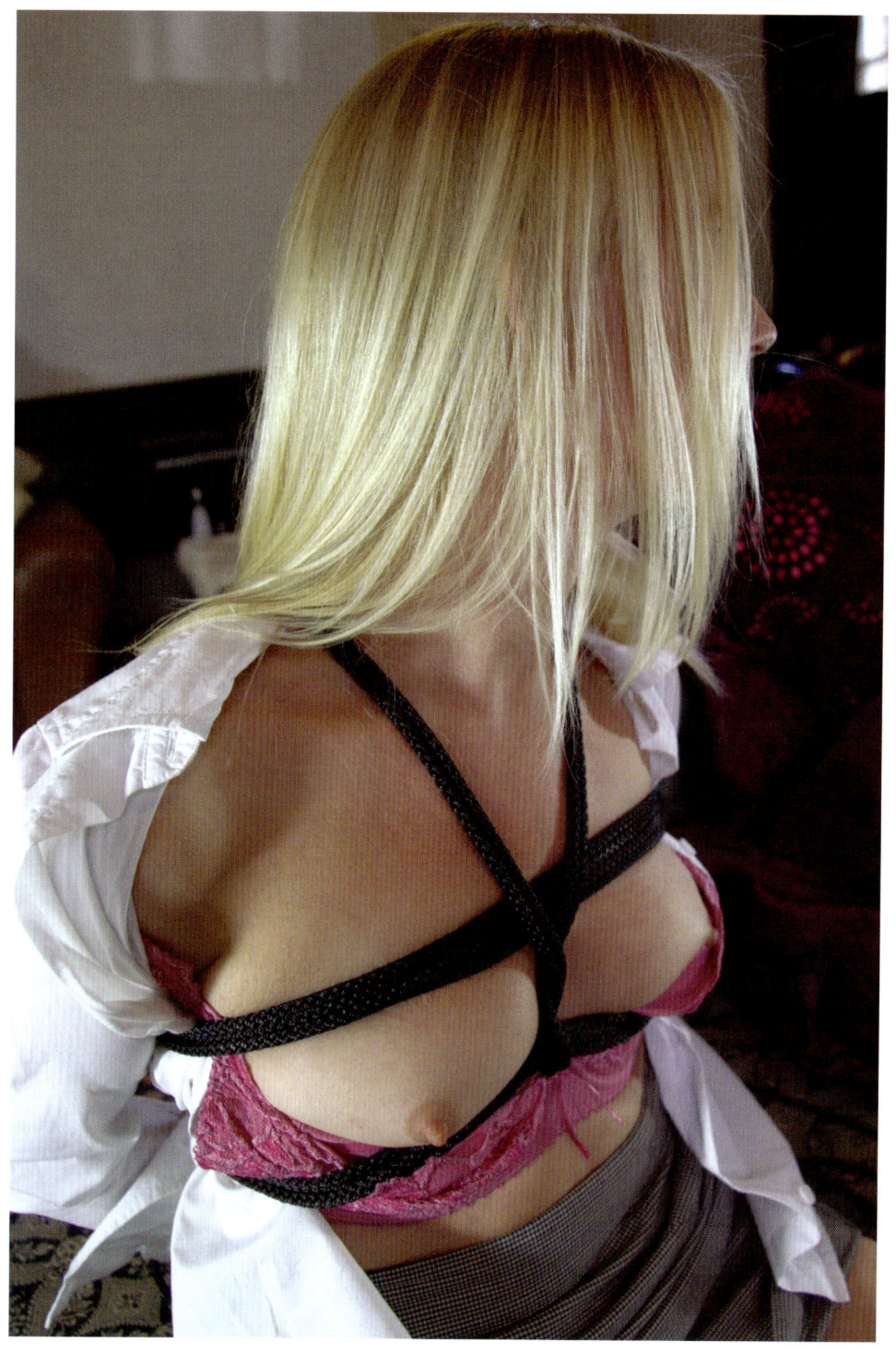

When she was naked and suspended in a storeroom full of builder's rubbish, she was completely liberated. The beauty of this woman is enhanced by the mess beneath her.

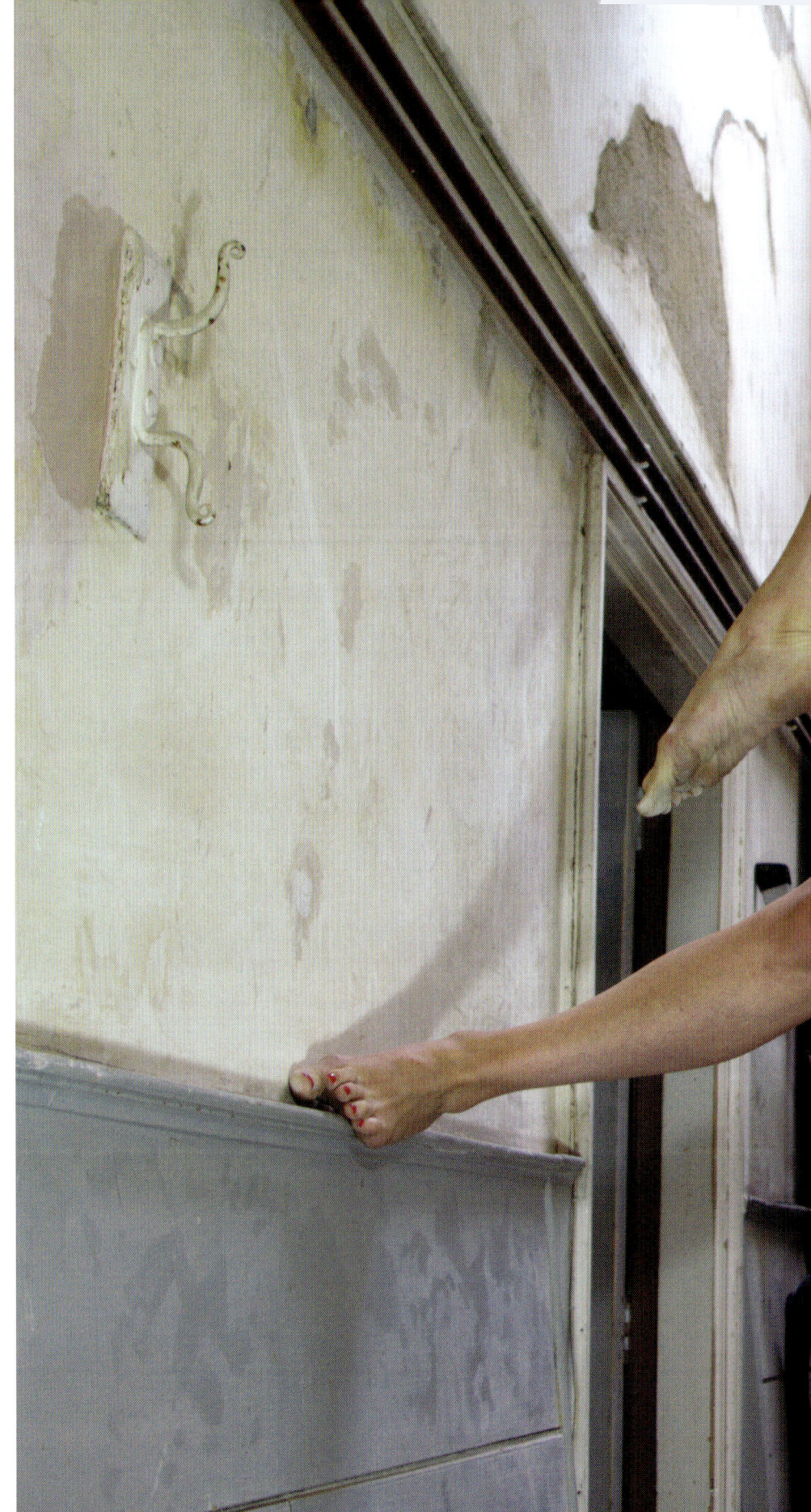

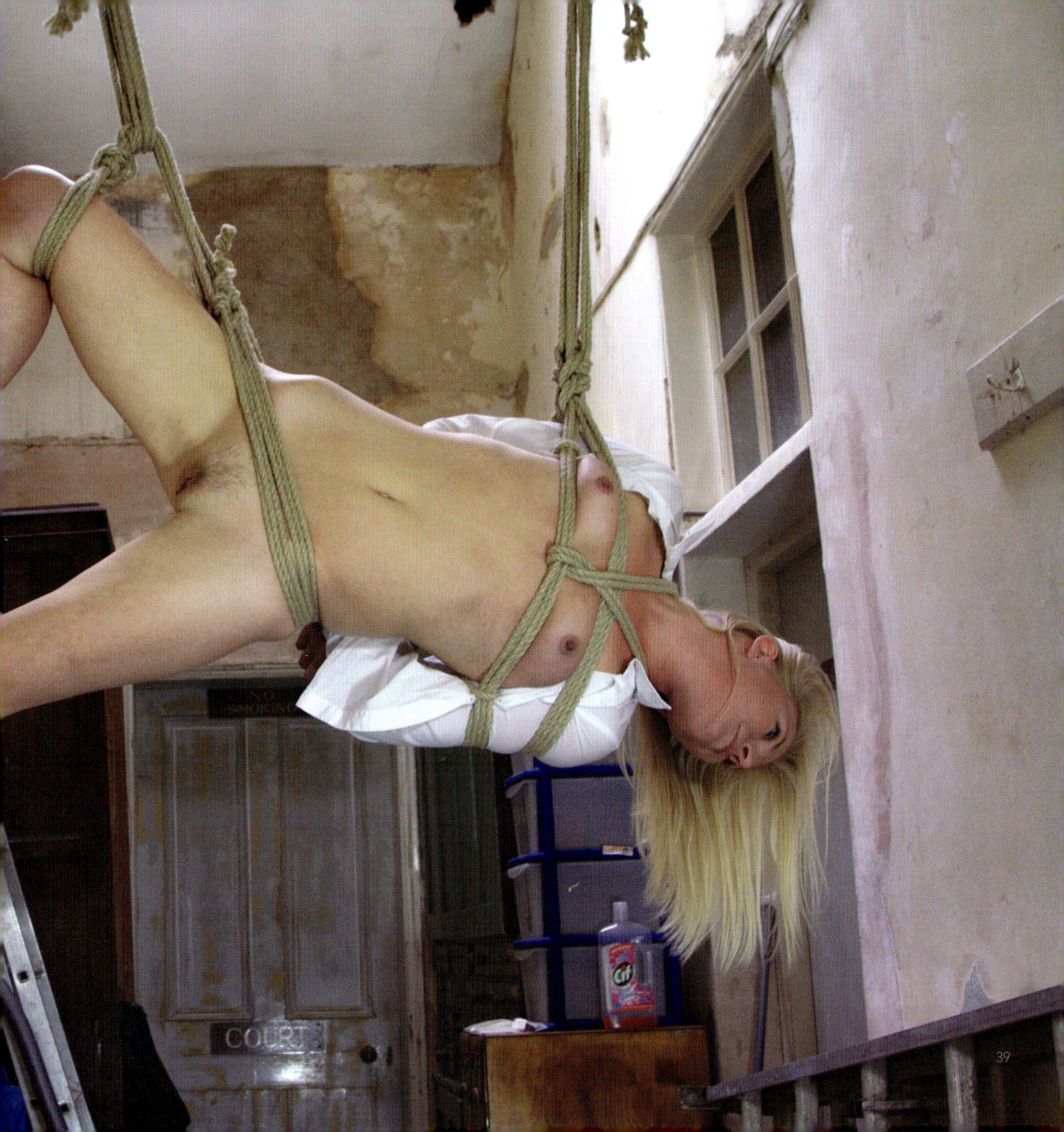

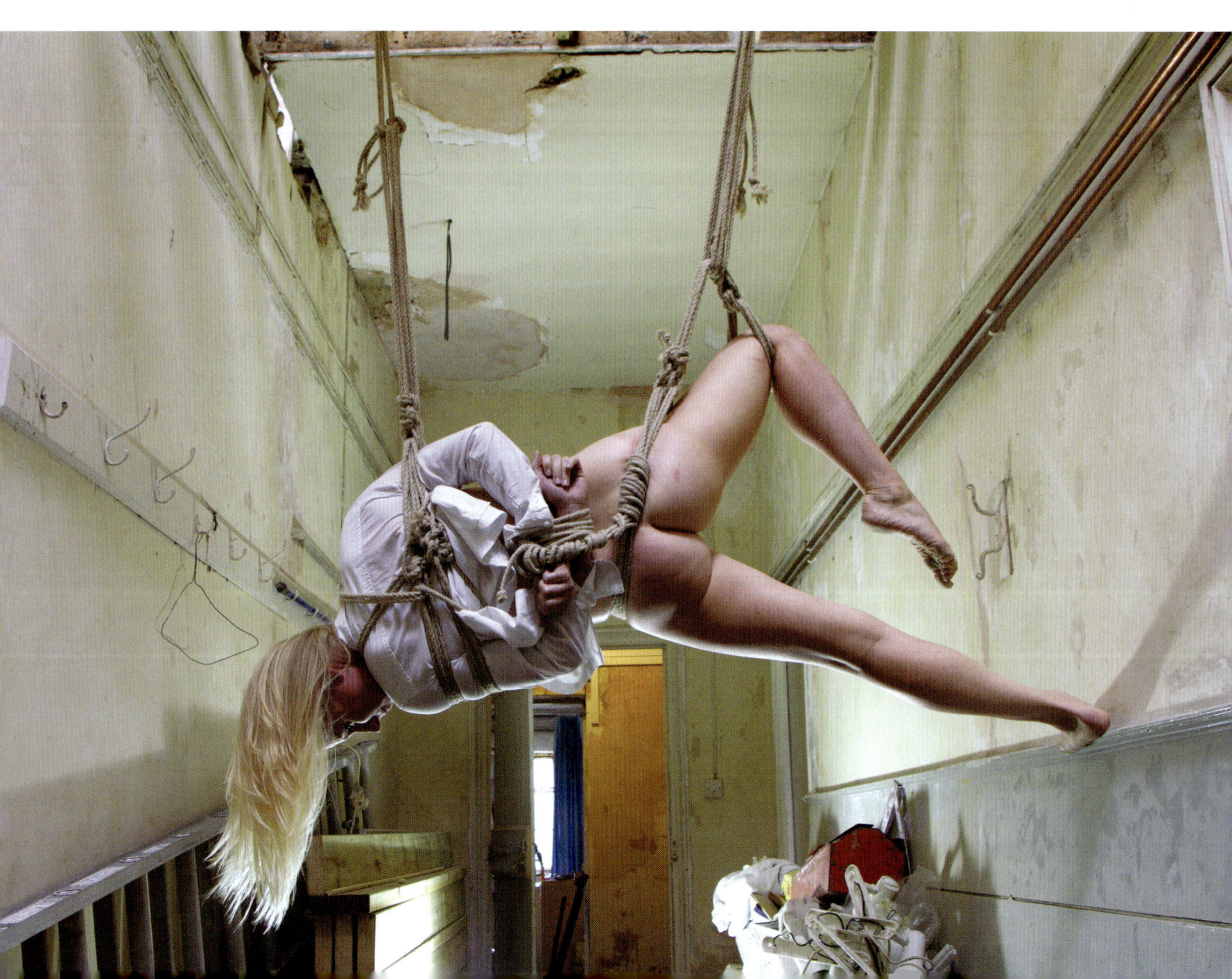

The nervous woman who arrived at the
Old Courthouse a few hours earlier was
experiencing the pleasure of the pain and
exposure of Kinbaku for the first time.

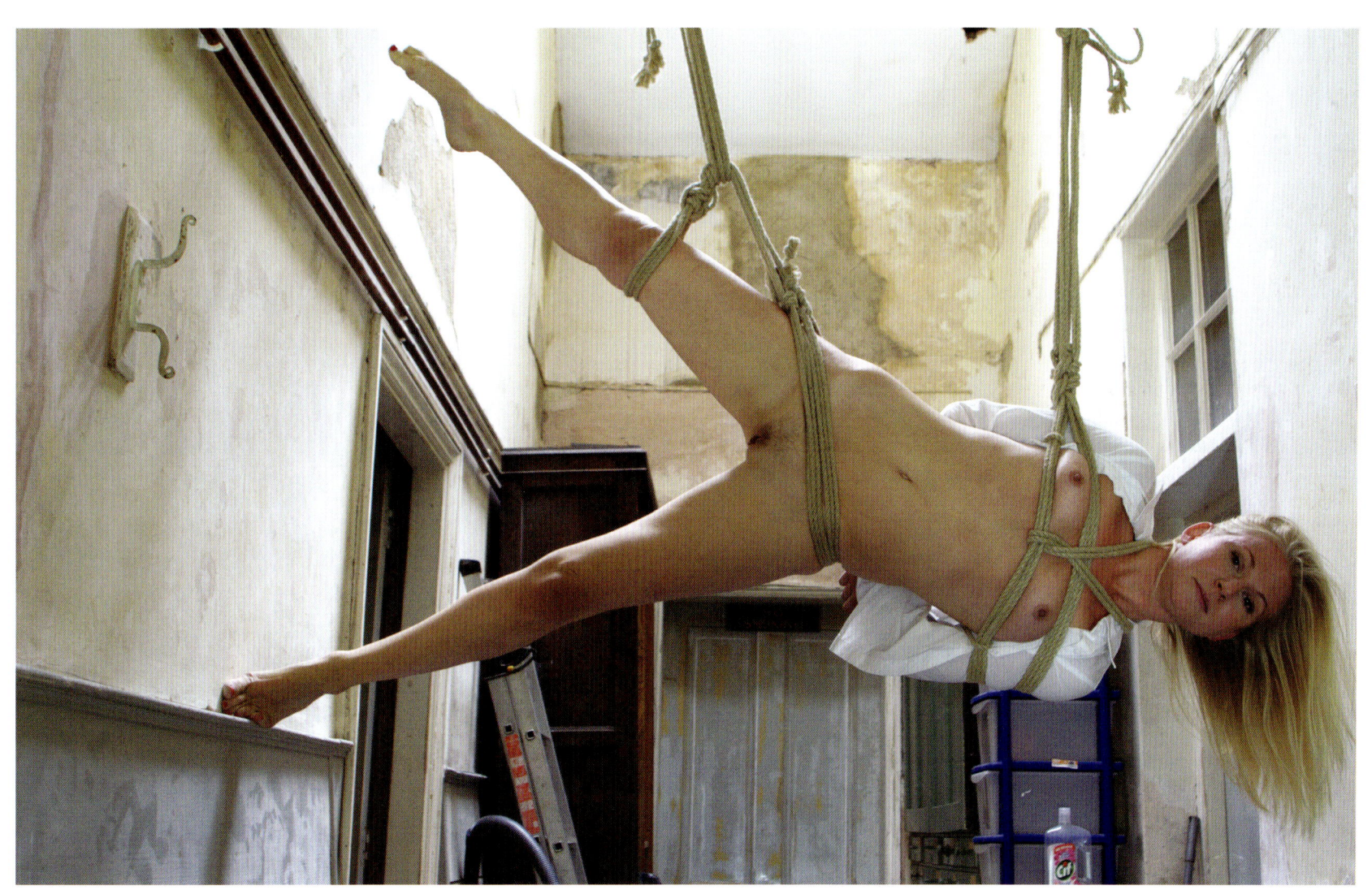

There was a special moment as she was tied and suspended: It was when I told her to let go. Up until then, she had at least one foot on a support, but there comes a time when the model has to let go and allow the ropes to take over.

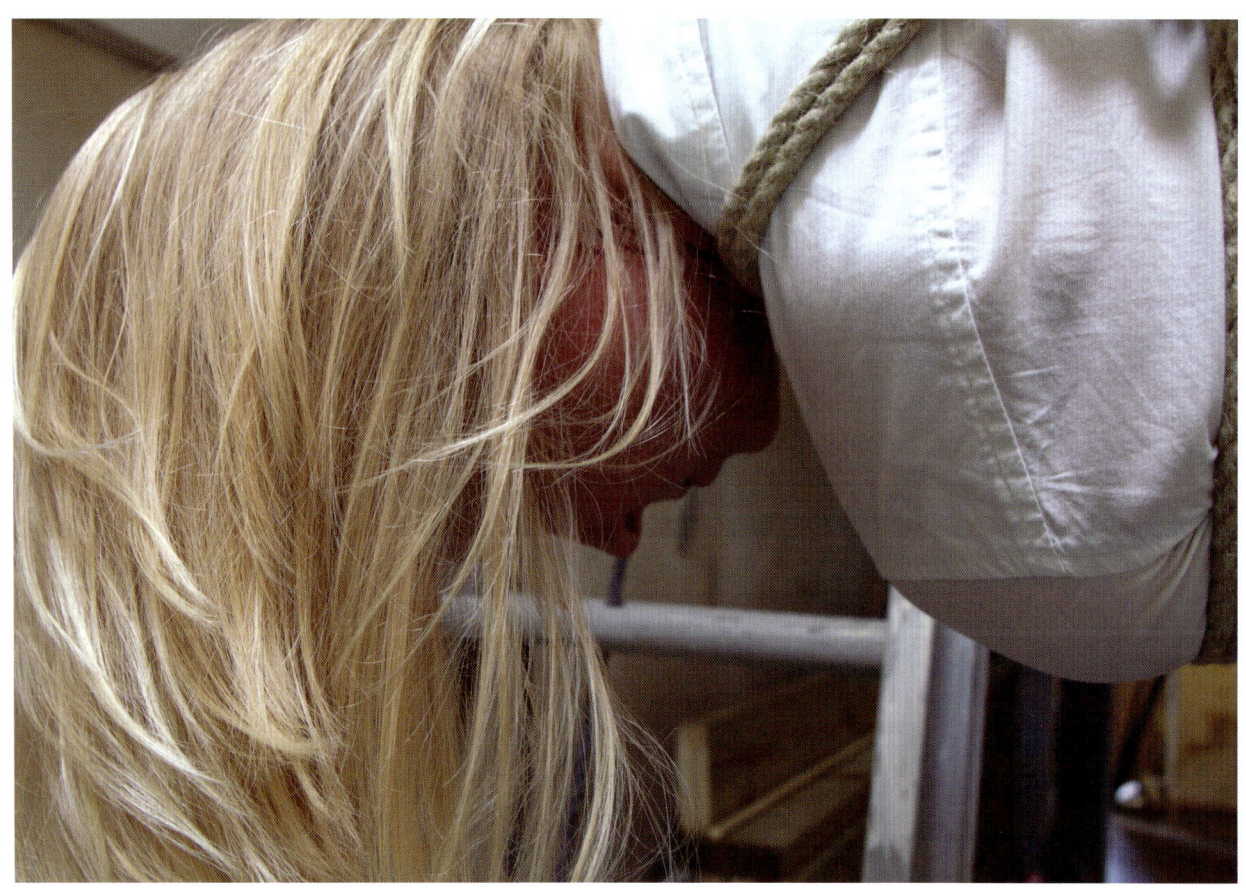

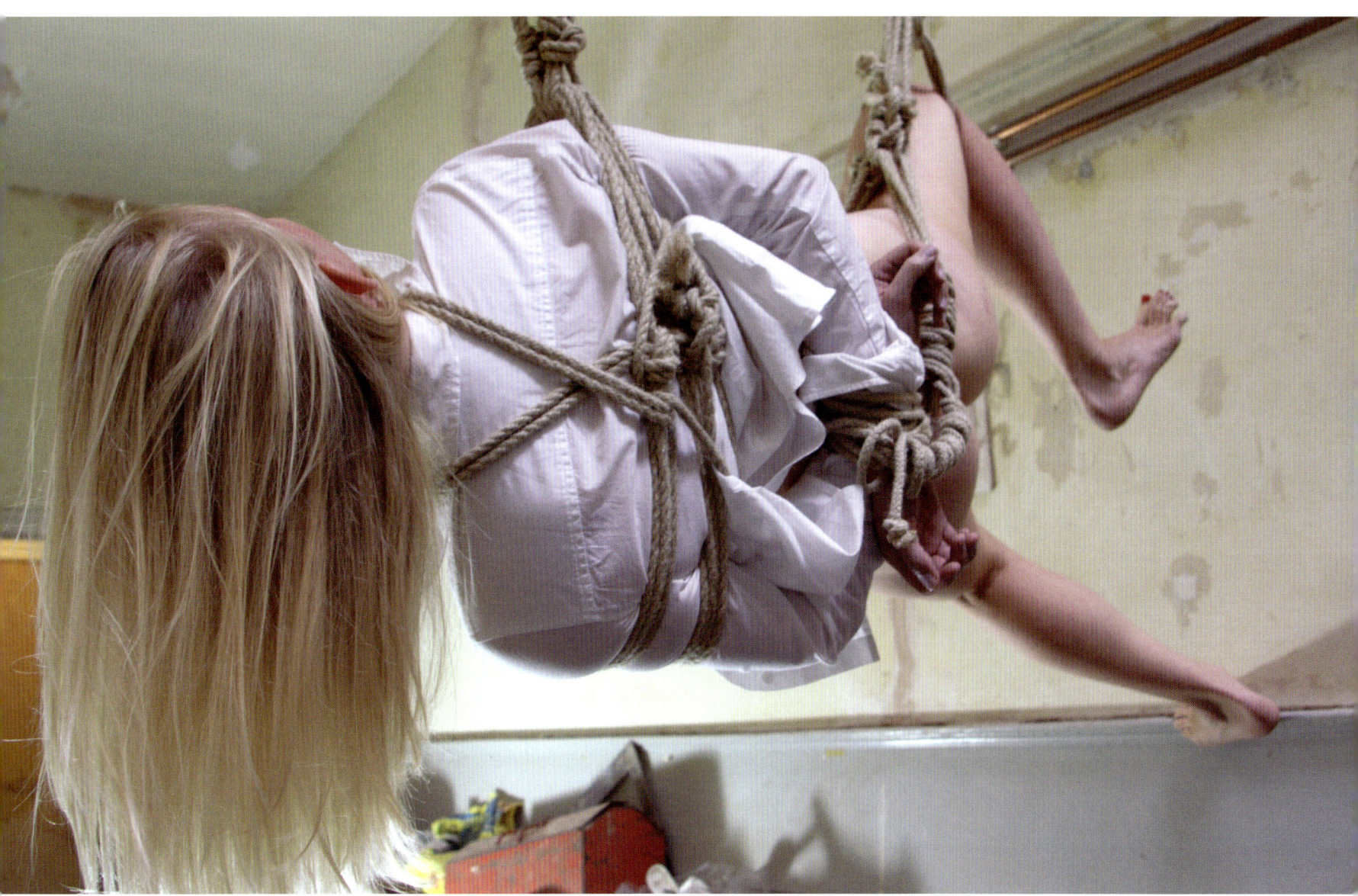

Then it is time to come back to Earth.

It is a time of exhilaration. A great feeling.

At the time, we can sense the new

pleasures that Sam had tasted.

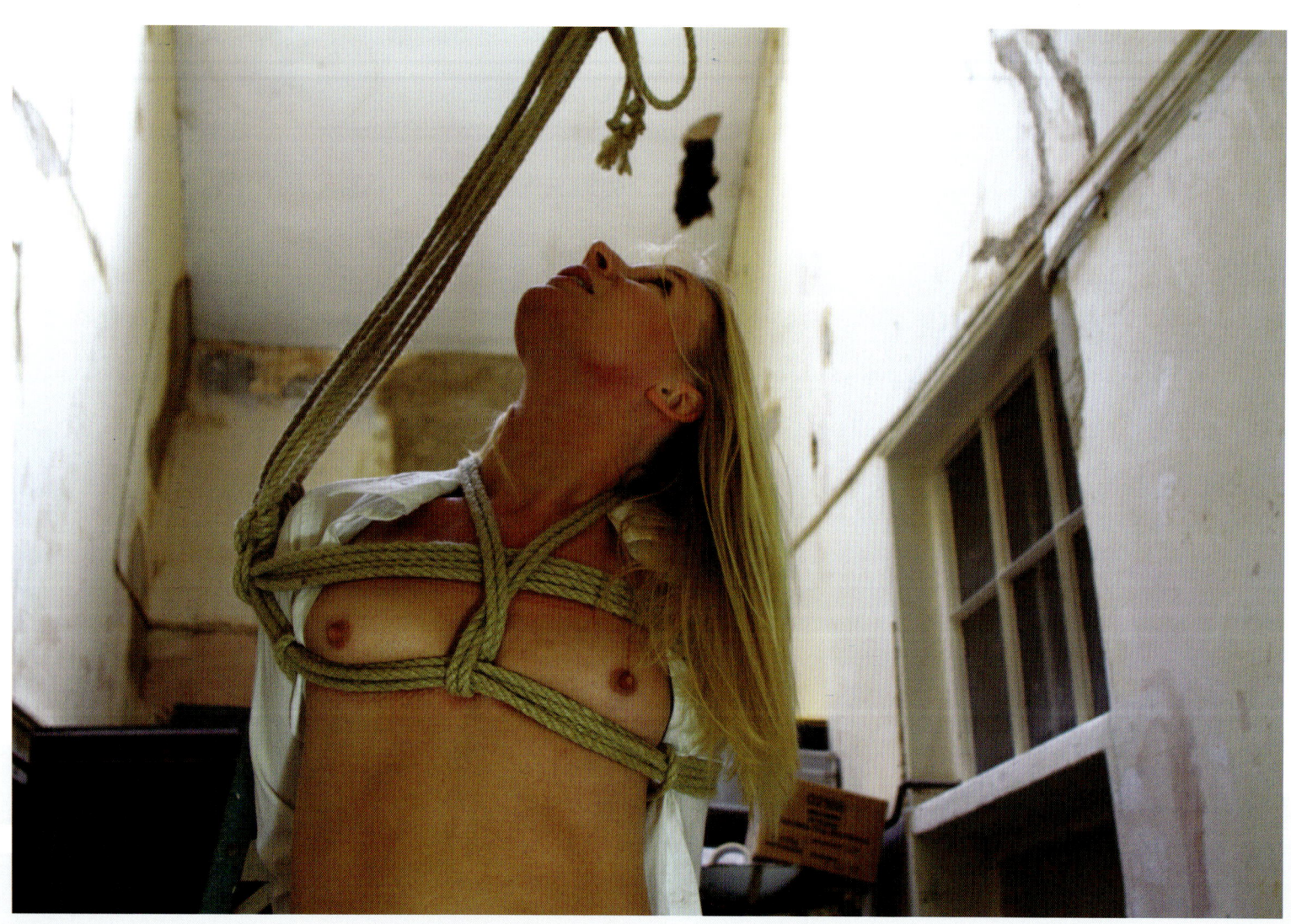

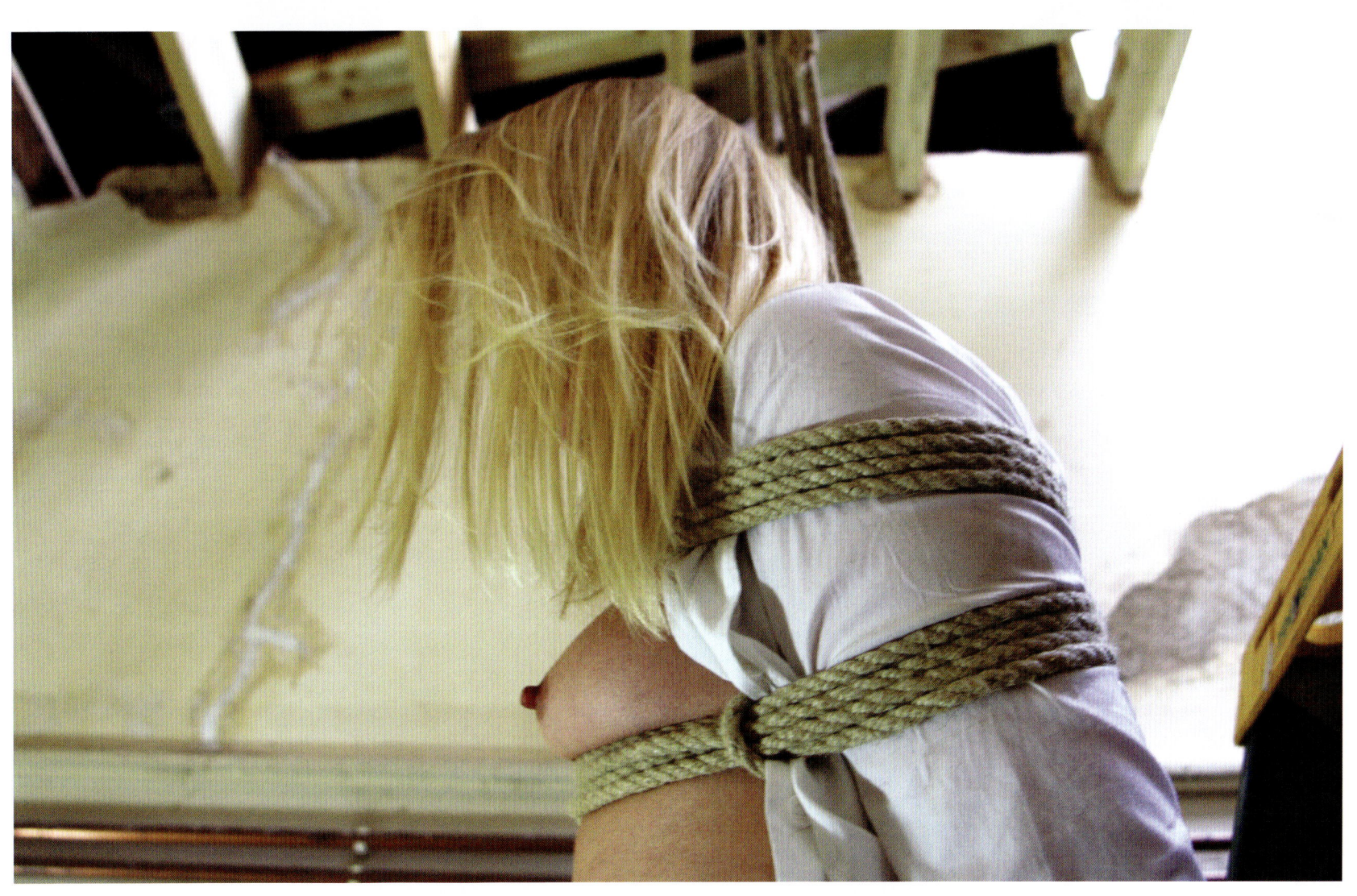

There is no rush to escape.
Maybe it is like climbing a mountain with
its reward of being above the world. There
is a touch of melancholy when it is time to
go back down.

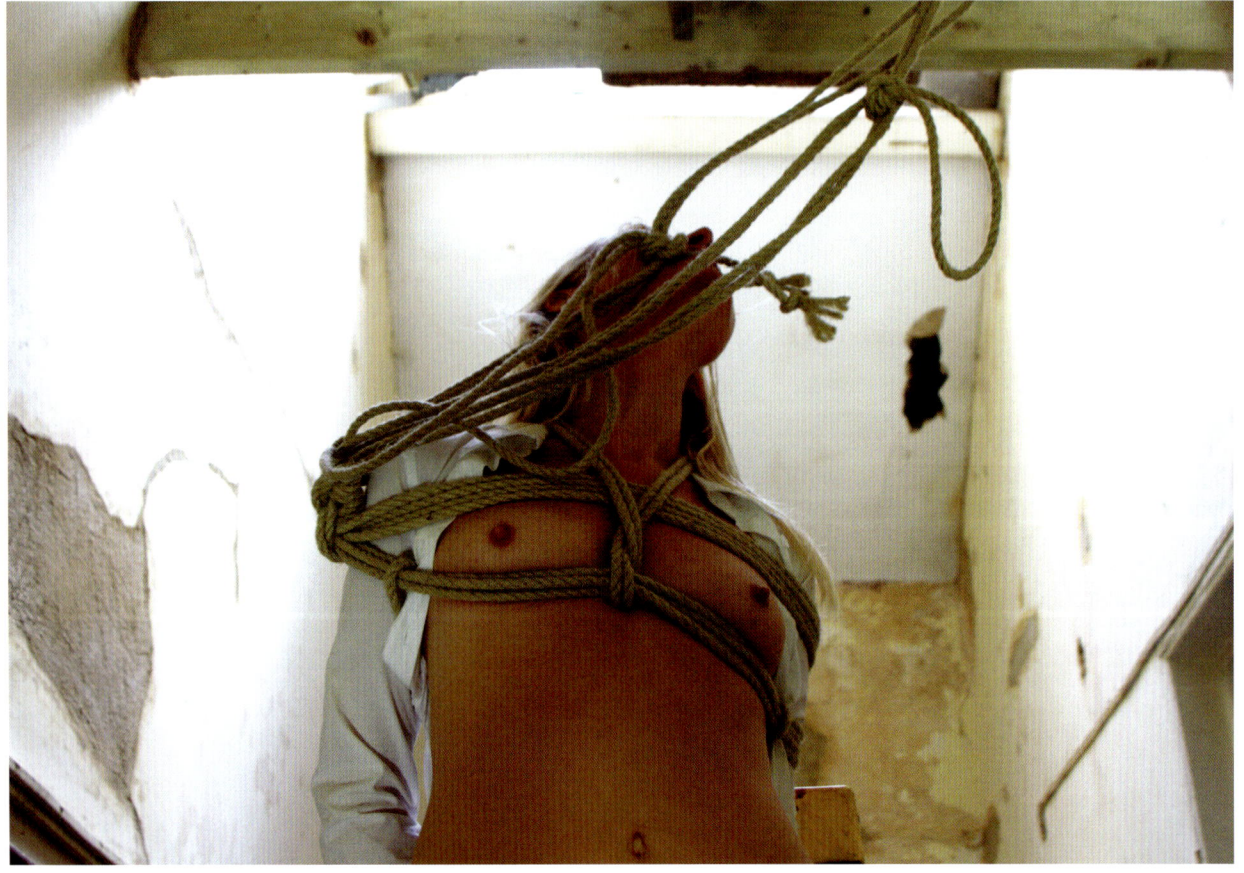

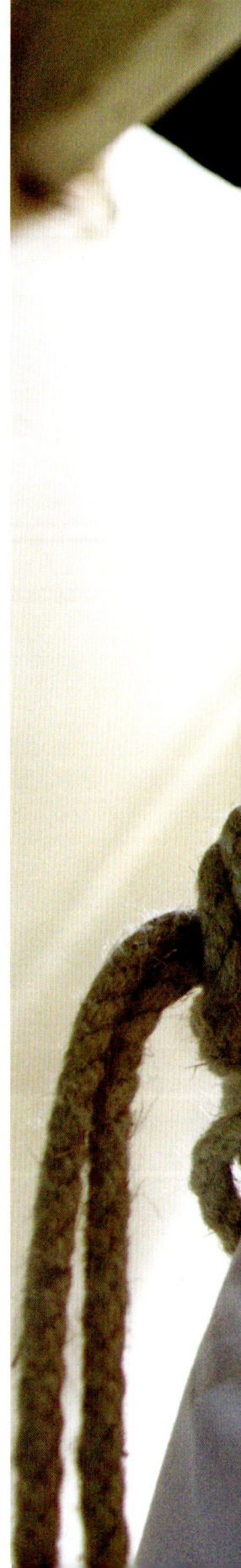

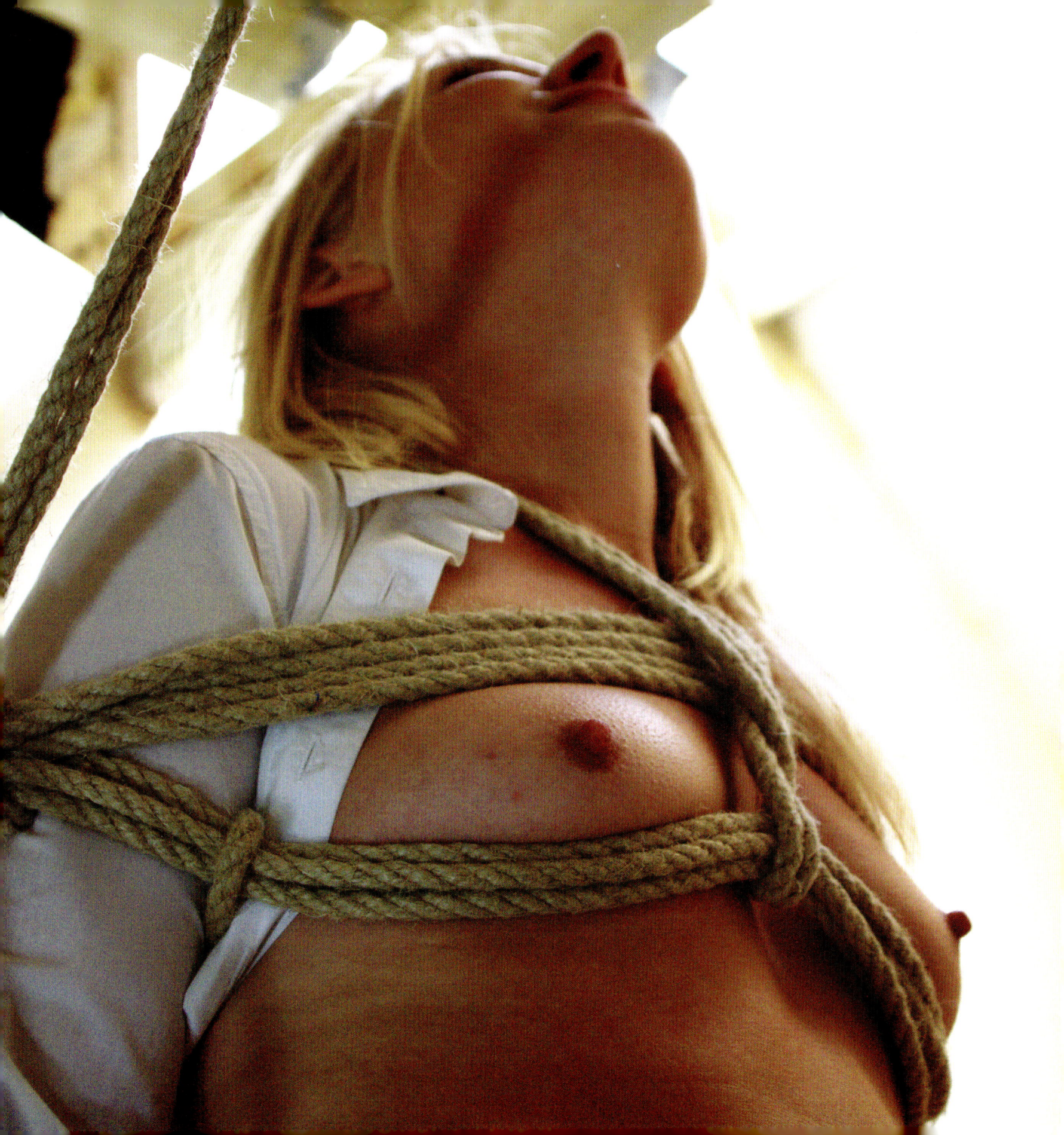

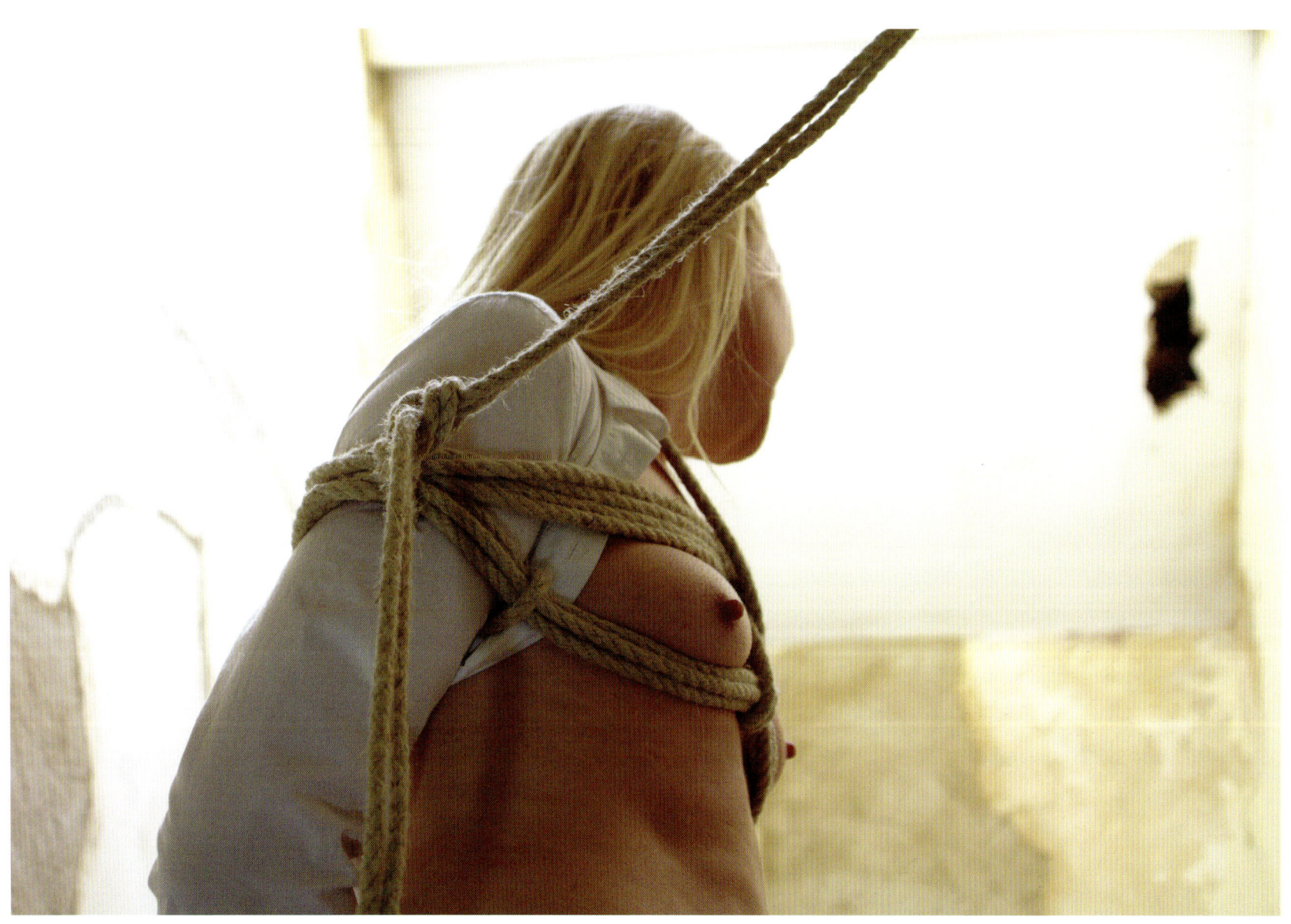

And so I win freedom
from all that controls me.
I'm proud in my body
and free to feel pleasure.
By tight tied restriction
I'm freed for completion.

The friction is lessened.
The ropes are all loosened
The pressure releases
its build up of steam.

My body relaxes
my needs they are sated,
my senses are quietened
to whisper from scream.

I return to the real world
the real but mundane world
the transports of pleasure
deposit me here.

The now is the present
I'm back to the normal
but always I'll know
the place where I've been.

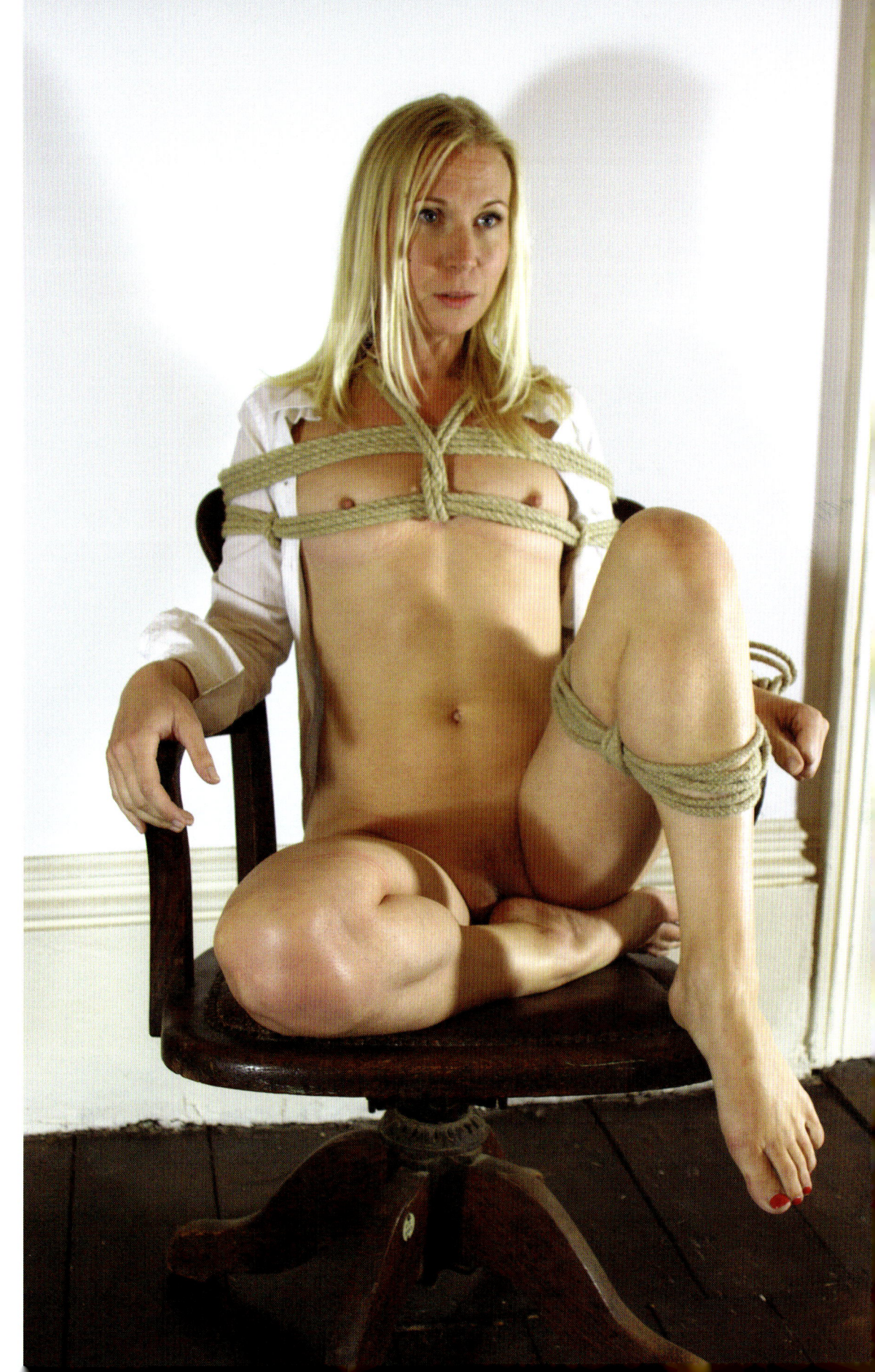

I've been hung
and.I've swung
like ripe fruit
on life's tree,
been open and helpless
and totally free.

I've been tied
and been bound
to be handled
however
restrained and constrained
and now I'm just me.

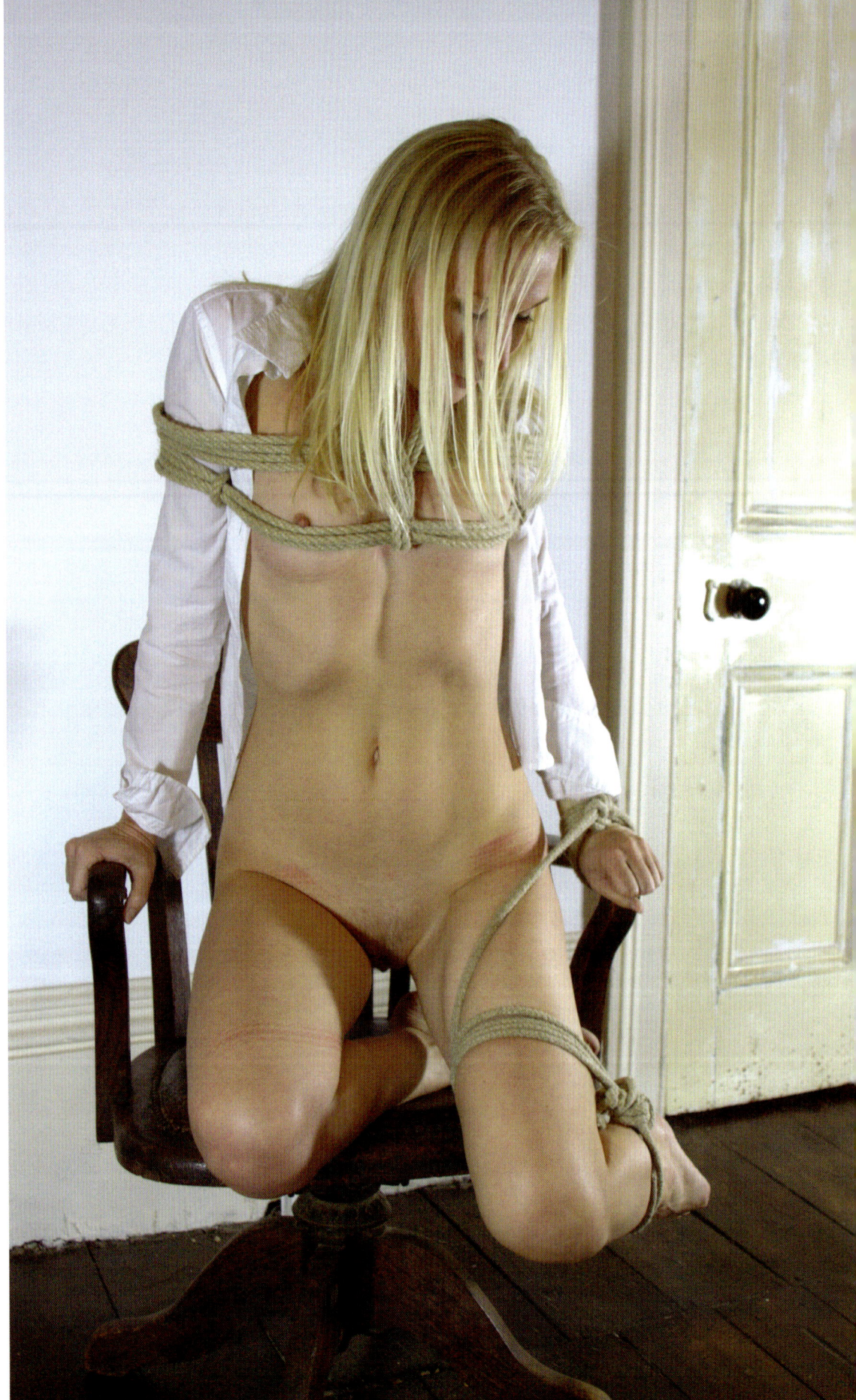

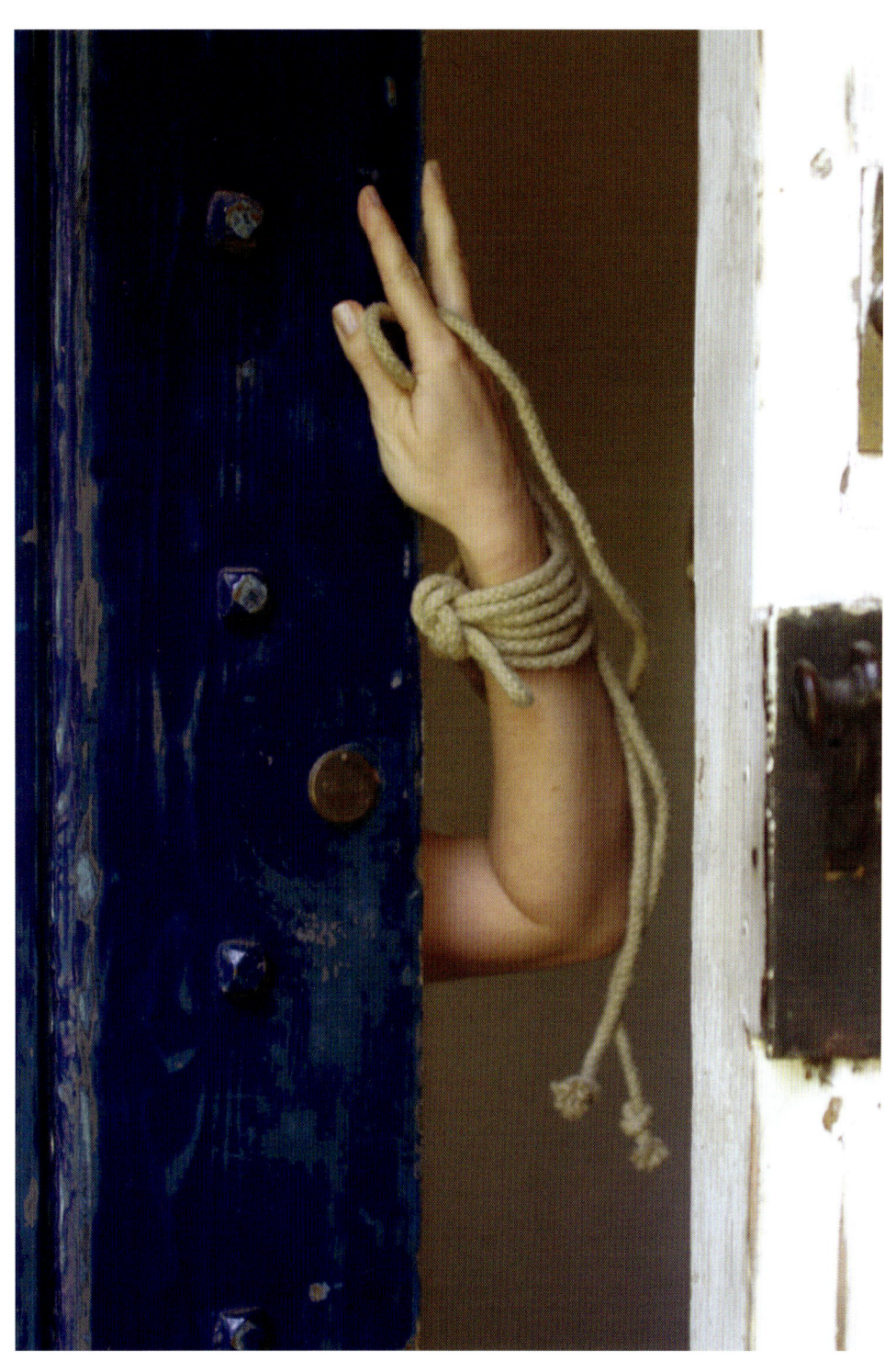

Chapter 4

Happy Friday

Taken from a performance by Miumi-U in Tokyo

Photography by Ero o-ji

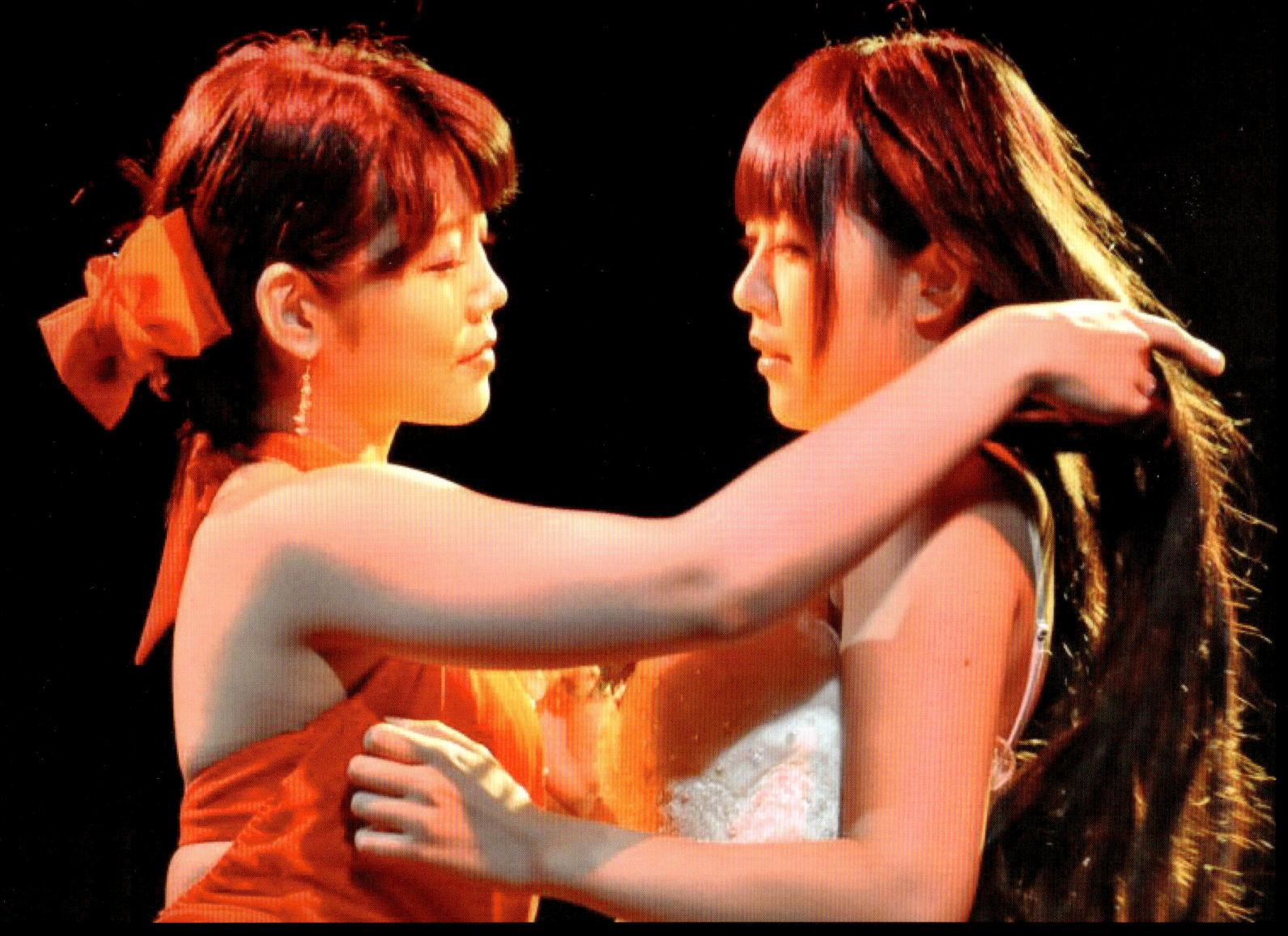

I became interested in Kinbaku because it was simply beautiful. I do like women and it is a way of having complete attention and ownership of a woman during the performance.

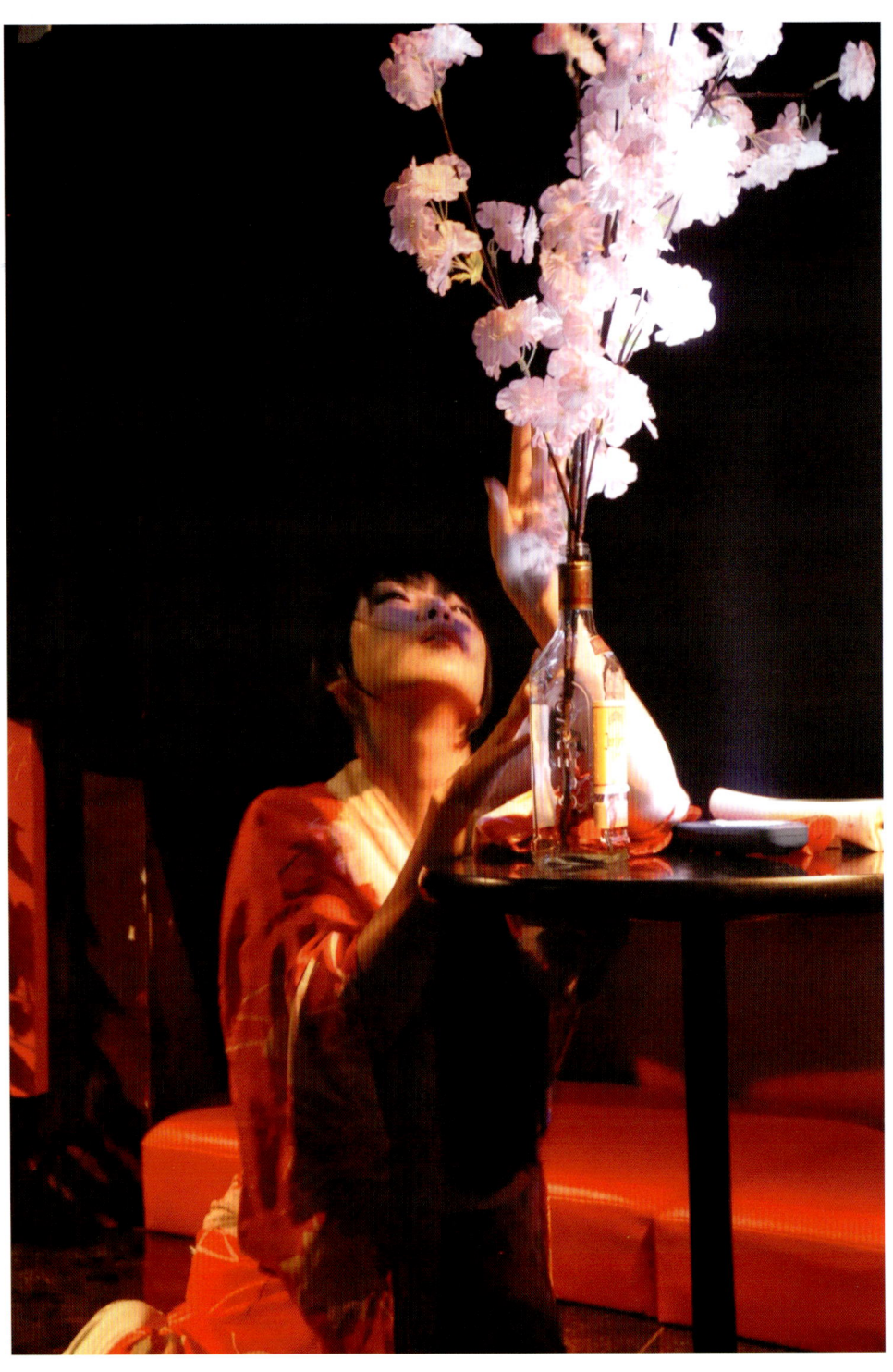

緊縛を始めた理由…それは単純に綺麗だったから…元々
女の子が好きな私は、昔好きだった子を独占したくて縄
を始めたのかもしれません。

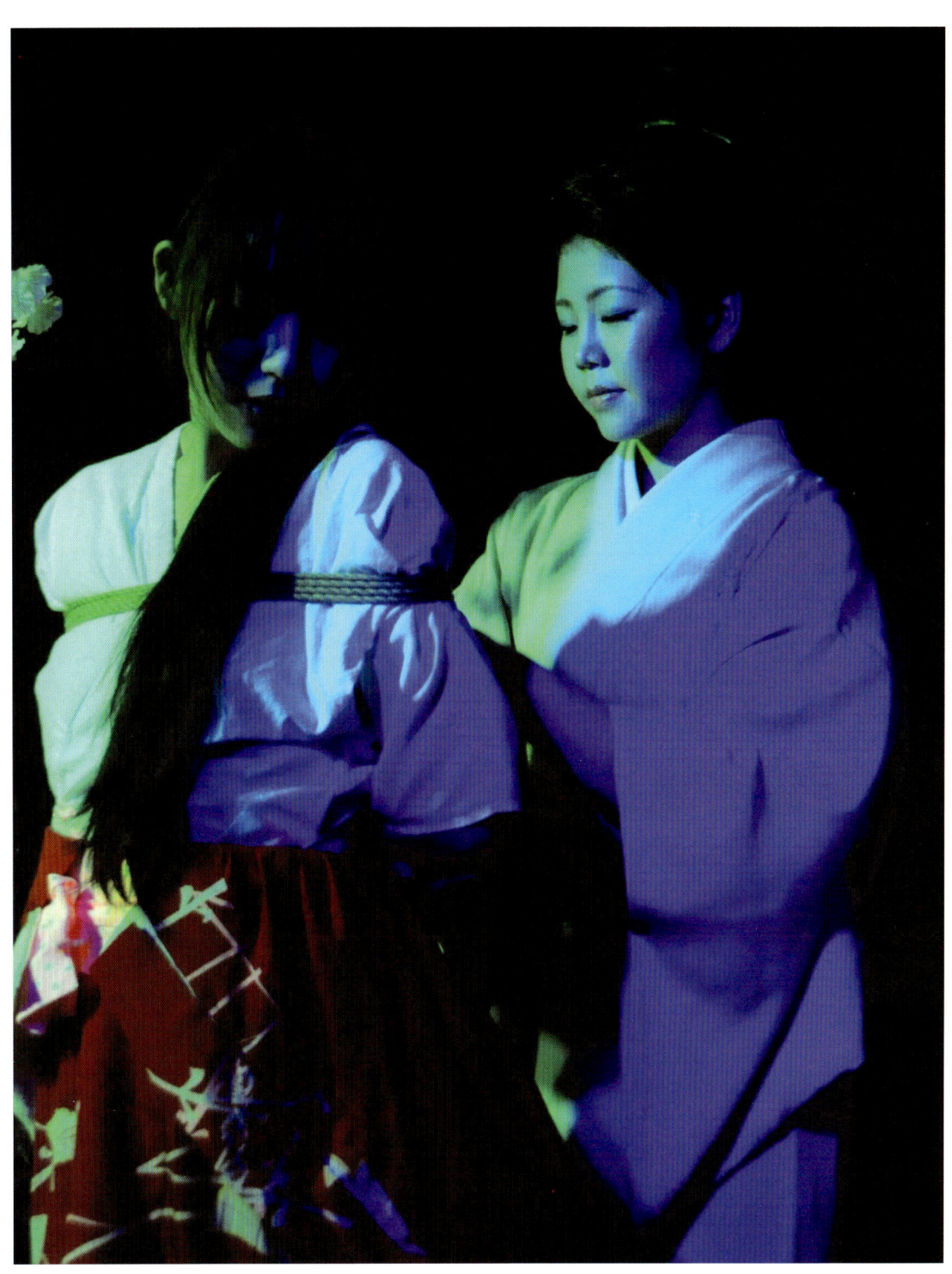

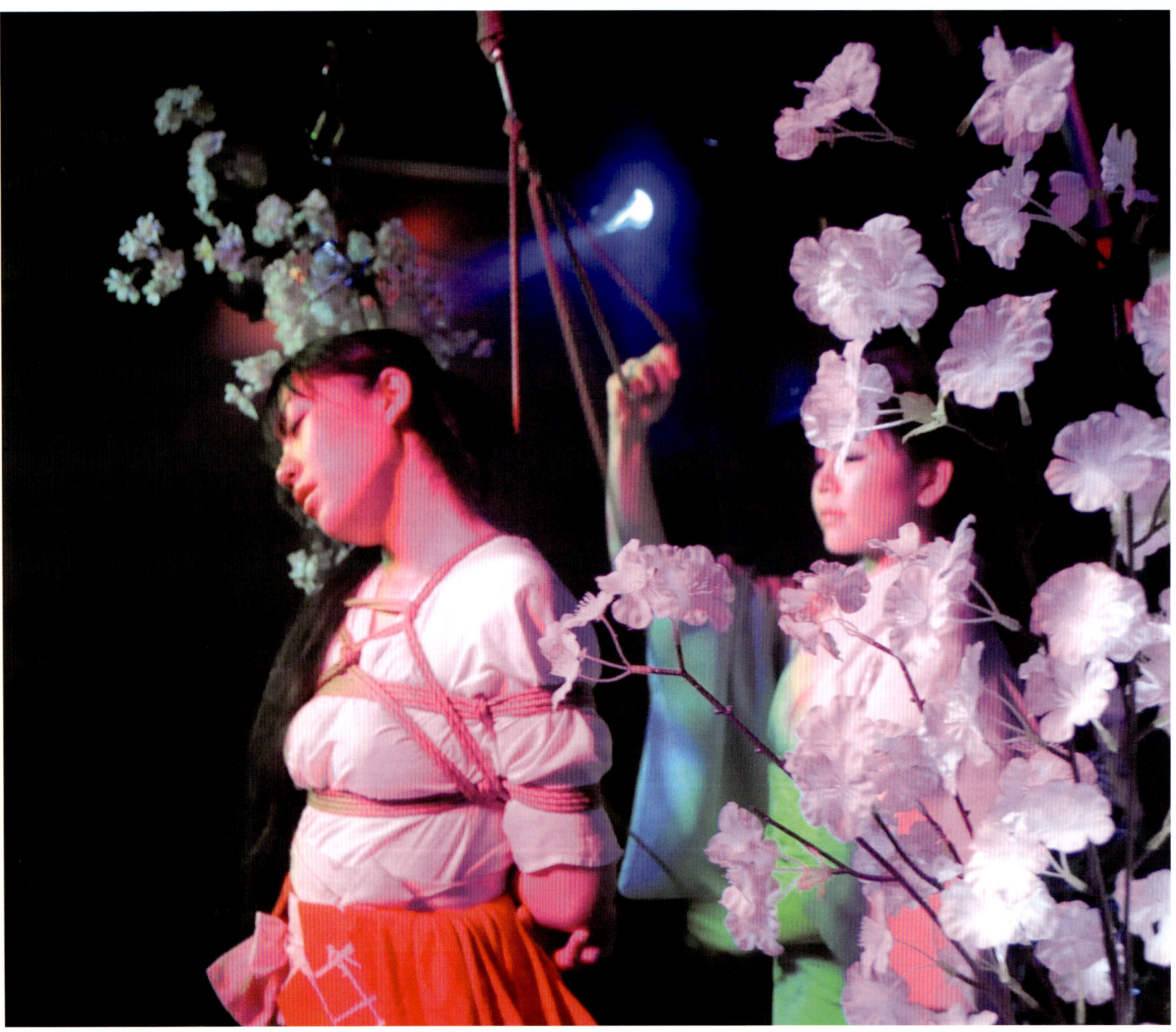

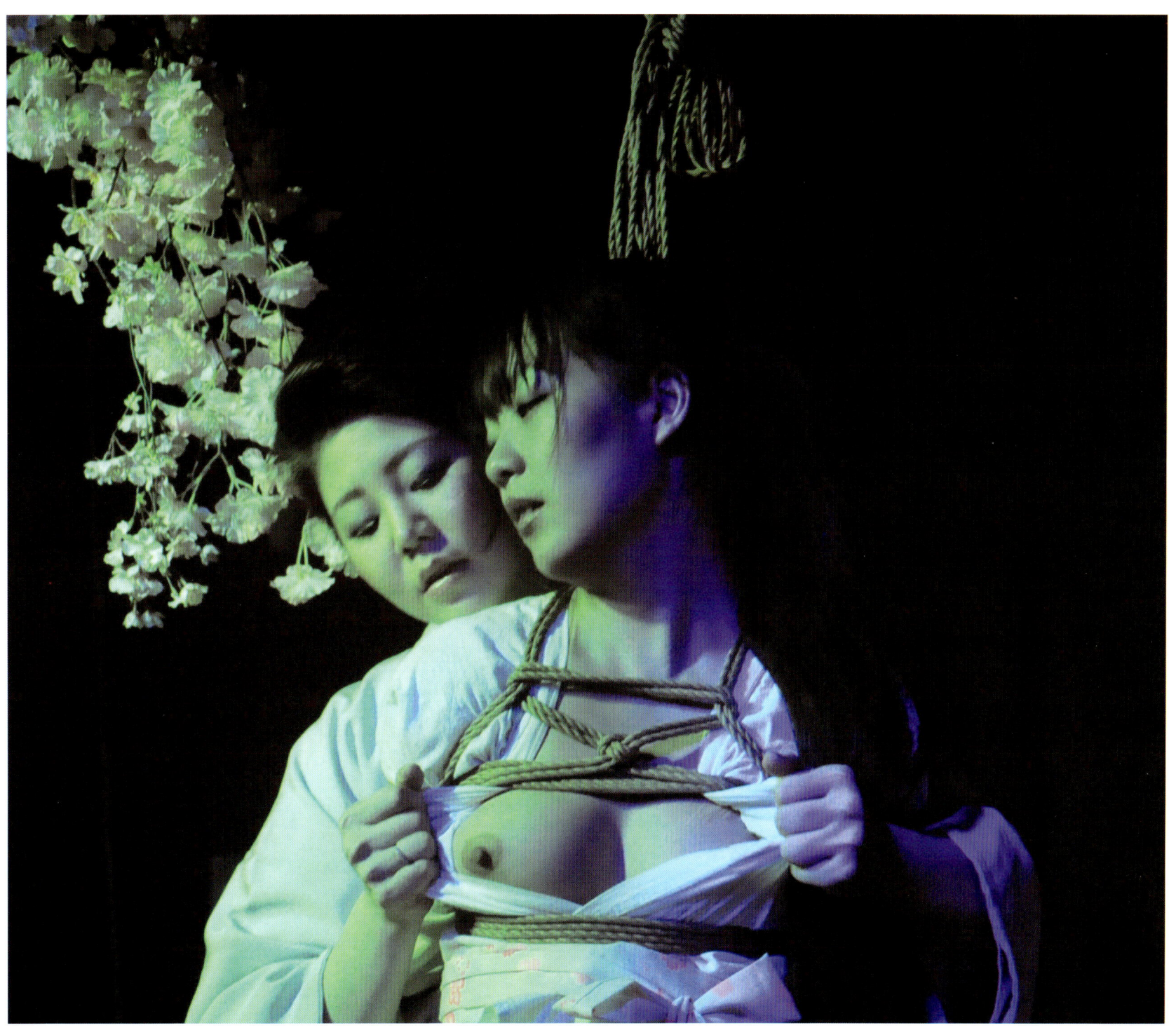

I like the time taken in tying up the model. I can think... "When I am tying, you are mine" because I have a longing to completely own her. It makes me very happy when I tie her and she gives her heart to me and she gives me her smile.

So, I think only of her and she thinks only of me when we do Kinbaku. I think that is Kinbaku's fascination.

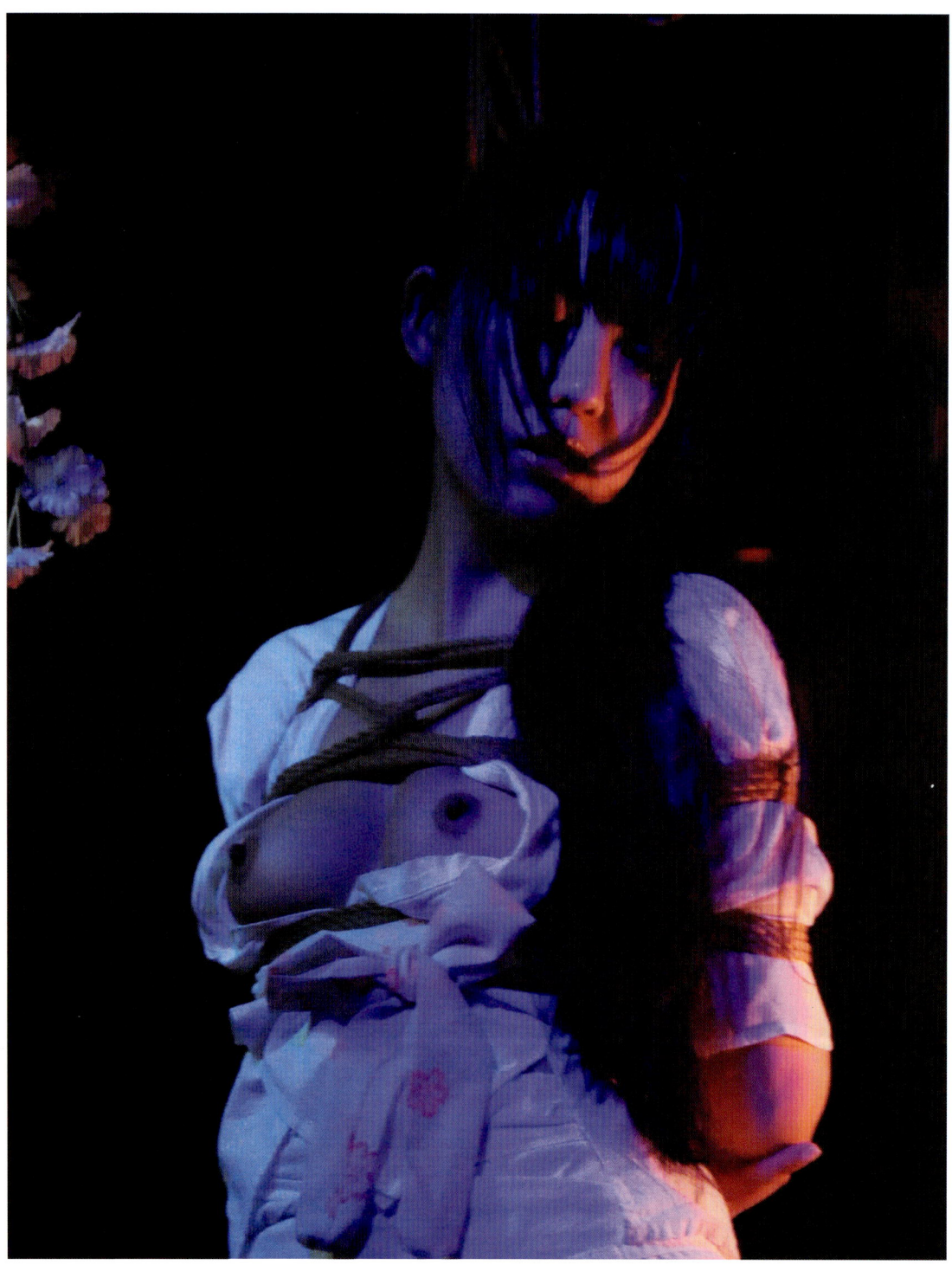

私は独占欲が人より強く、〞縛っている間だけは私だけ
の彼女〞と思えるその時間が大好きなのと、私の縛った
縄によって心を解放してくれたり笑顔になってくれる女
性達を見ると私も嬉しい。

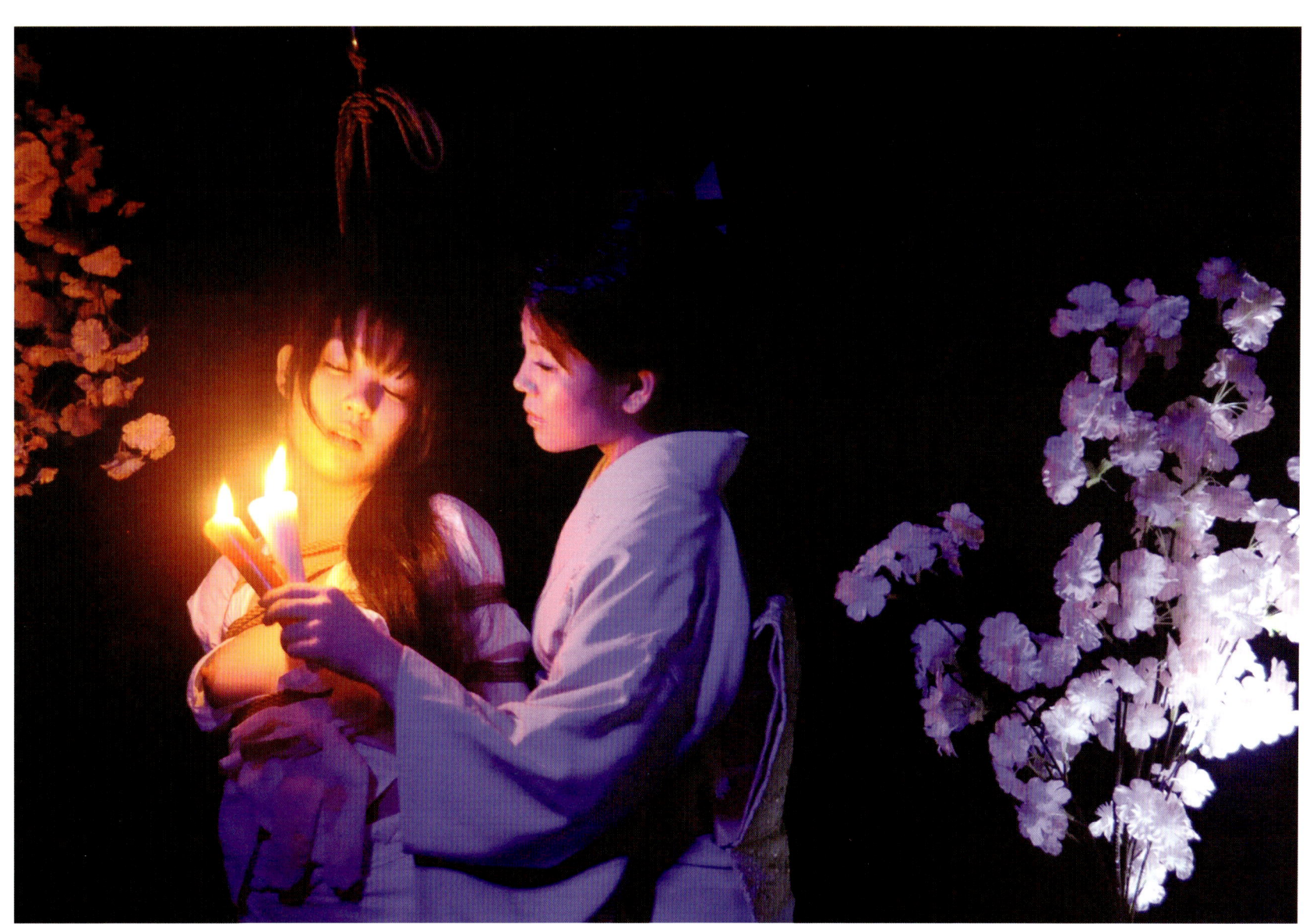

I can't take over control of her like a
mistress. I always have a hard fight in
my mind about this thought. But I enjoy
every moment that we do Kinbaku together.

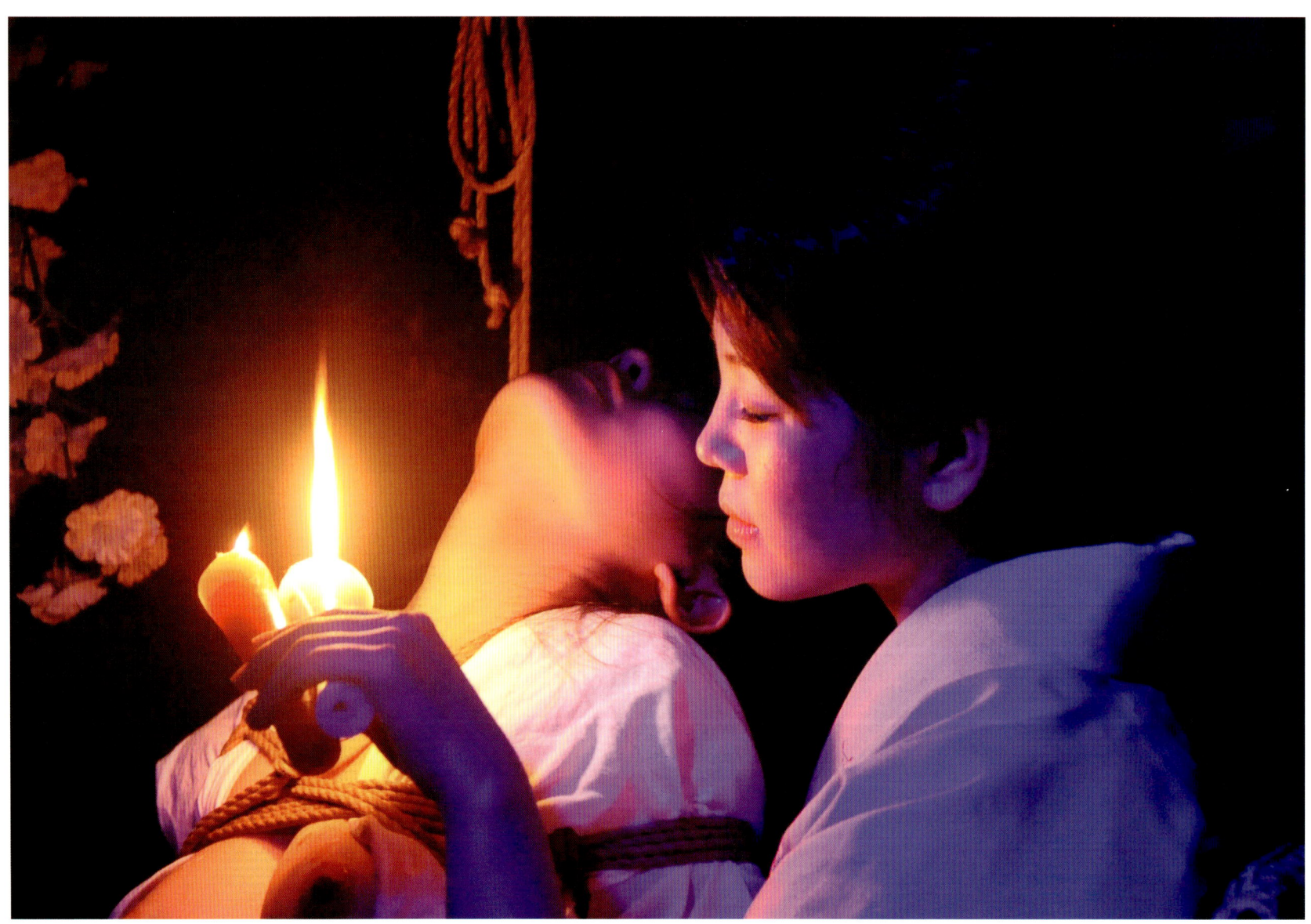

好きな女の子を縛っている間、私は、その子だけを想い、

縛られている彼女は、私だけを見て見つめて考えてくれる…

緊縛の魅力の一つだと思っています。

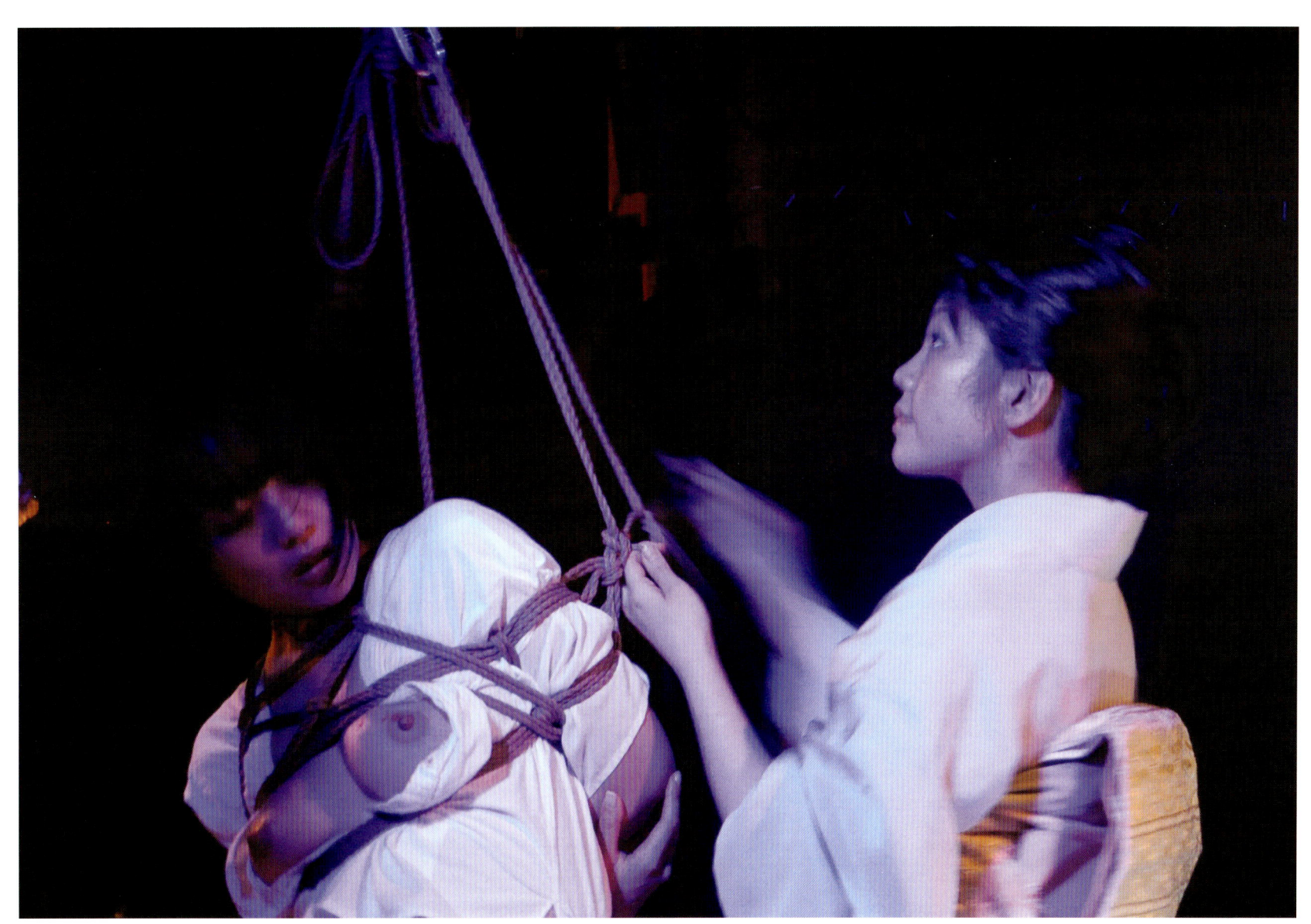

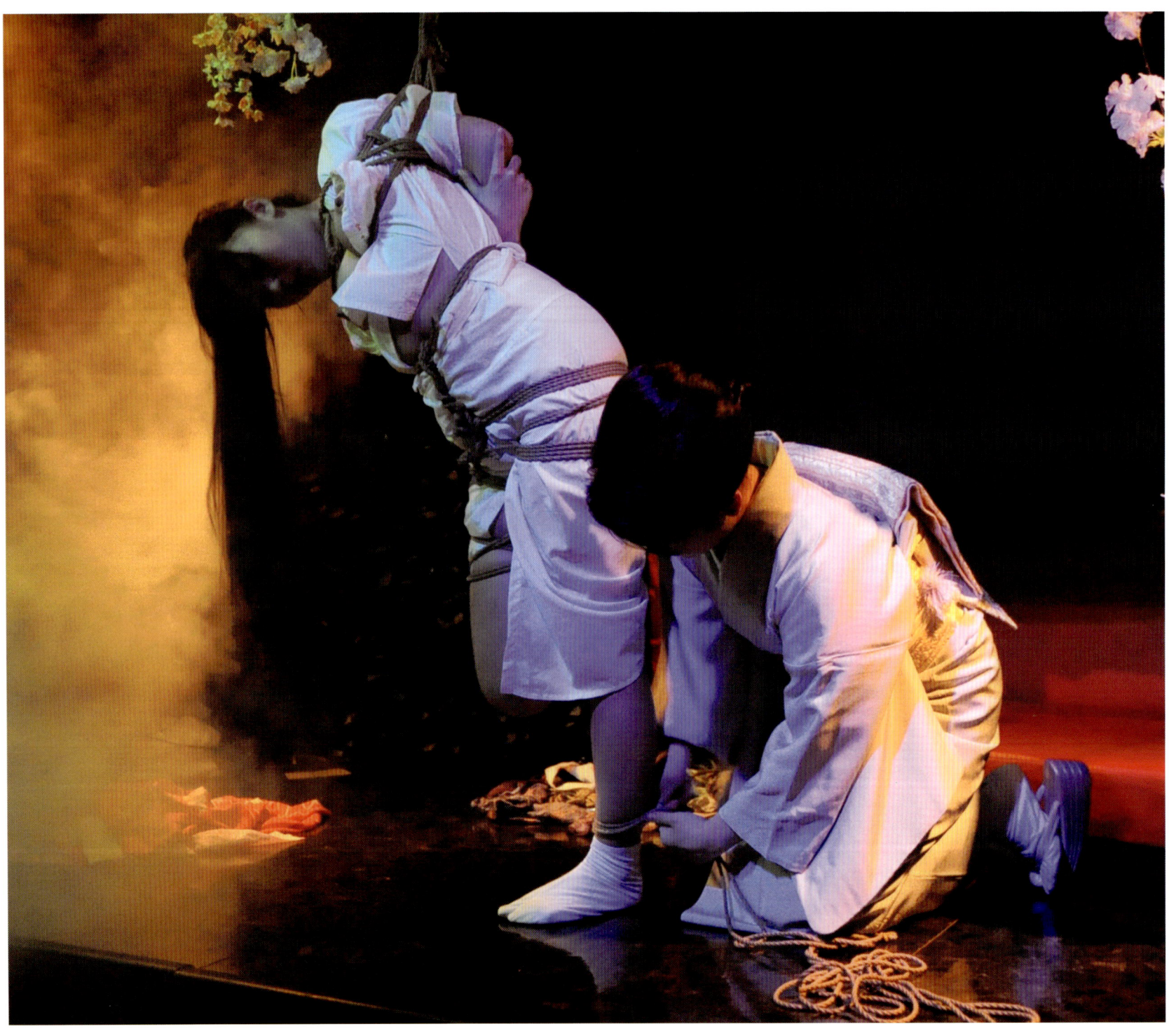

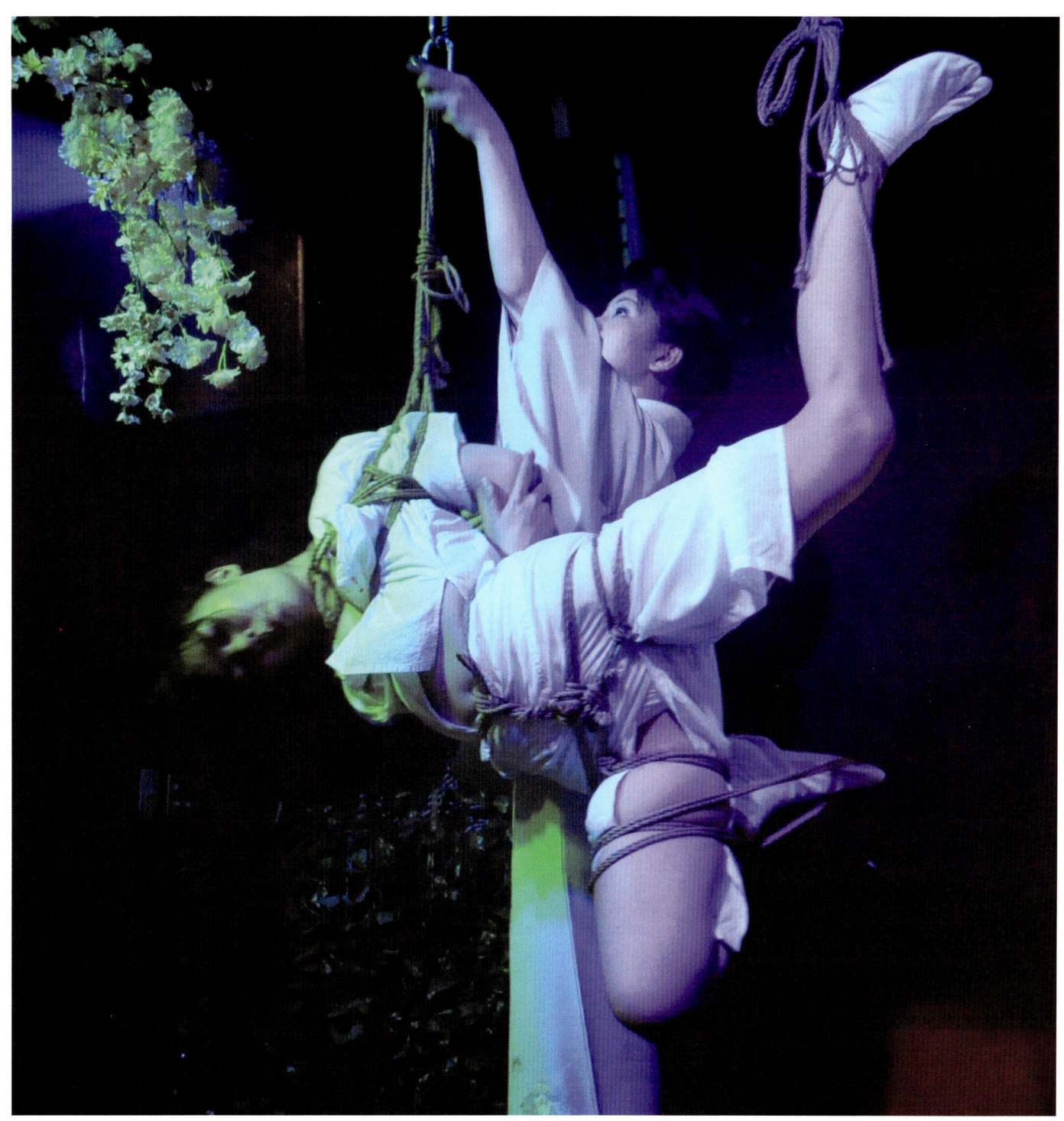

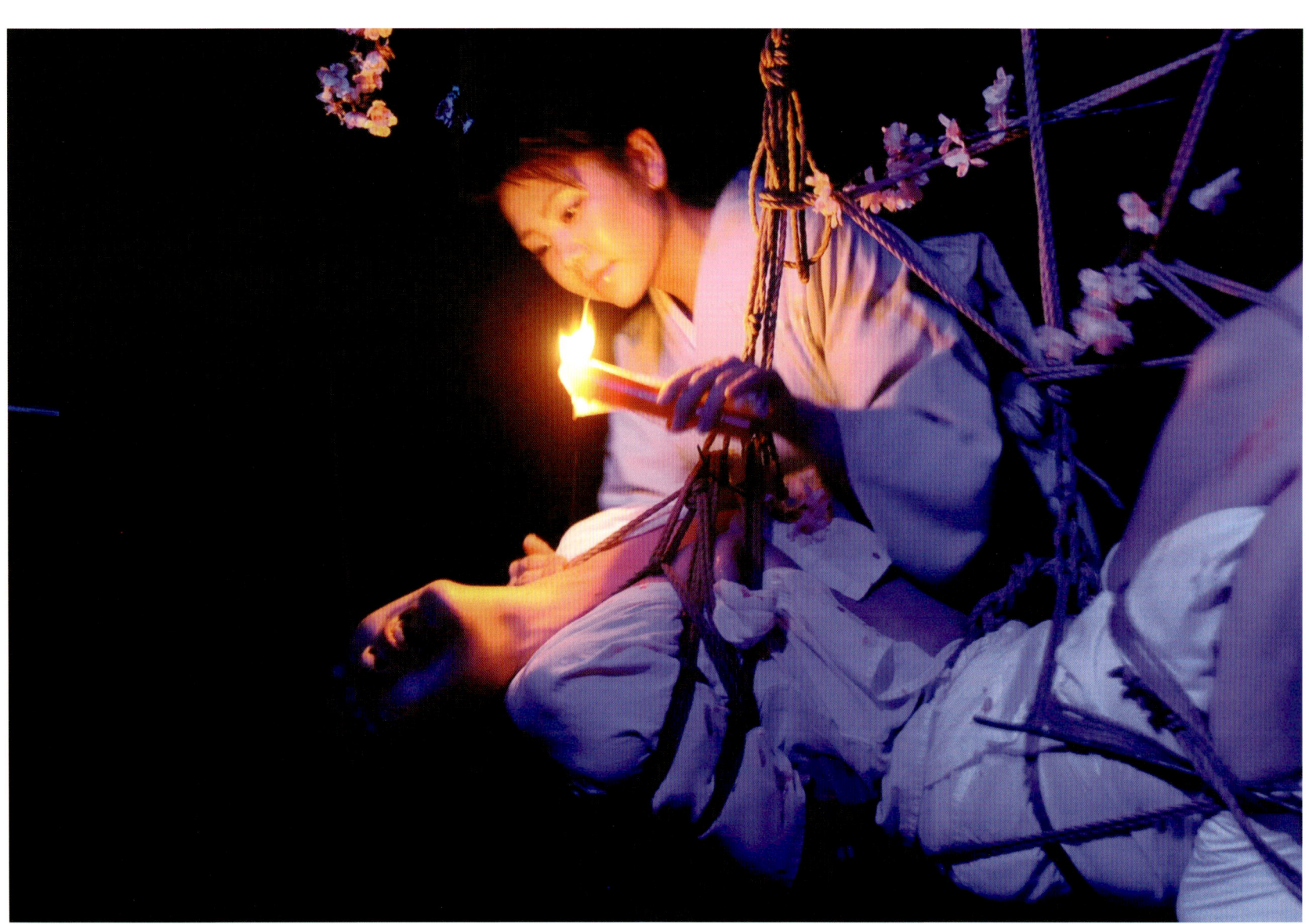

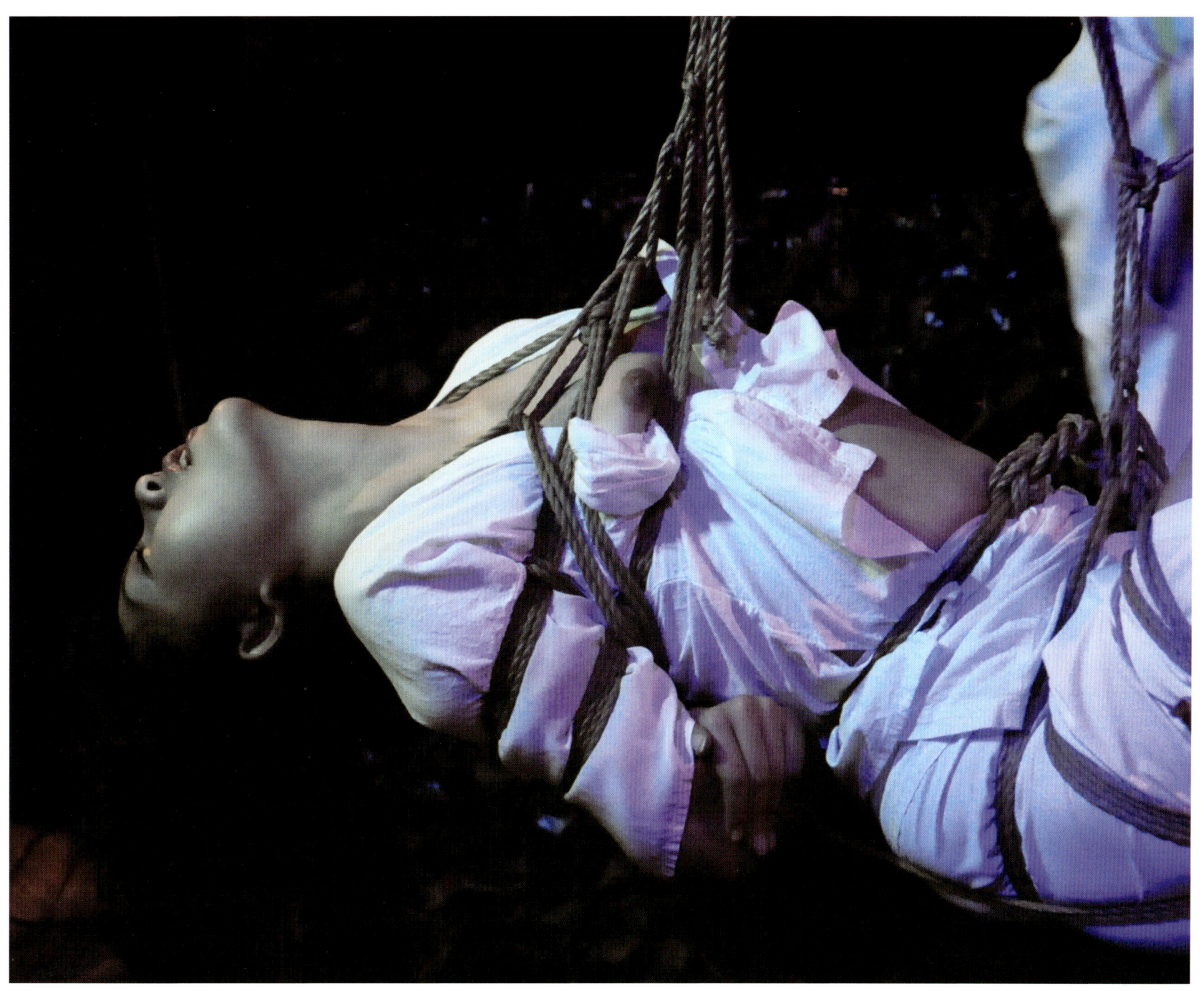

I think that it is important that both the Kinbakushi and the model should be able to enjoy the time spent together in being tied up.

Even if you have limited skill and your rope work doesn't look so good, be it in public or private, I think that it is important for everyone involved to enjoy it.

I thought recently when I came in UK ... I might not enjoy it simply because I did not speak English and could not talk with the model. But speaking is not important and you don't need language and words for Kinbaku. Only the heart and feelings.

Thank you.

Miumi-U

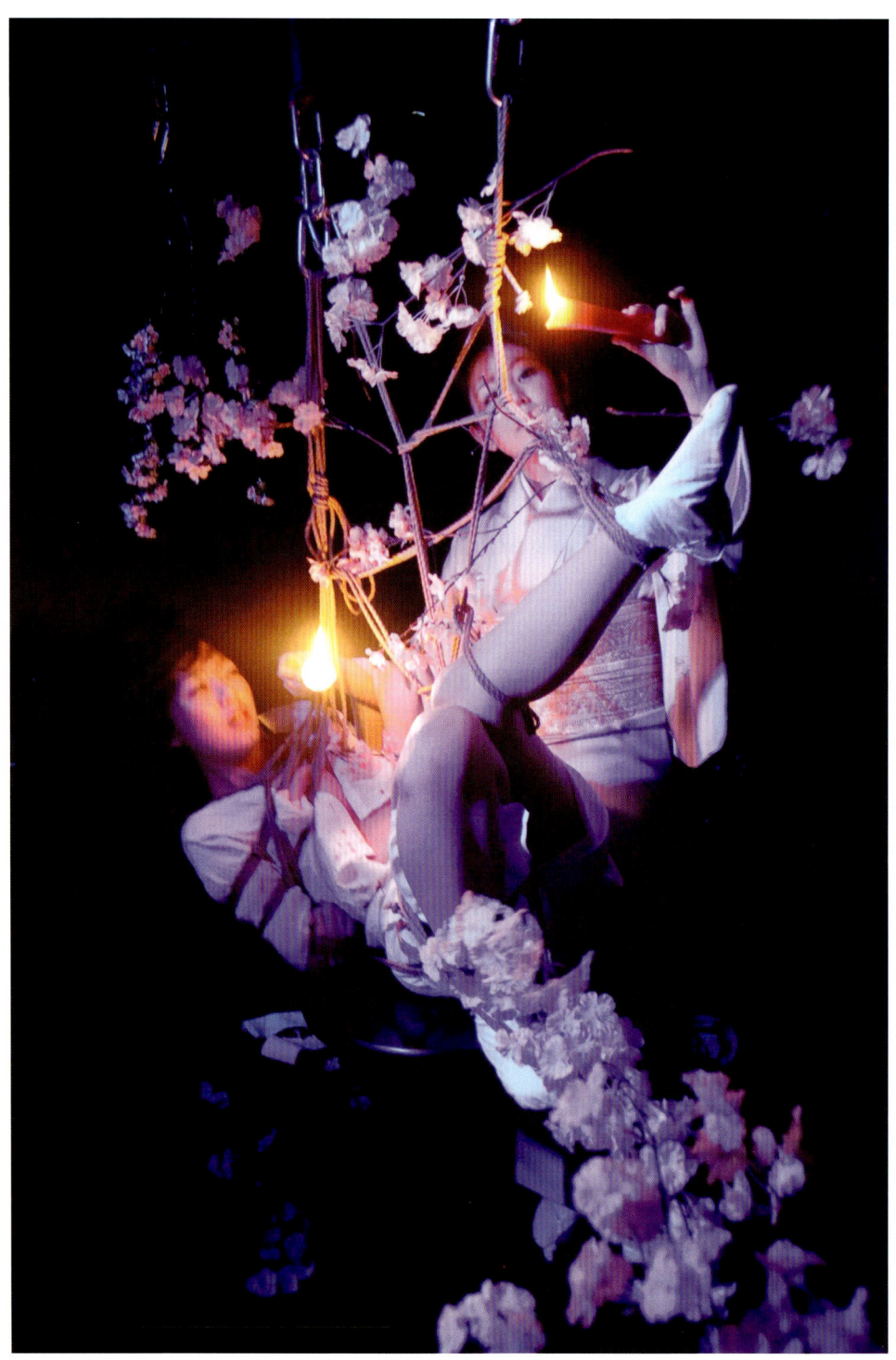

女王様みたいな事は、私には出来ないし、日々苦戦して
ますが楽しんでいます。緊縛はお互いが自分達なり に
楽しめればいいと思ってます。

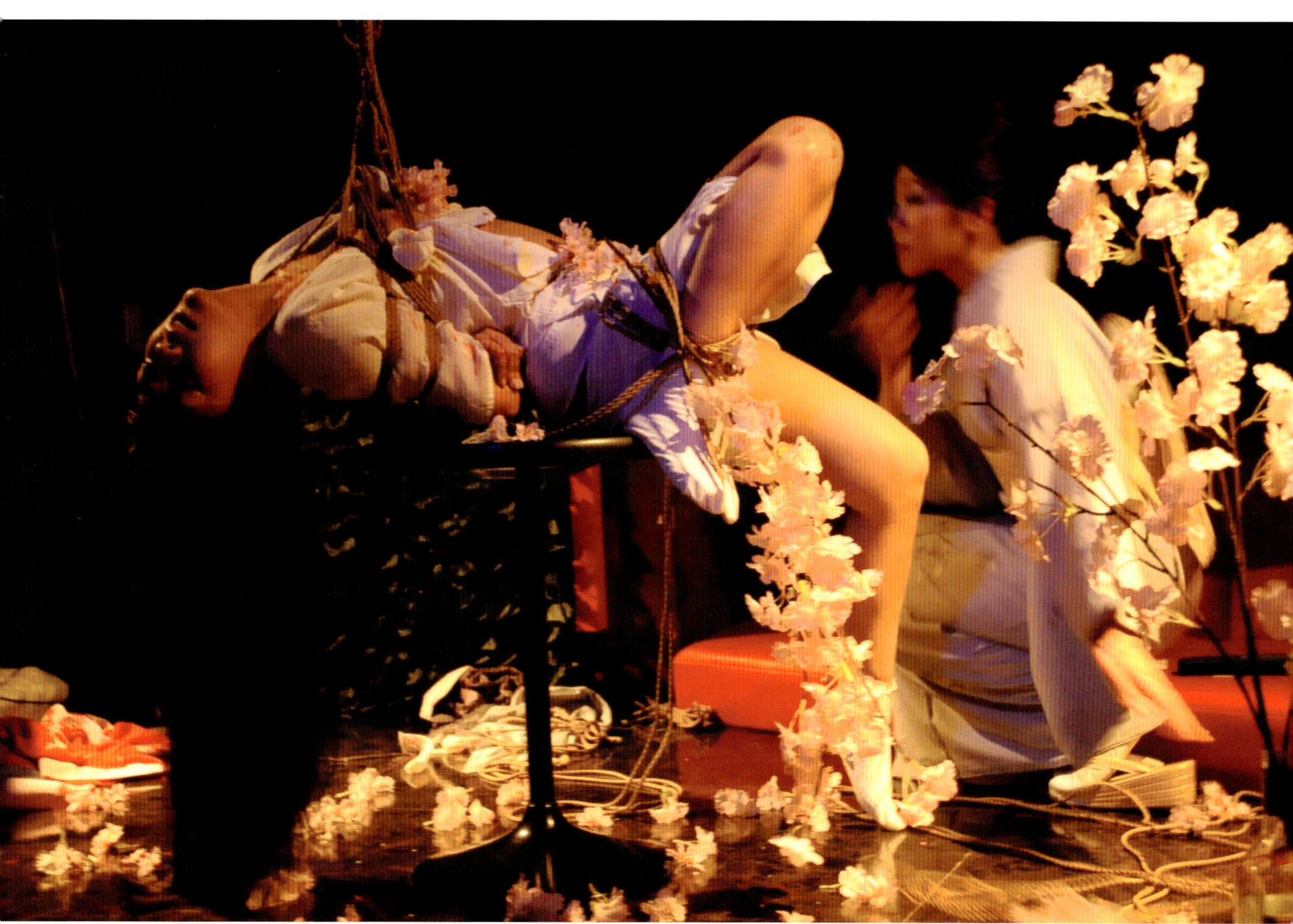

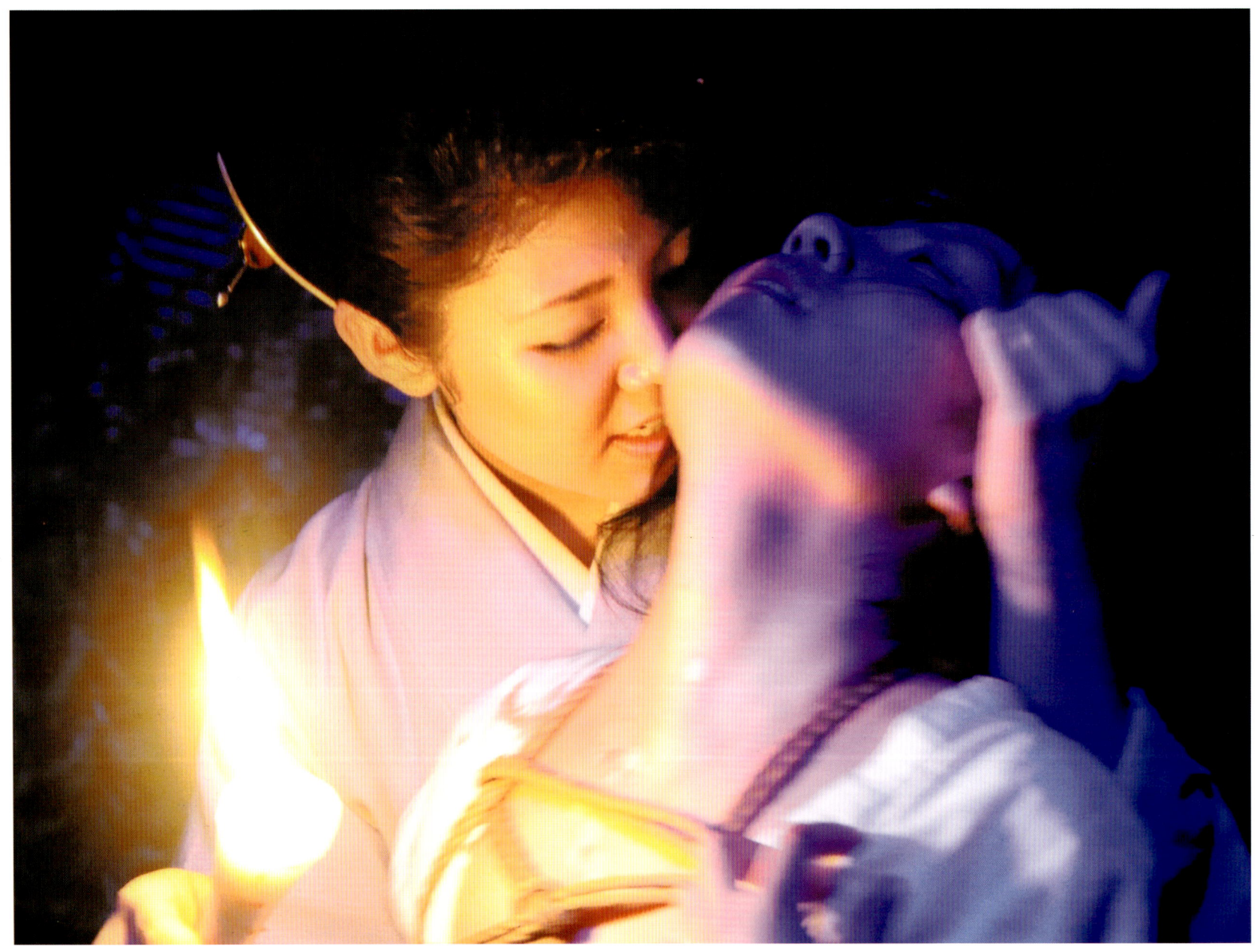

見た目が悪くても技術がなくても、プライベートでも
ショーでも、縛り手さんと受け手が2人で楽しんでいれ
ば。

そして、イギリスにいて最近思った事は言葉が通じない
からこそ緊縛で楽しめる事もあるのだと思いました。

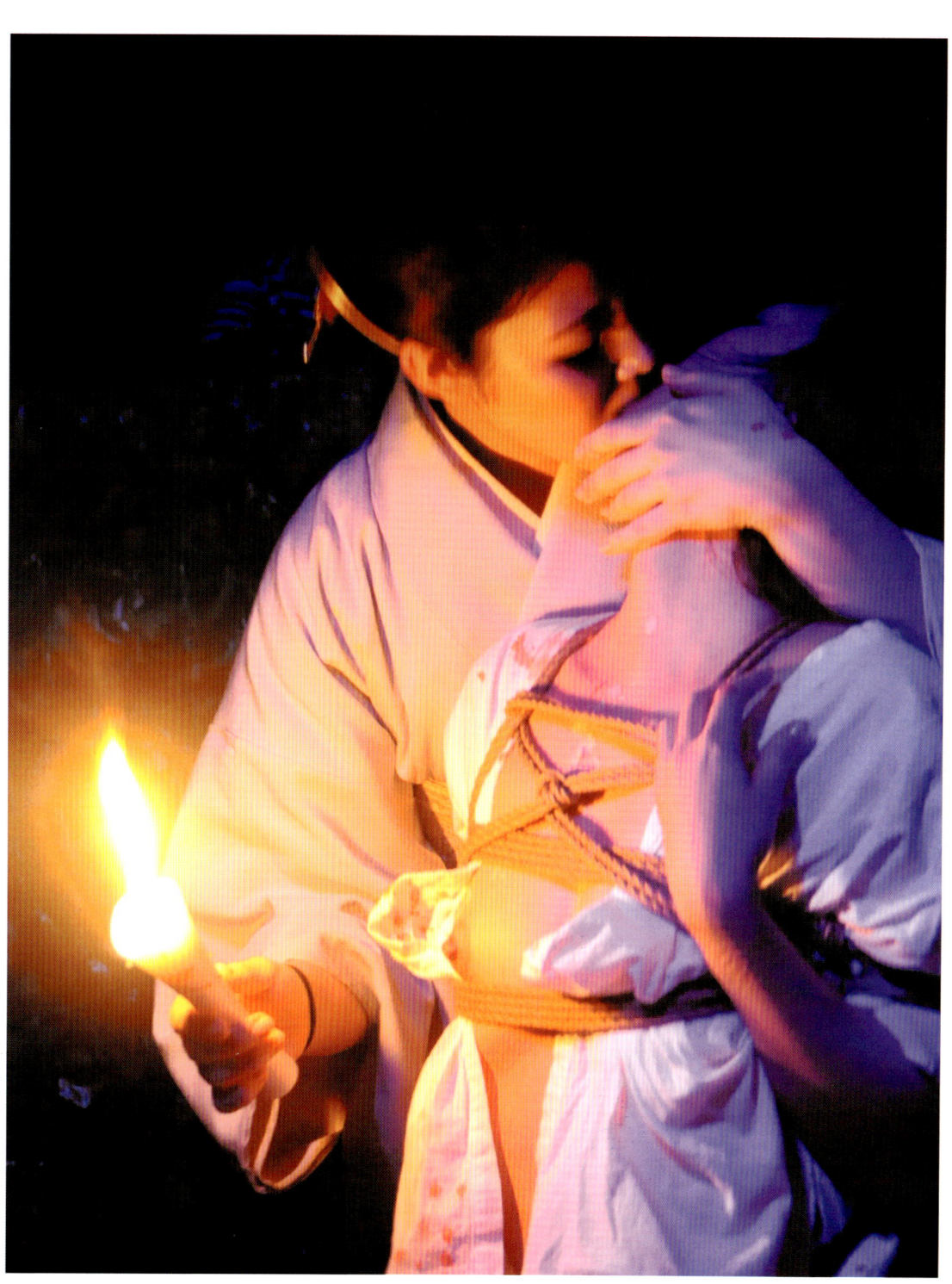

Chapter 5

Shibari in San Francisco

Creating sensual and erotic photographs fuels my creativity like
nothing else. The models provide a new story with each photo.
Exploring everyone's fetishes and fantasies has been an exciting
adventure that has changed me and my work.

I started to incorporate shibari in many of my images several years
ago. Rope, with its fibers and twists, and shibari, with its intricate
knots and ties, provide a visually rich setting to highlight and interact
with the models. Depending on the pose and the way the rope is
used, the results can be sensual, erotic, or provocative.

I also find that most models really enjoy the feeling of rope.
Reactions to the rope's texture ranges from sensual to sexual.
This is easily seen in the intense and intimate expressions of the
models who are bound and tied.

Chi lives in San Francisco, where he shoots most of his work. His
work can be seen in local and national exhibitions and has received
critical recognition and awards.

Photography: Chi

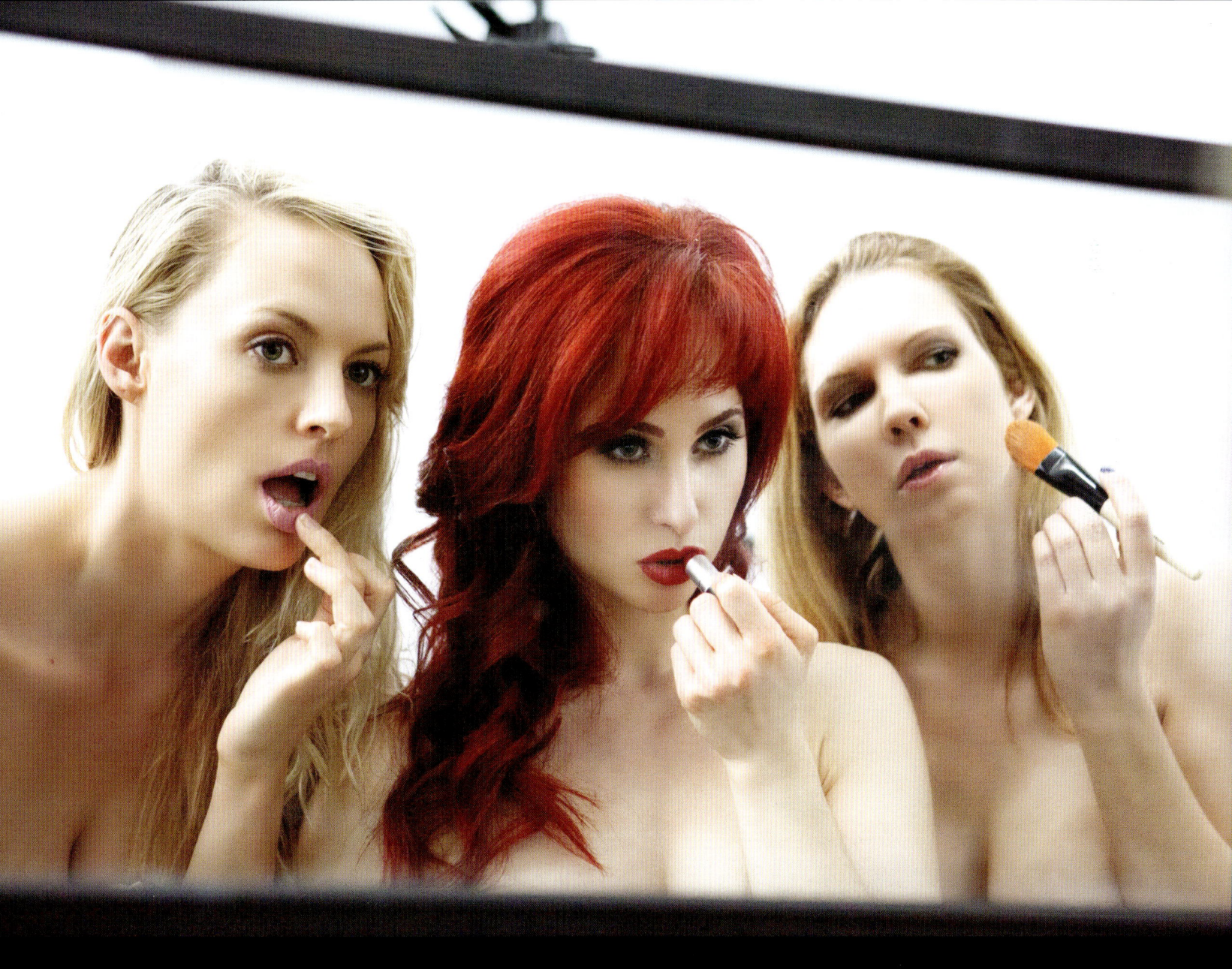

In the model's words:

I feel that rope is an entity that must be respected, something that is powerful and dangerous.

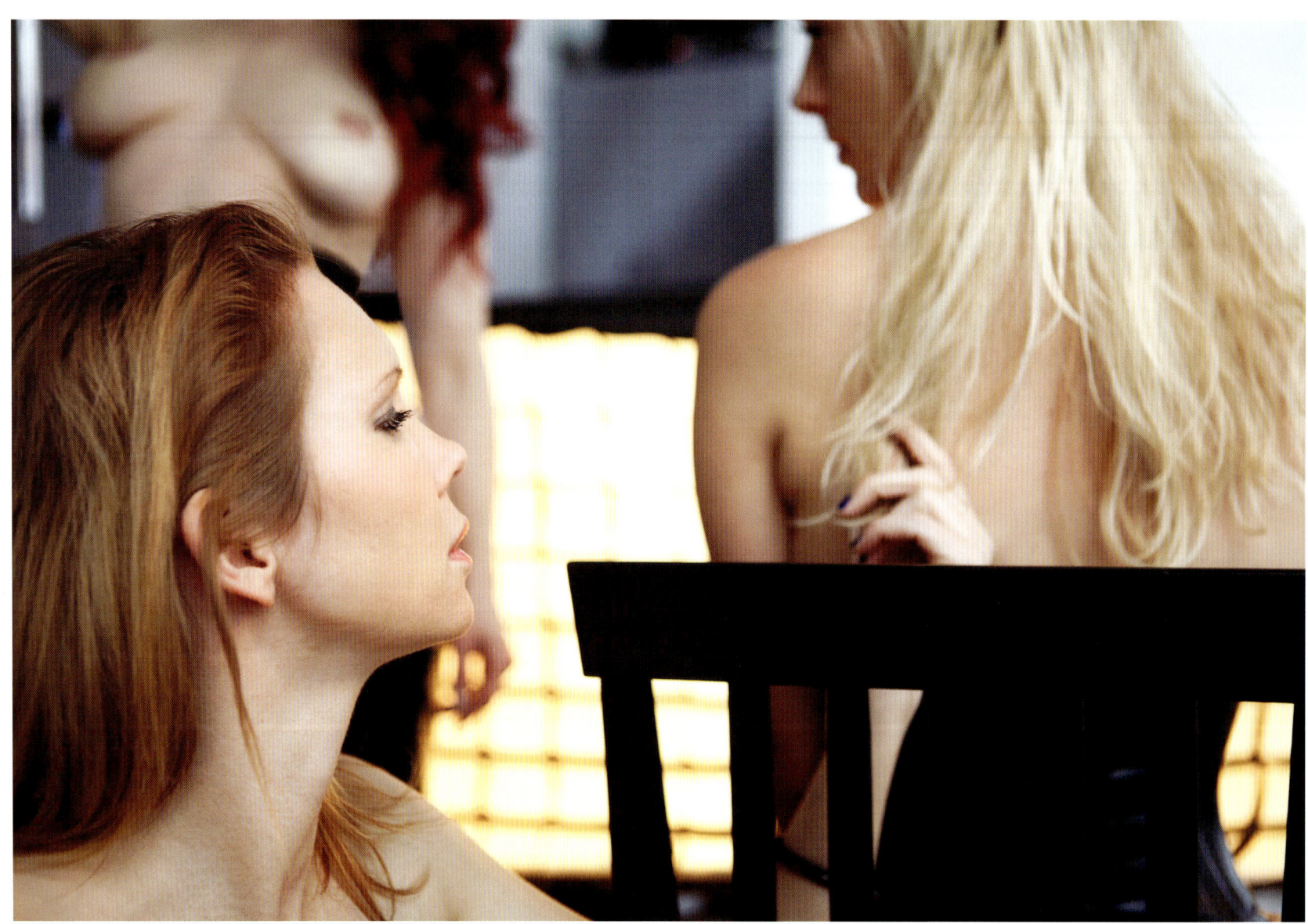

Rope binds and restricts movement,
including basic functions such as breathing.
For those reasons I like to feel connected to
it and to the person who is tying me.

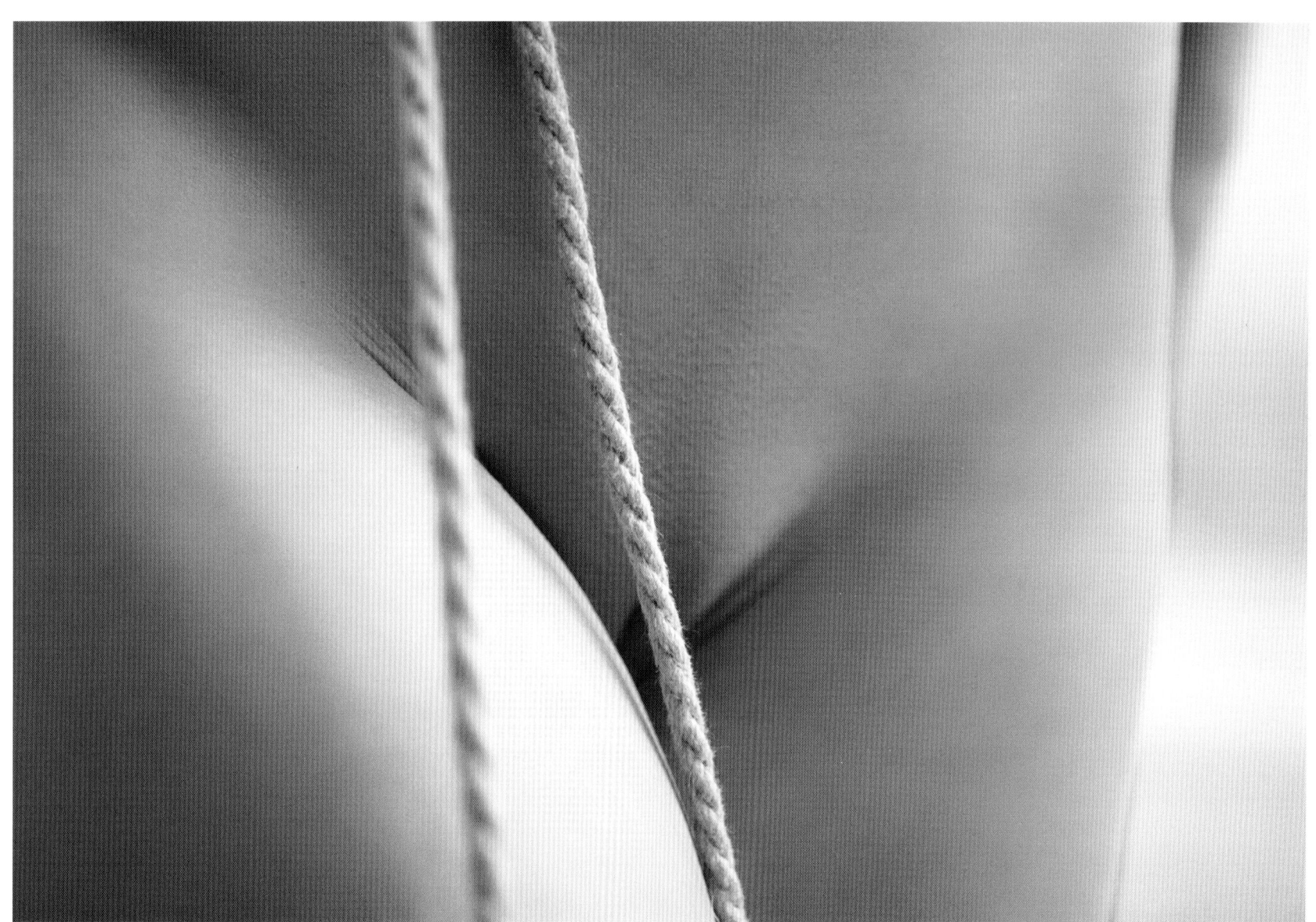

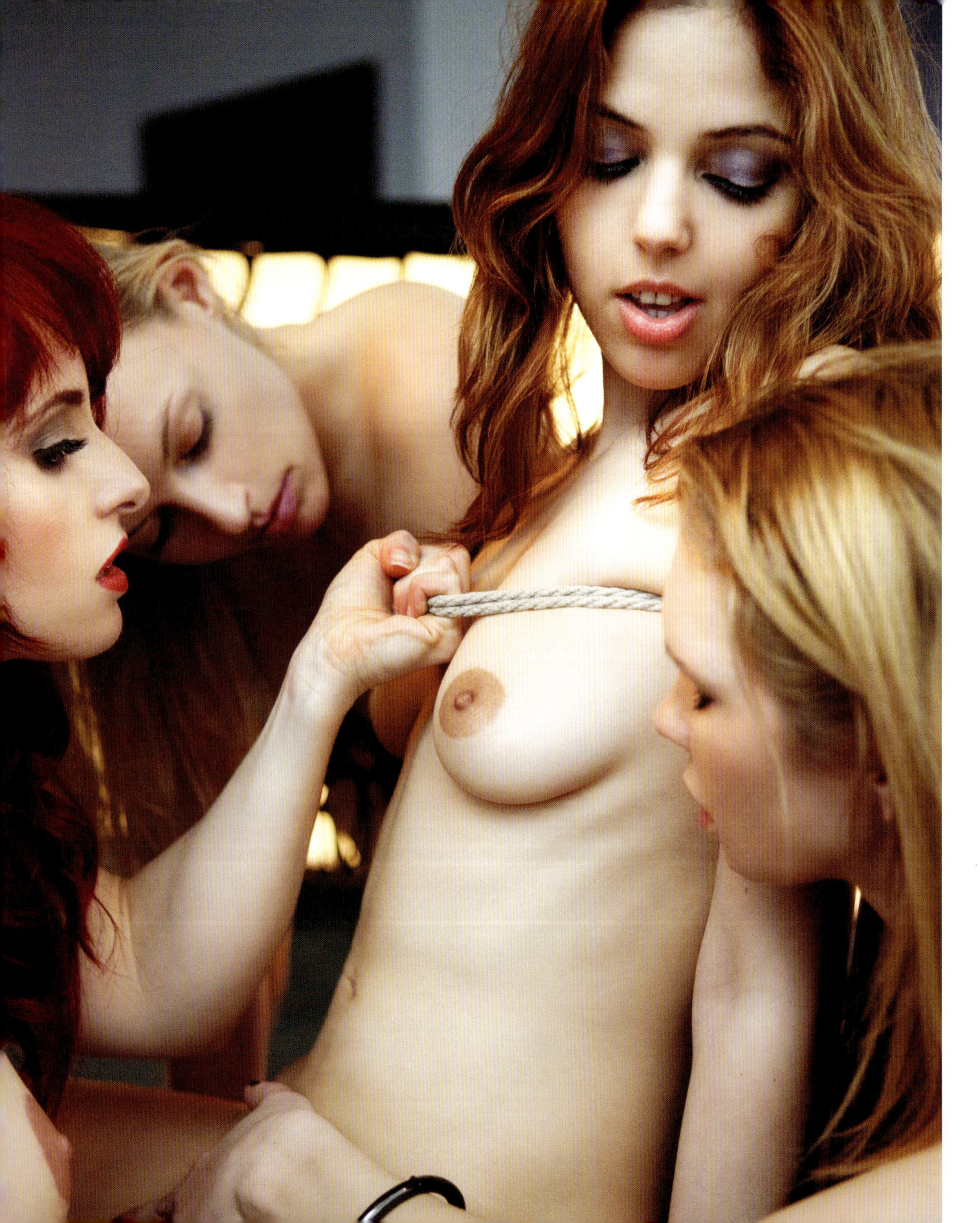

I enjoy feeling the rope on my skin. I enjoy feeling it drag across me. I enjoy feeling its caress as it binds me. Being in rope is a sensual, almost spiritual experience.

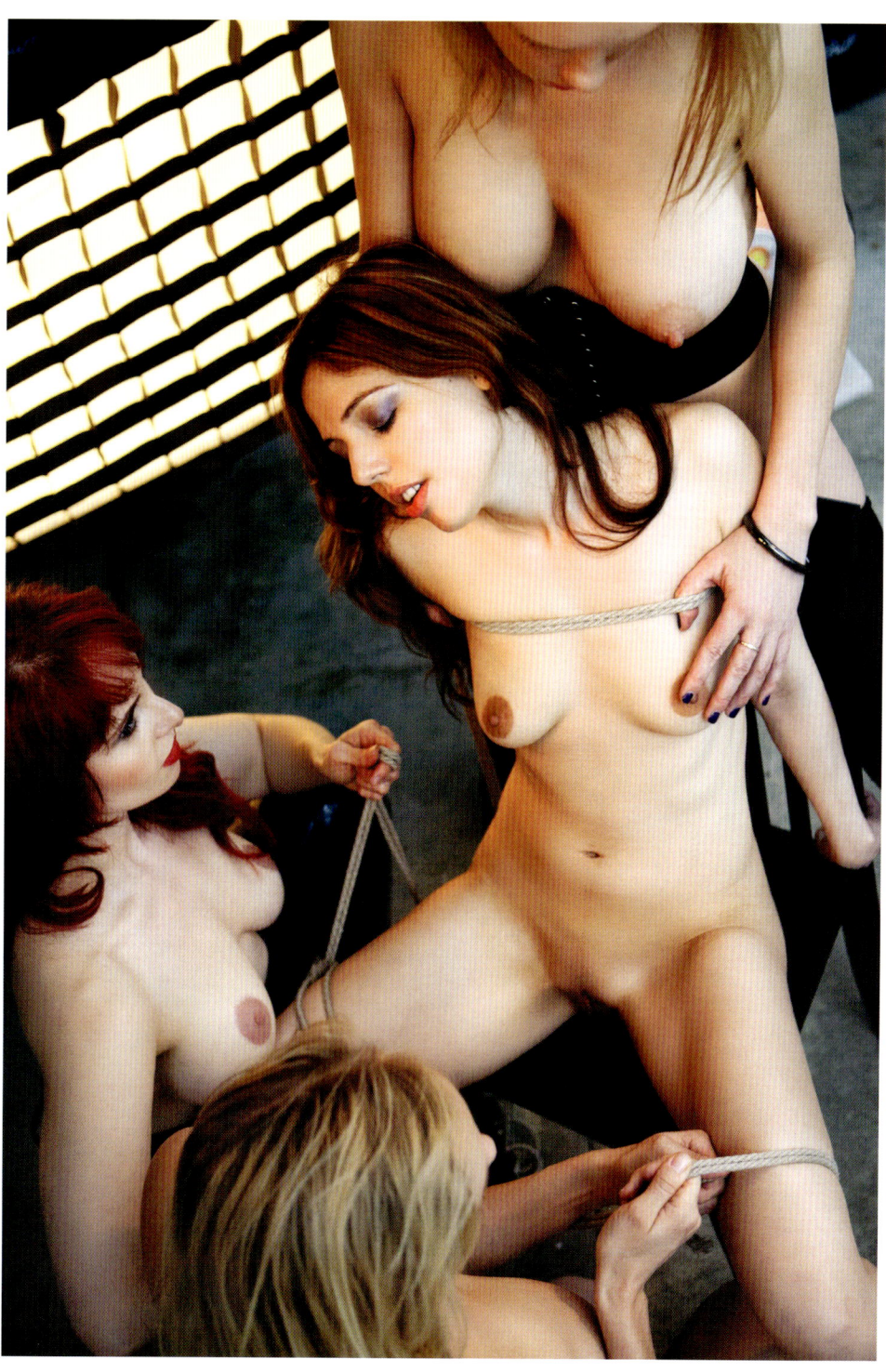

This experience is one shared by the model, rigger, and photographer. A successful rope shoot cannot happen without these three people and each plays a vital role. I feel that it is important to communicate with the rigger while being tied because I know that my comfort and safety depends on them.

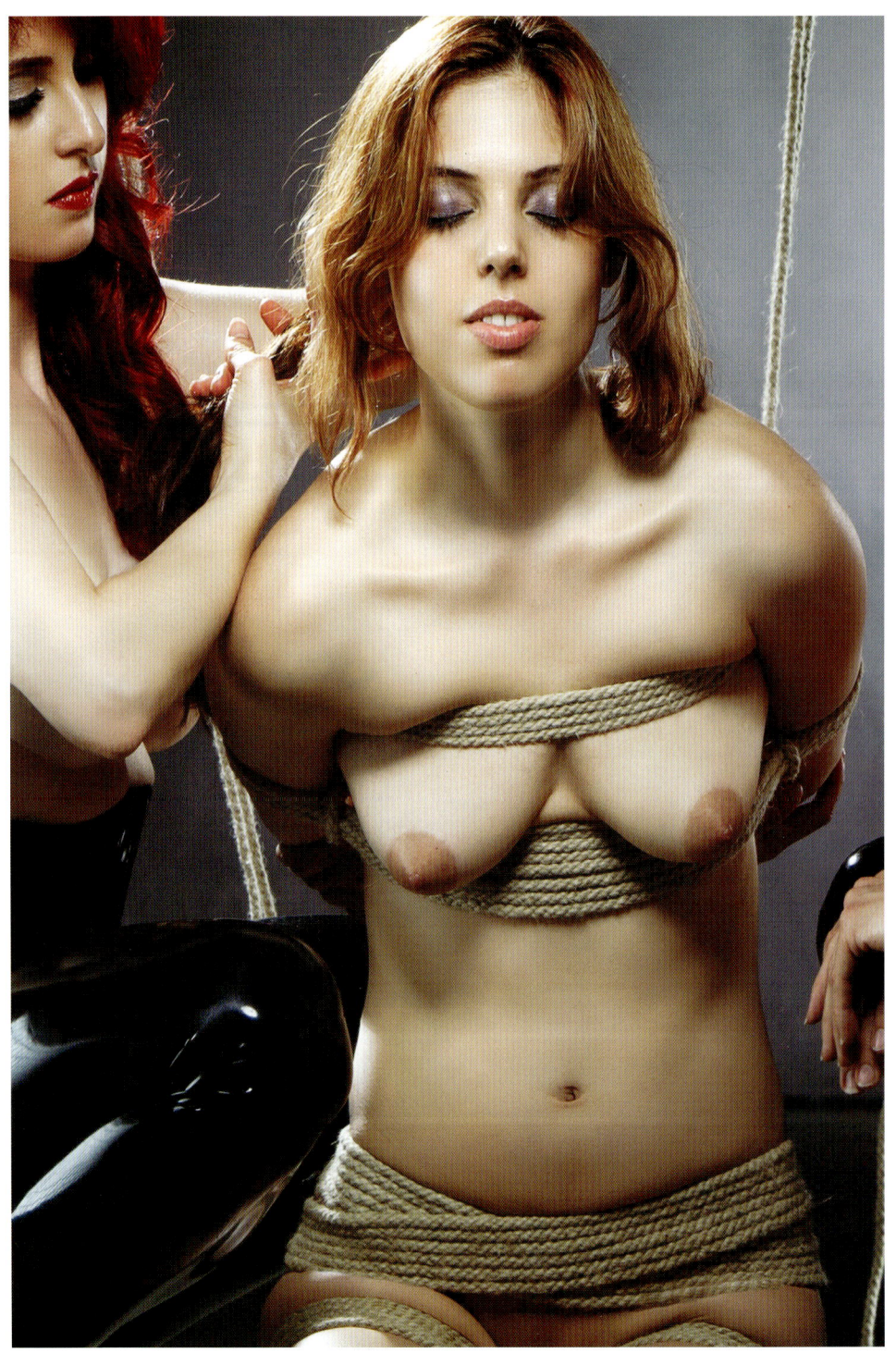

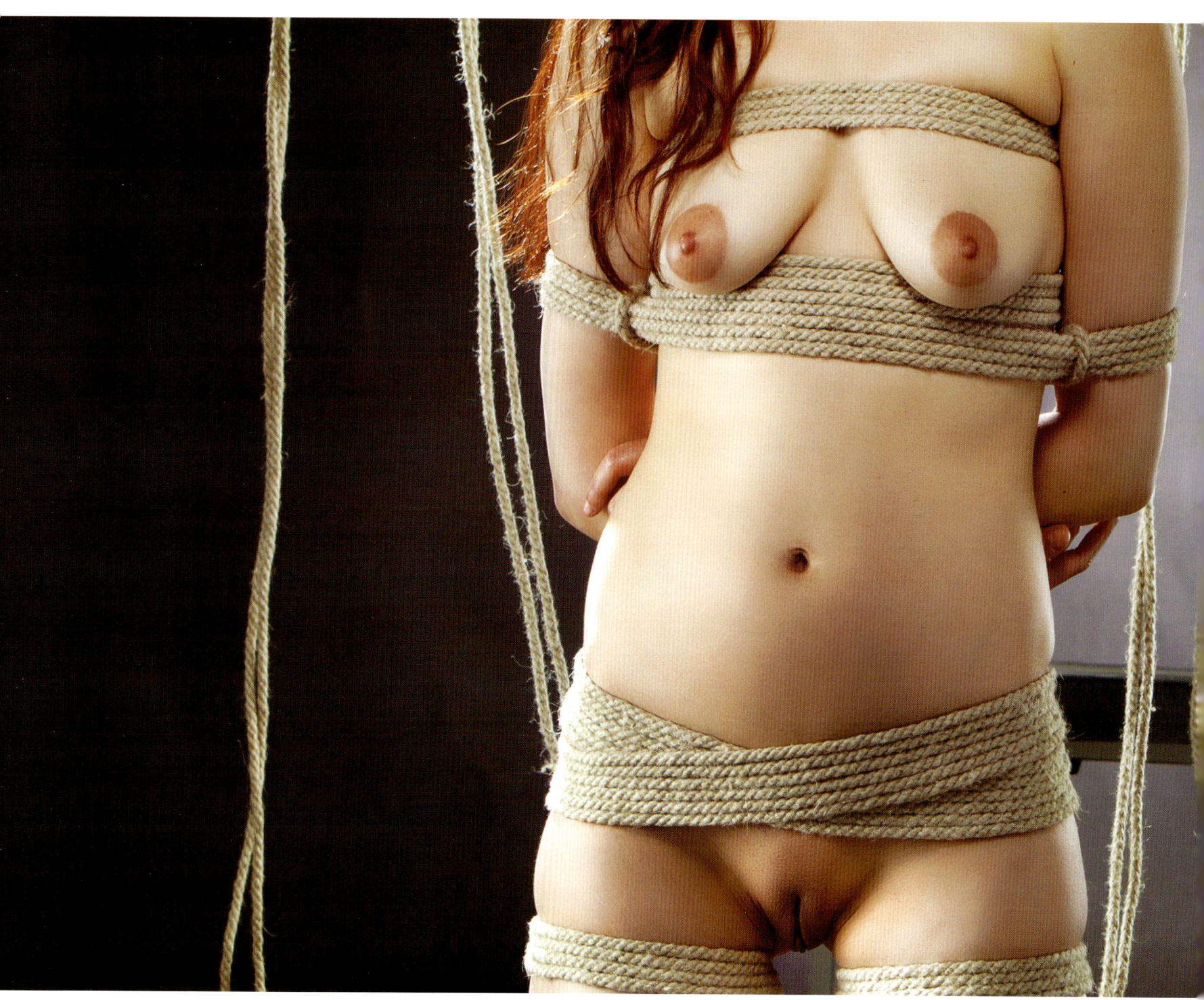

I have been truly lucky to work with many wonderful riggers who put emphasis on the safety and maintenance of their rope. For those not familiar with the art of rope in all of its forms, it can be hard to understand all that goes into making a rope scene a safe and enjoyable experience.

A shibari shoot requires a lot of thought and planning, with both aesthetic and strenuous positions. For this reason, being a rope model is not for everyone and requires a lot of patience, ability to handle discomfort, and a little bit of bravery!

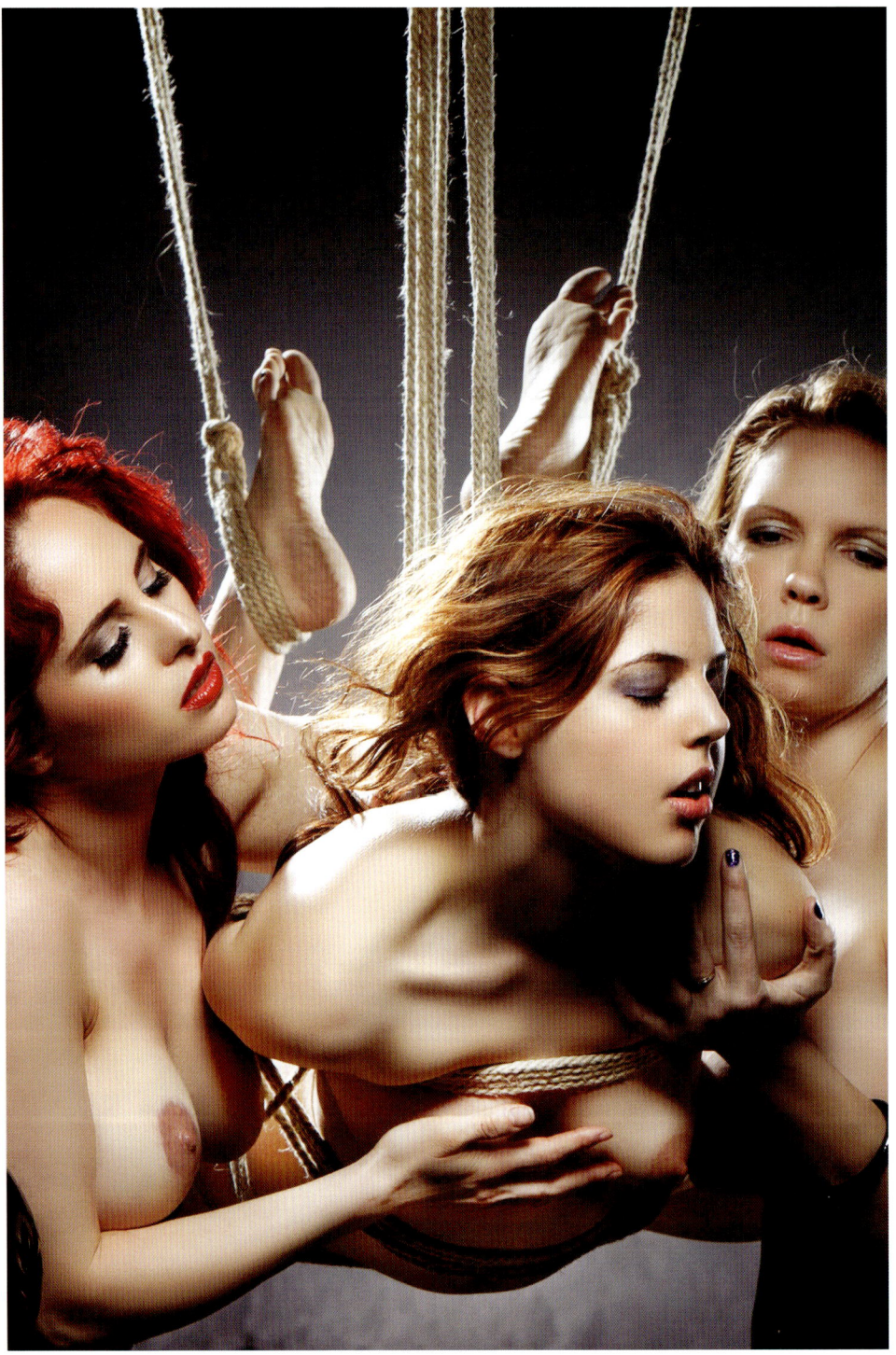

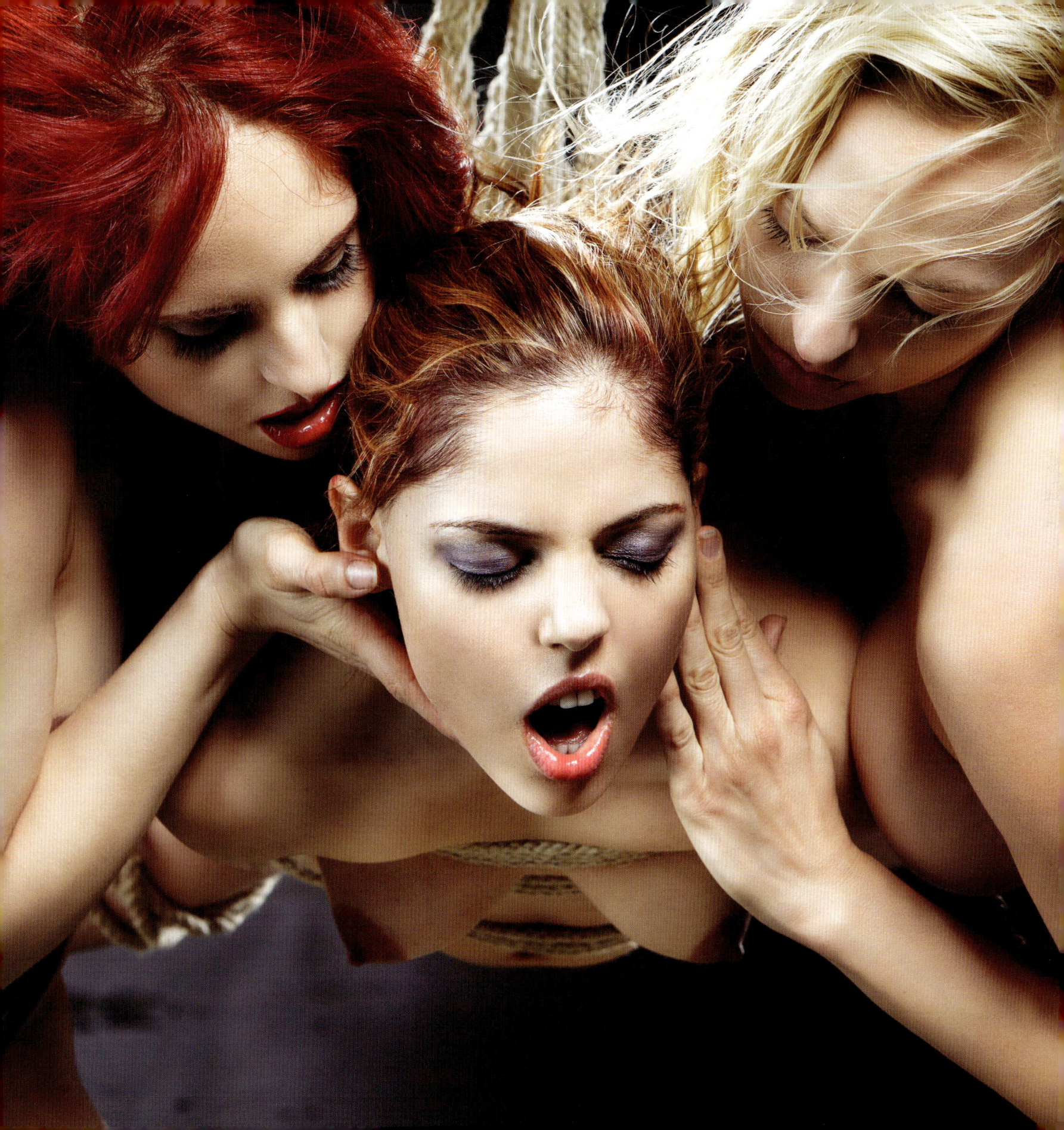

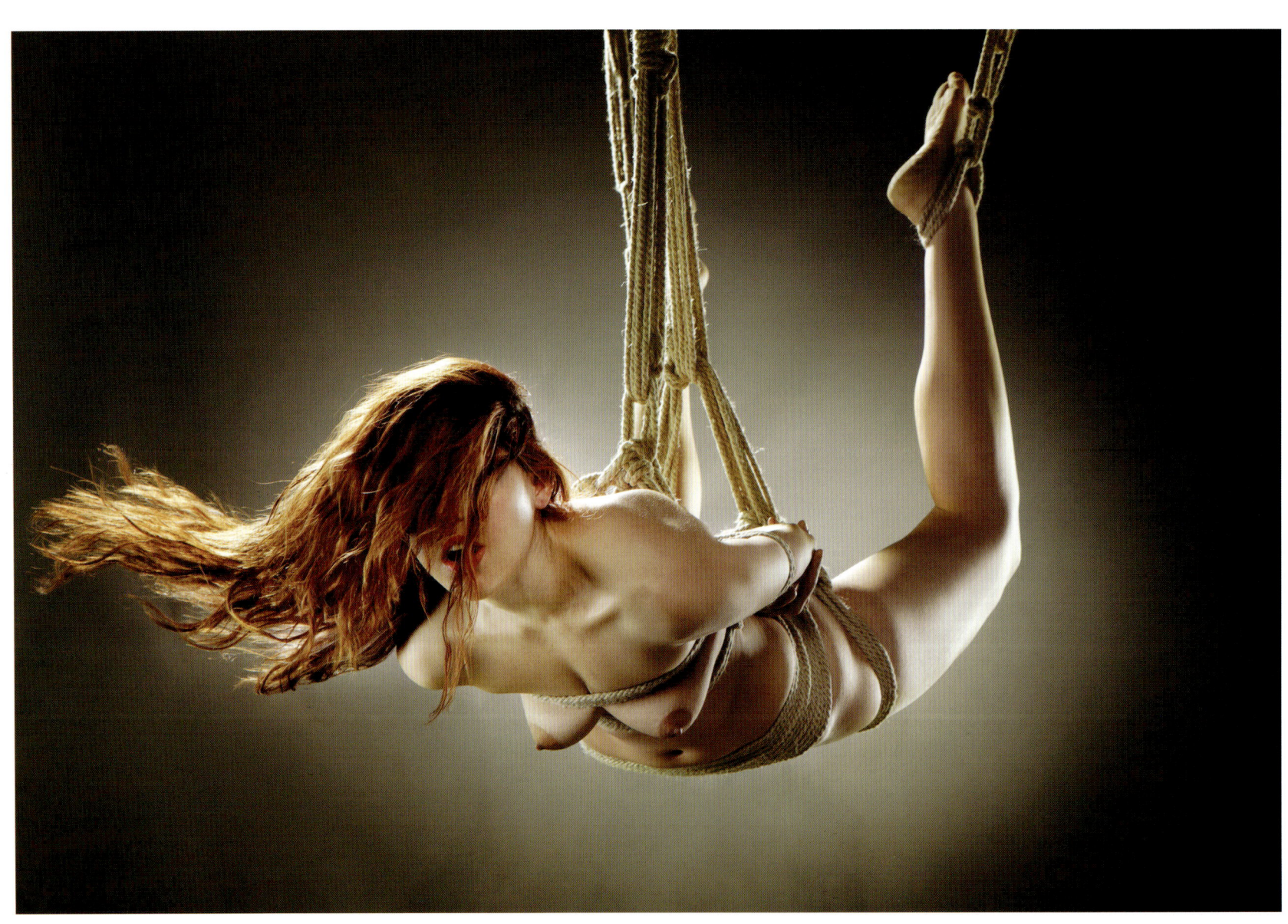

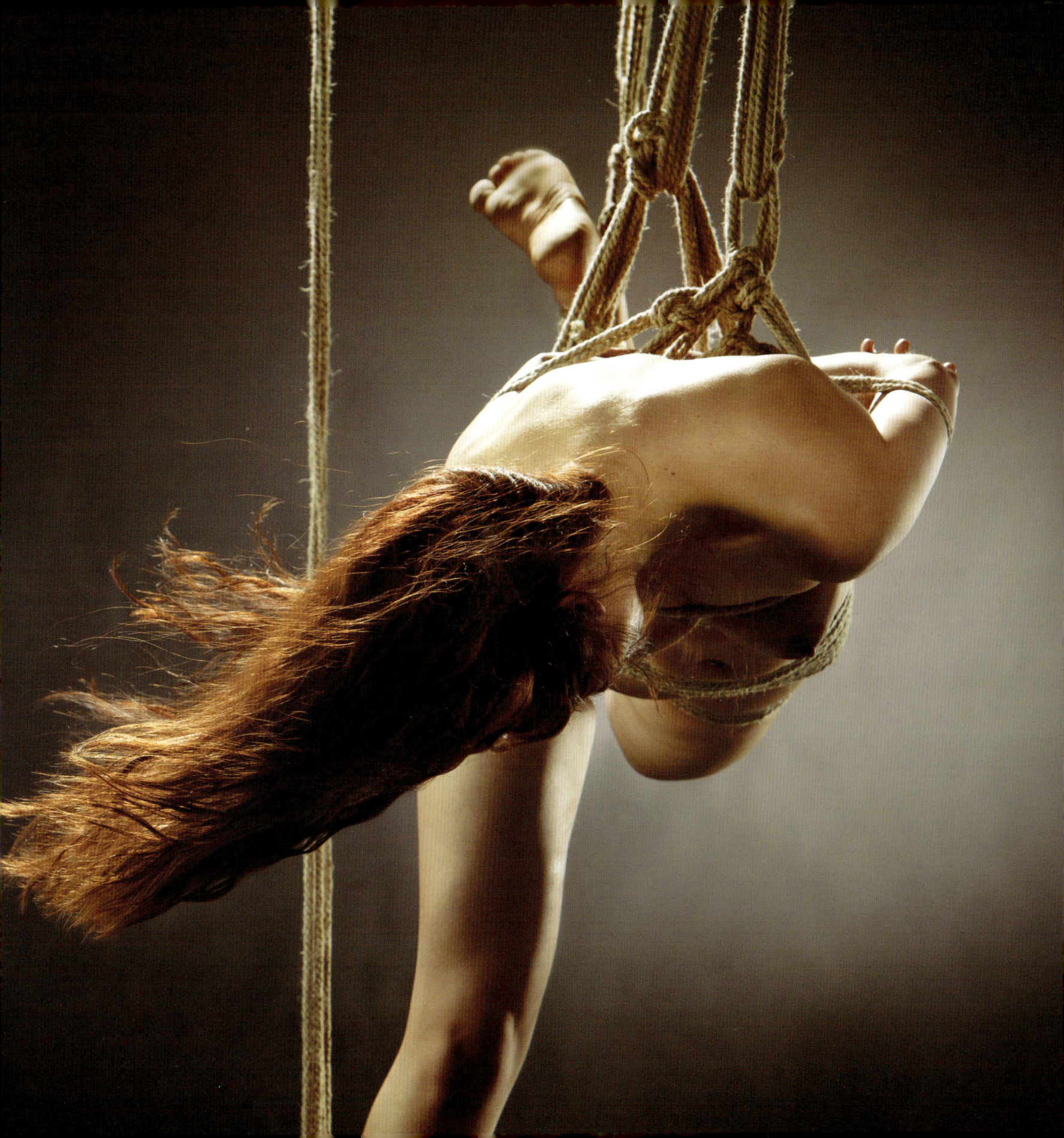

The model must be in a good place mentally and physically before being tied. I remember not knowing what to expect the first time I was suspended. It was a painful and exhilarating experience and I was addicted to rope ever since. However, there were simple things I wish I had known before, such as stretching and relaxing your muscles, that would have saved me a lot of soreness in the days afterward.

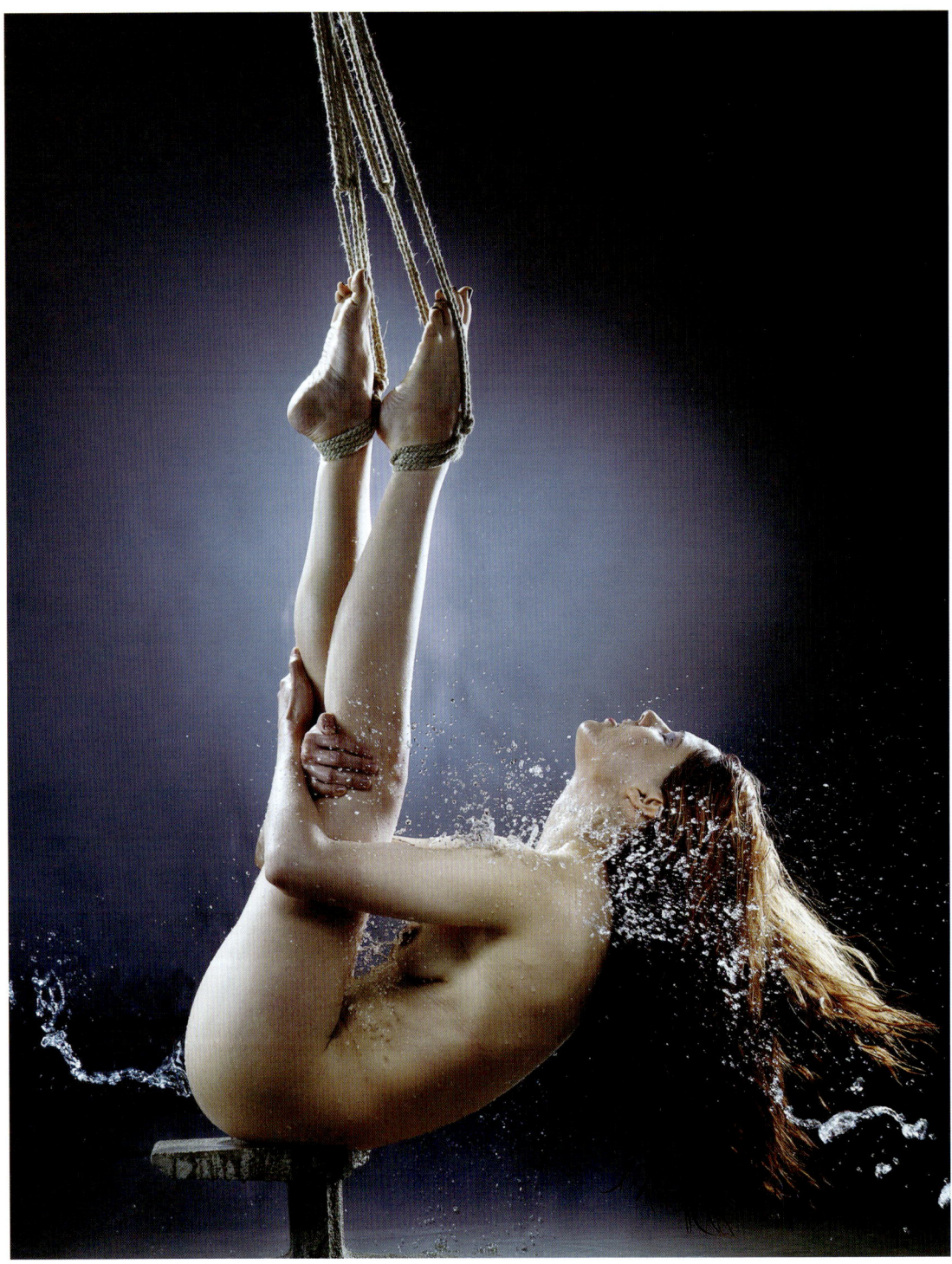

You do not want to be tense during a scene. That increases the chances of panicking or getting hurt, which is why it is important to have a rigger and photographer who you can trust and put you at ease. On this shoot for the book, the photographer, the rigger, and I all shared many good thoughts, ideas, and especially laughs. It was definitely an experience I will never forget.

Lily LeFleur
March 2013

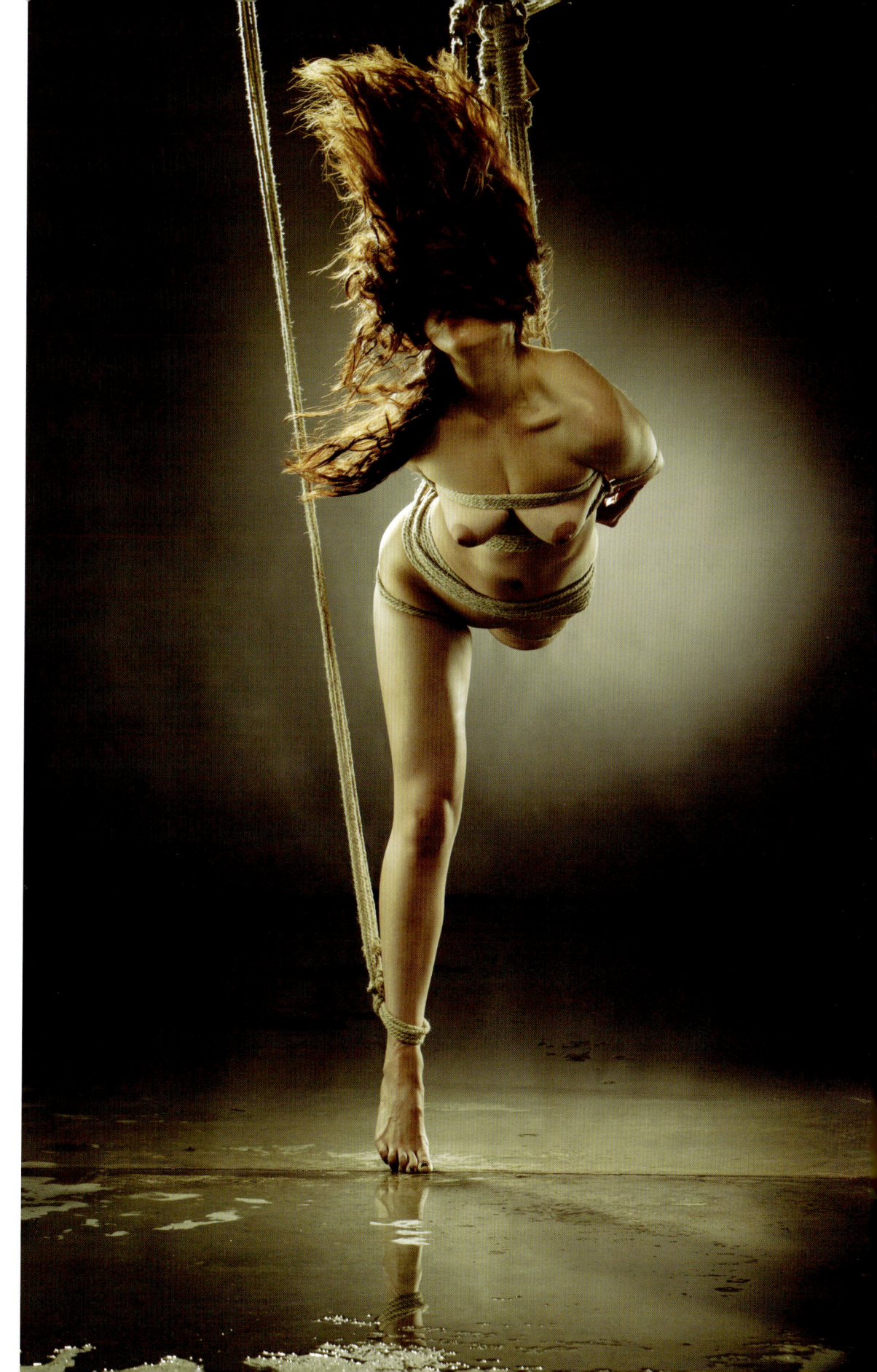

Chapter 6

Time for bed

Photography: Kahboom

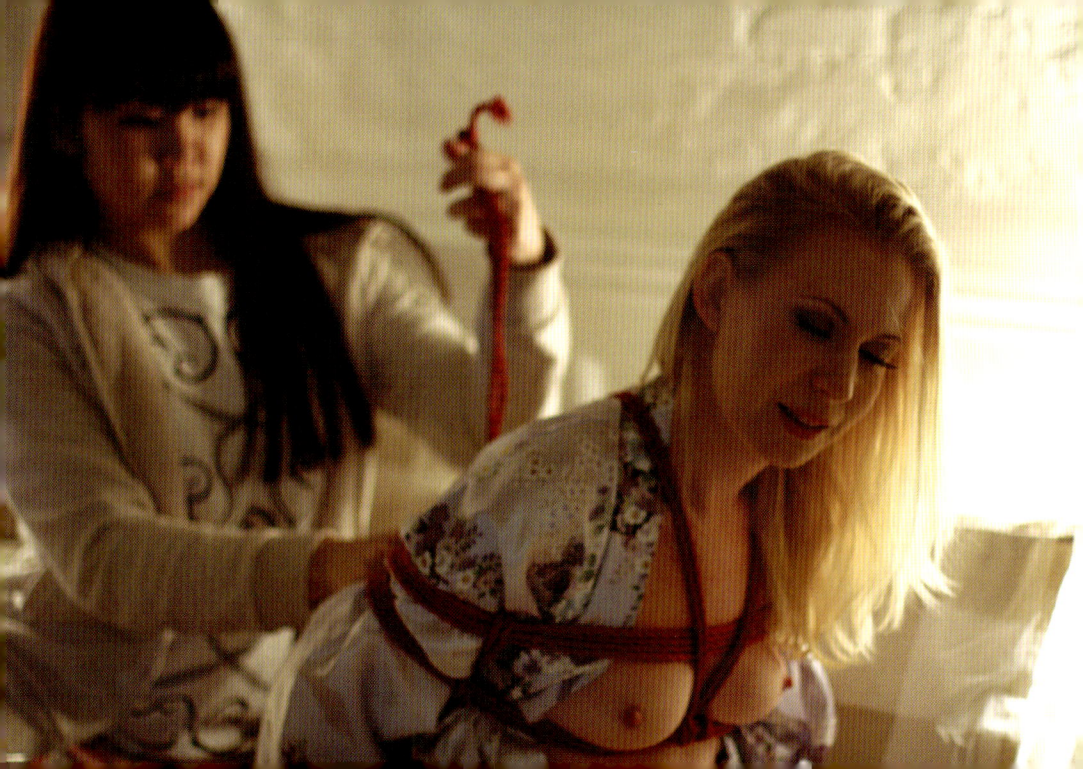

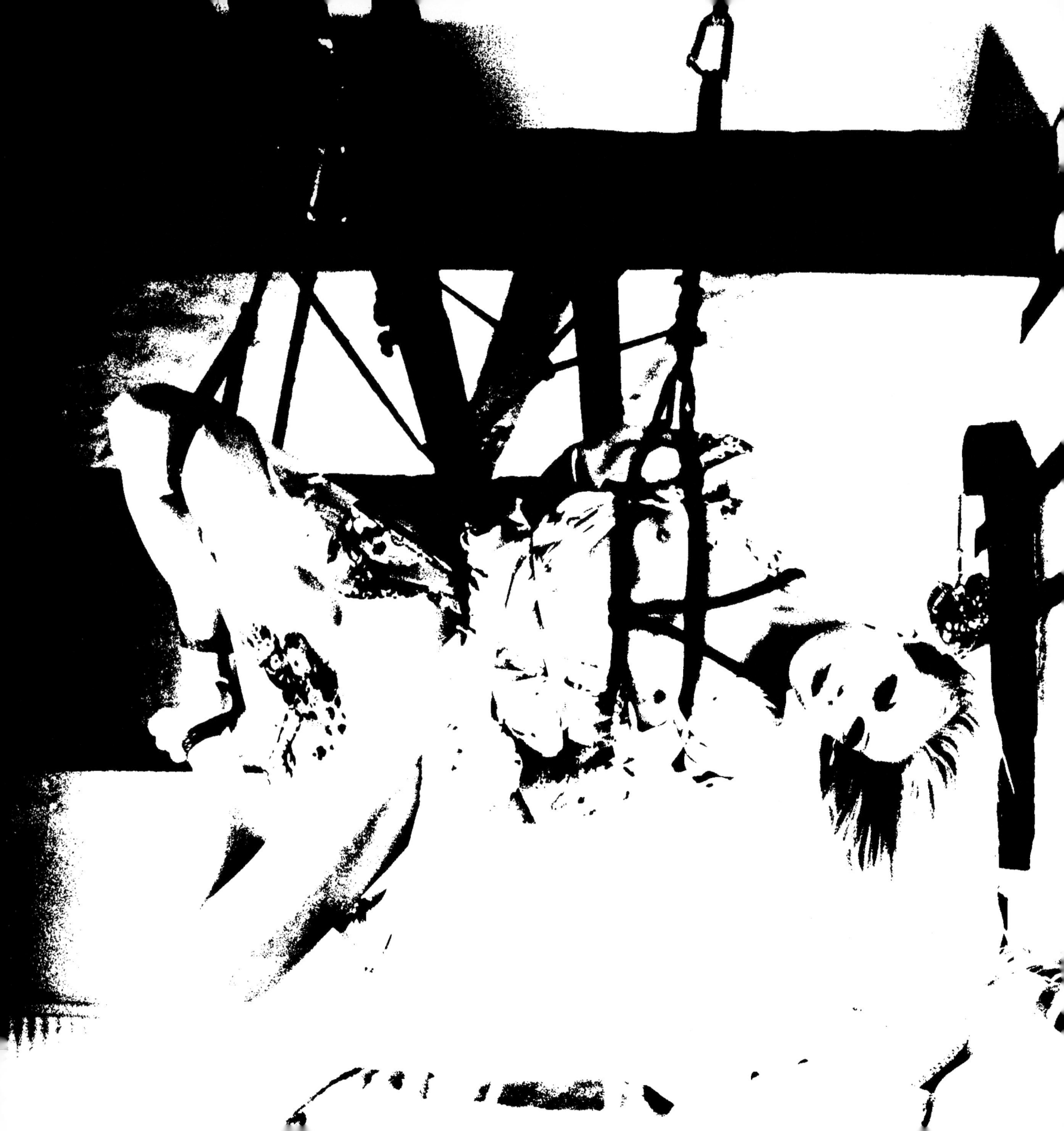

A long shower, then my silk robe

There is one thing bound to happen when he is here

But tonight he isn't

and my Kinbakushi sits and looks at me

Silently

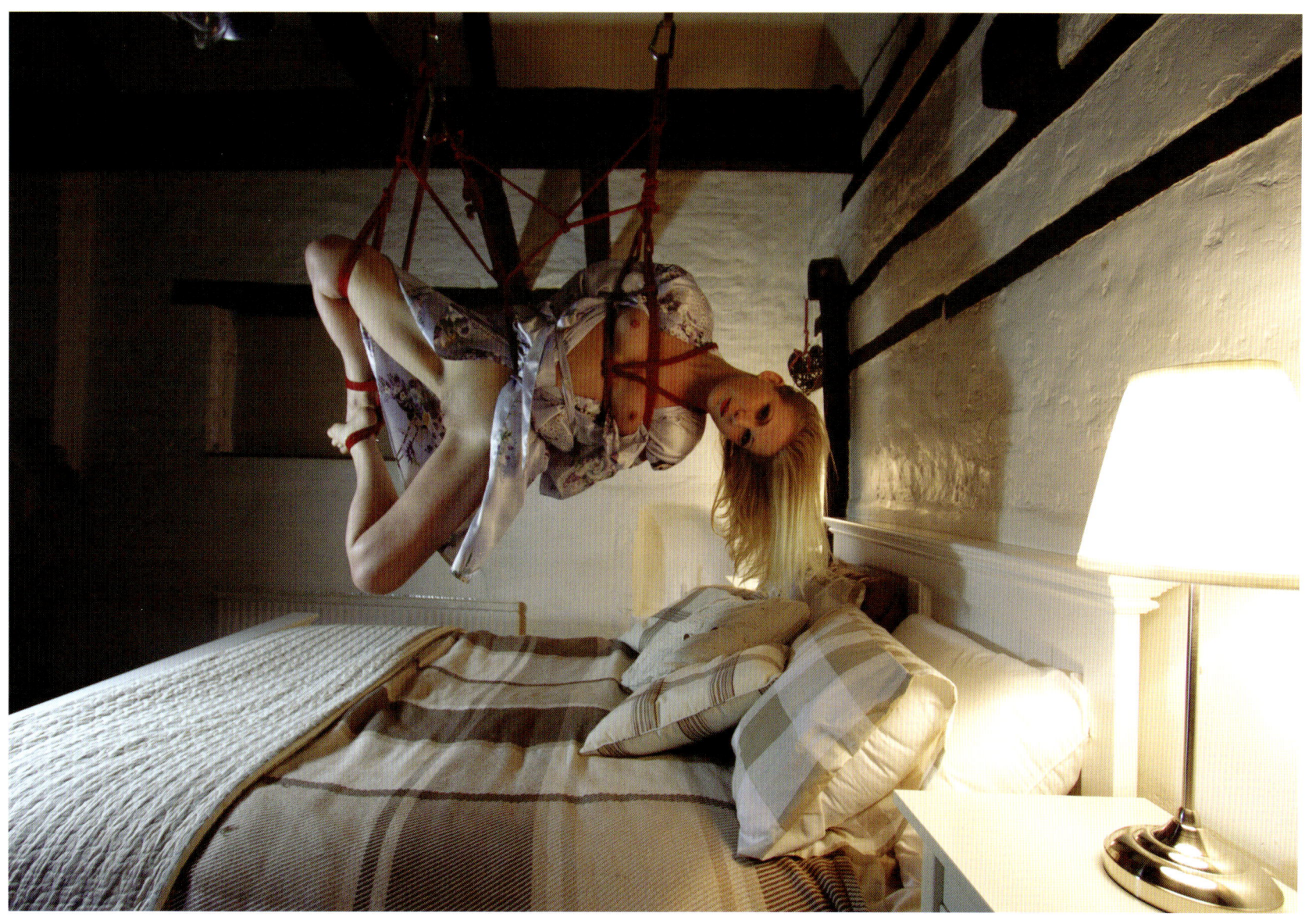

She is behind me now, and out of sight

Swift as the tongue of a Chameleon

Her red rope flicks around my breasts

No chance of escape

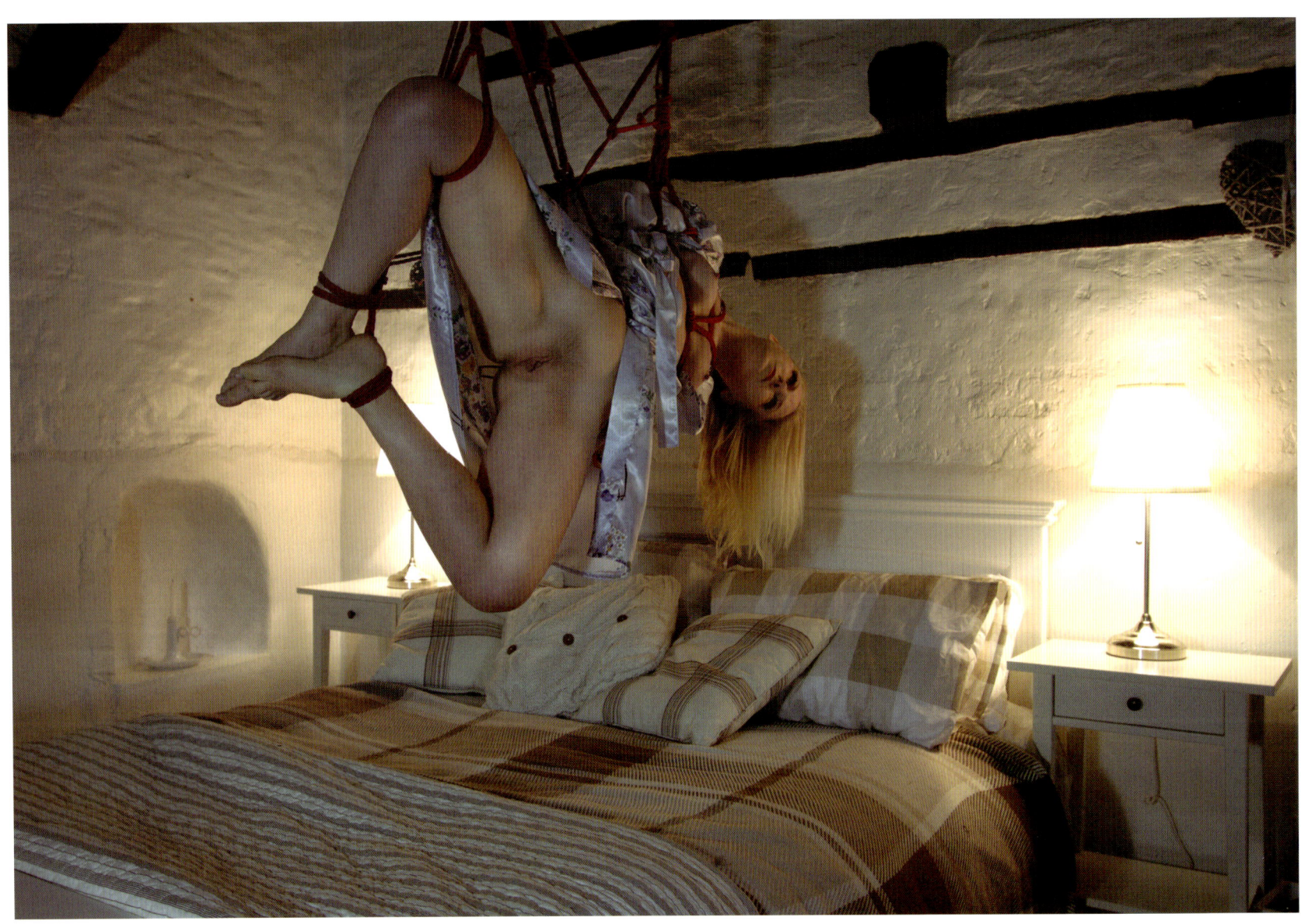

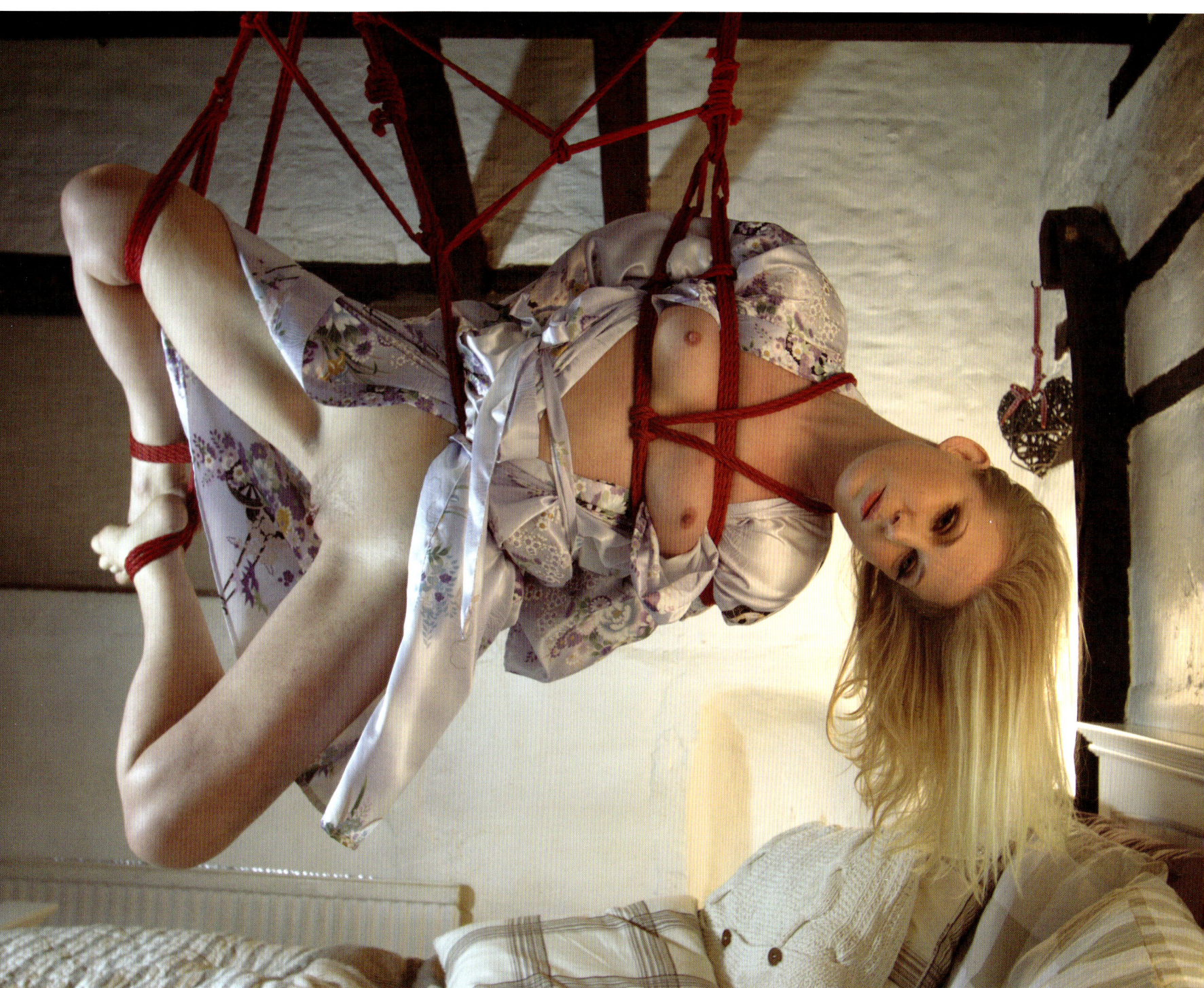

Is it her fingers or the red tendrills

that find the secret zones

known only to women?

Each wrap releases more of my inhibitions

Amazingly

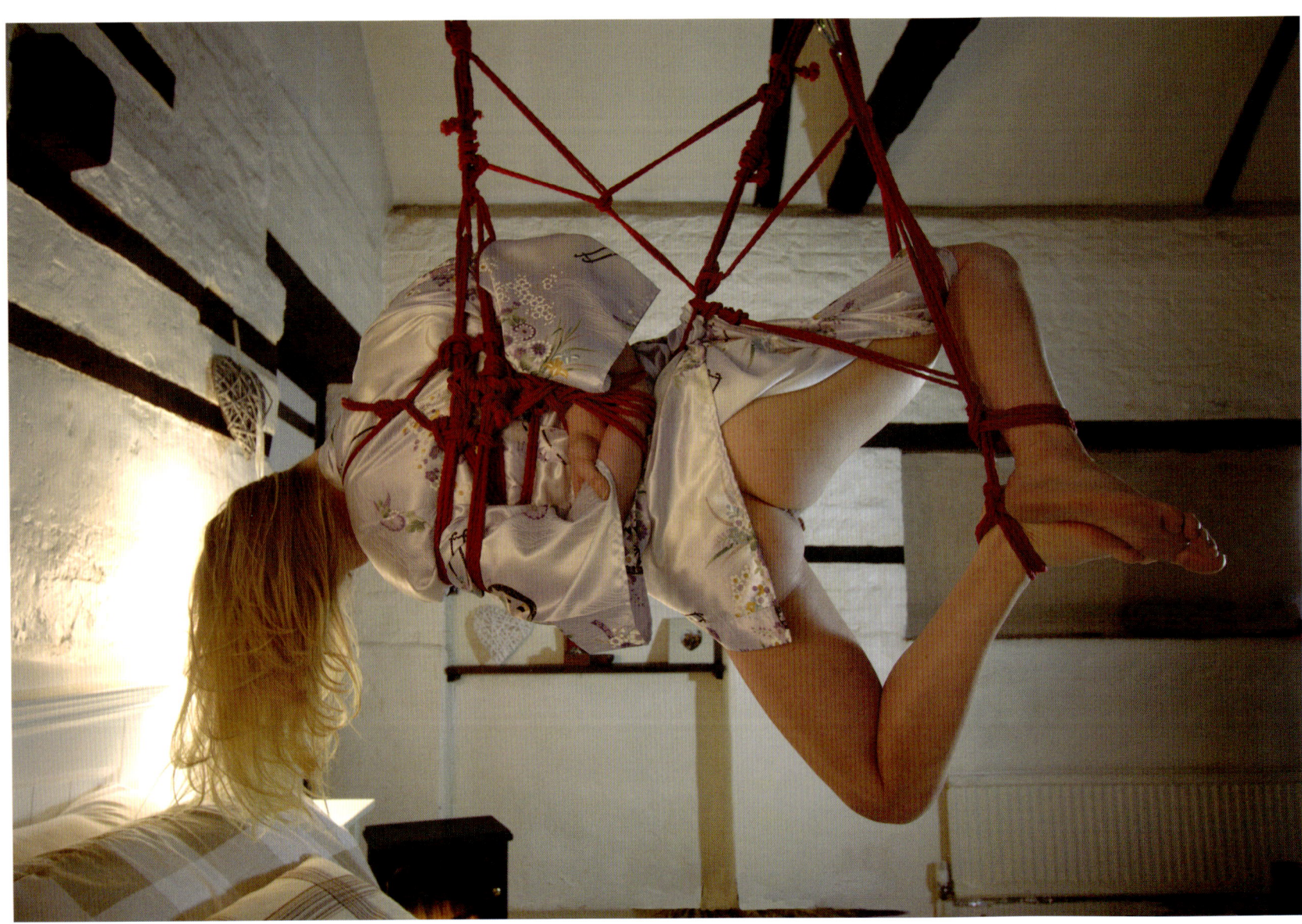

Now she adds pain to the pleasures

The ropes are tethered to high beams

I am lifted above mere comfort

To a place where I defy gravity

Erotically

Everything is exposed to my Kinbakushi

She reveals all parts of me; she knows me

We are bound together in trust

She knows the limits

Perfectly

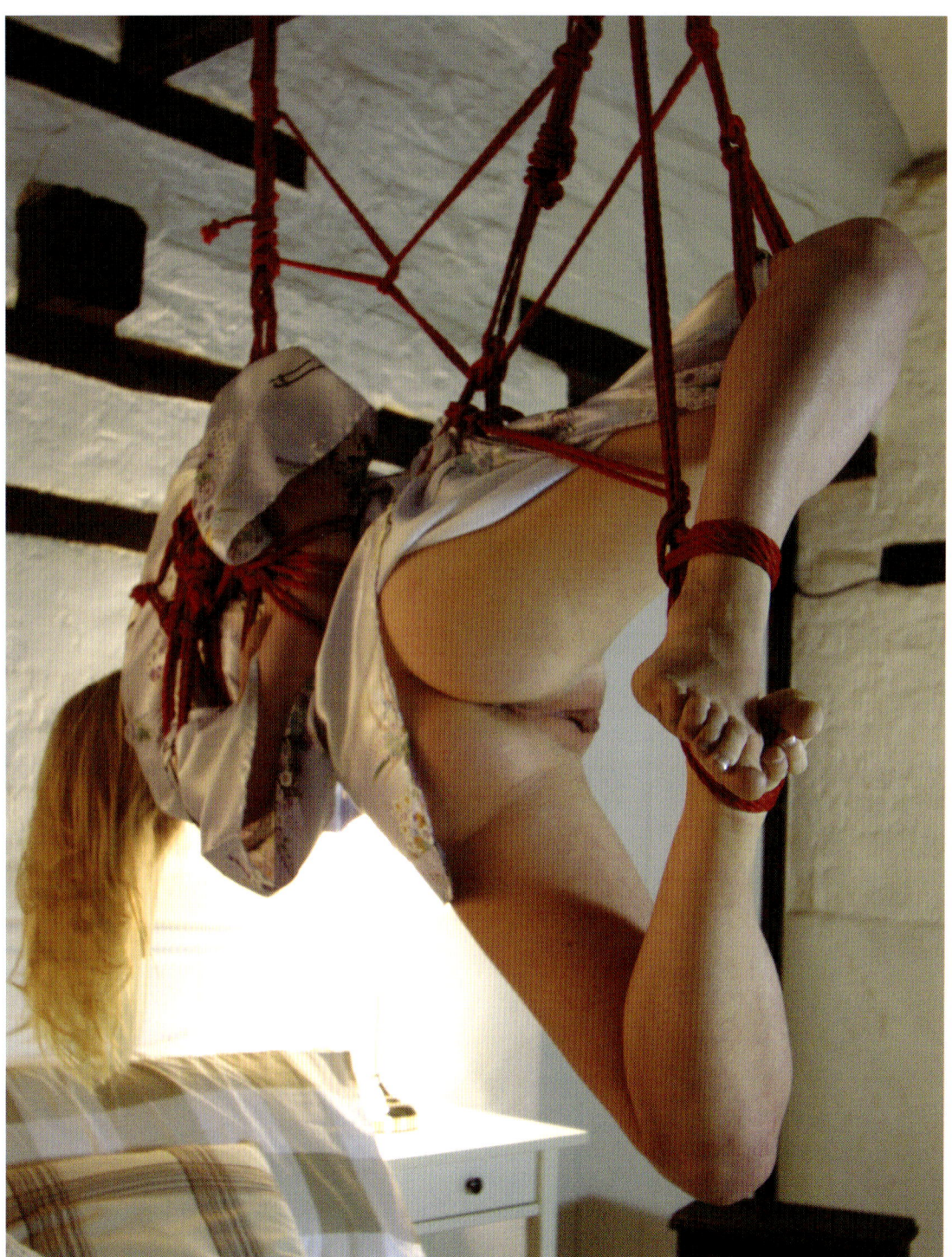

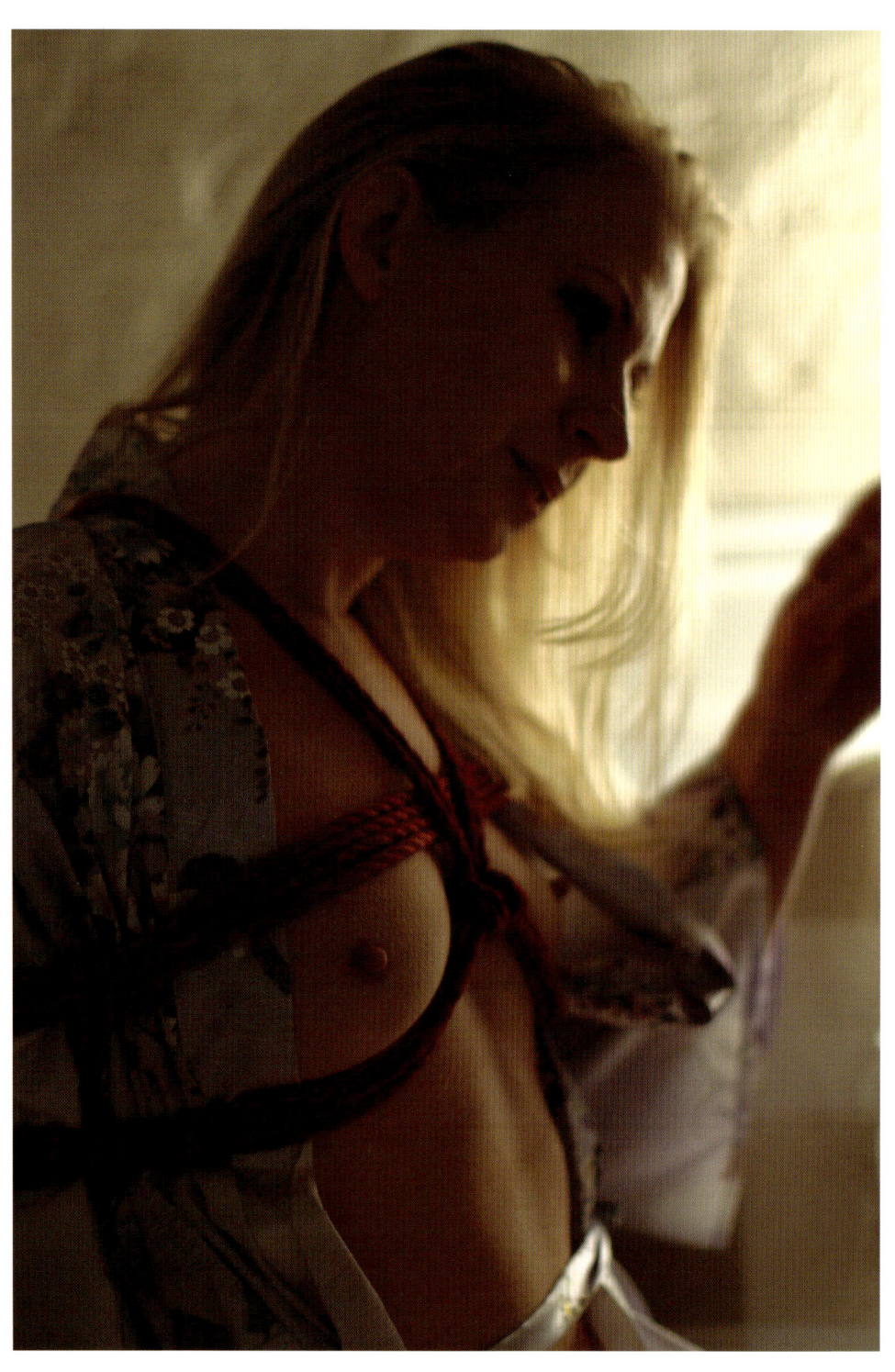

With him, le petit mort

Followed by relief and sleep

But my Kinbakushi takes her time

To bring me back to Earth

Heavenly

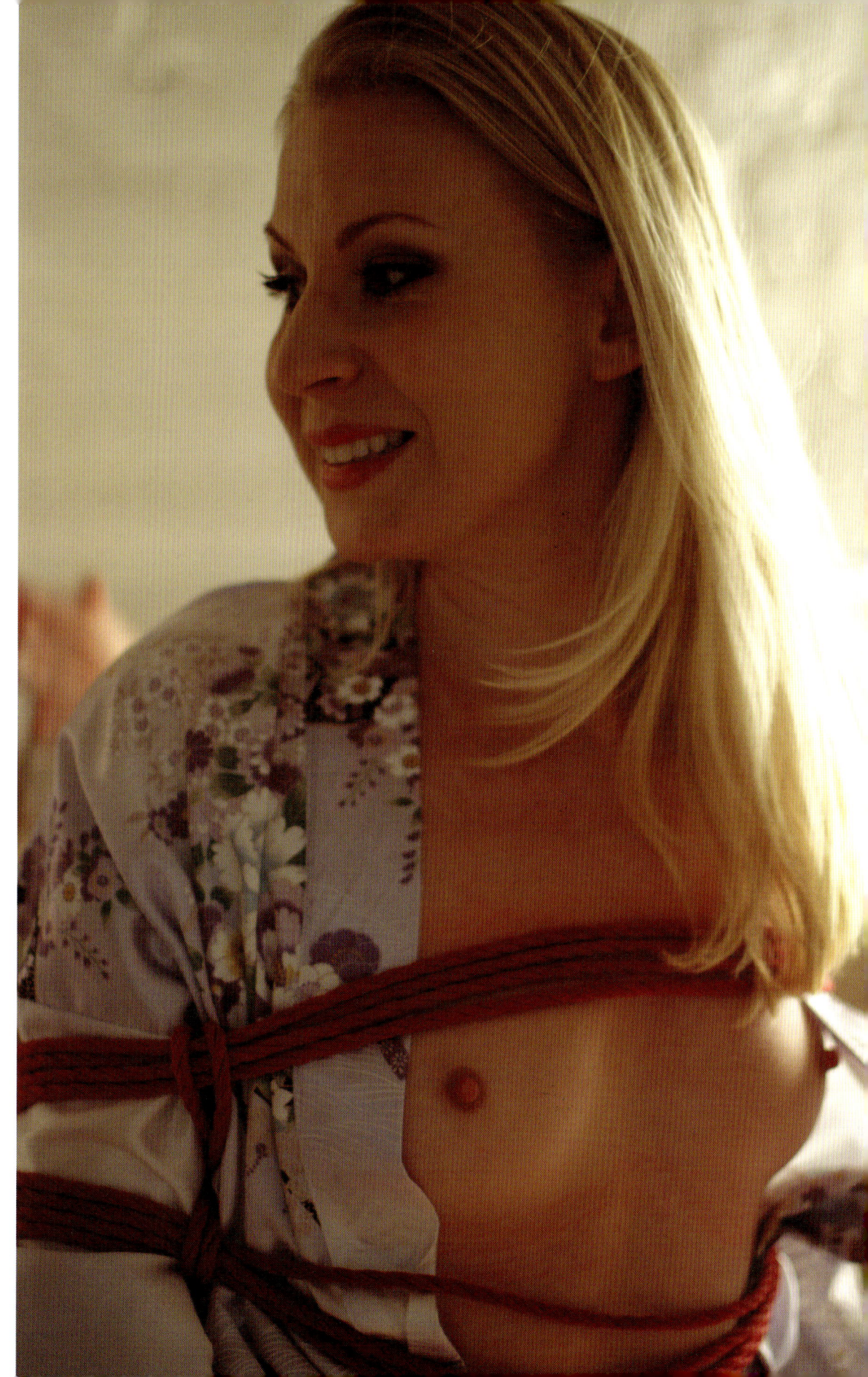

Chapter 7

Elissa is hung

Photography: Kahboom

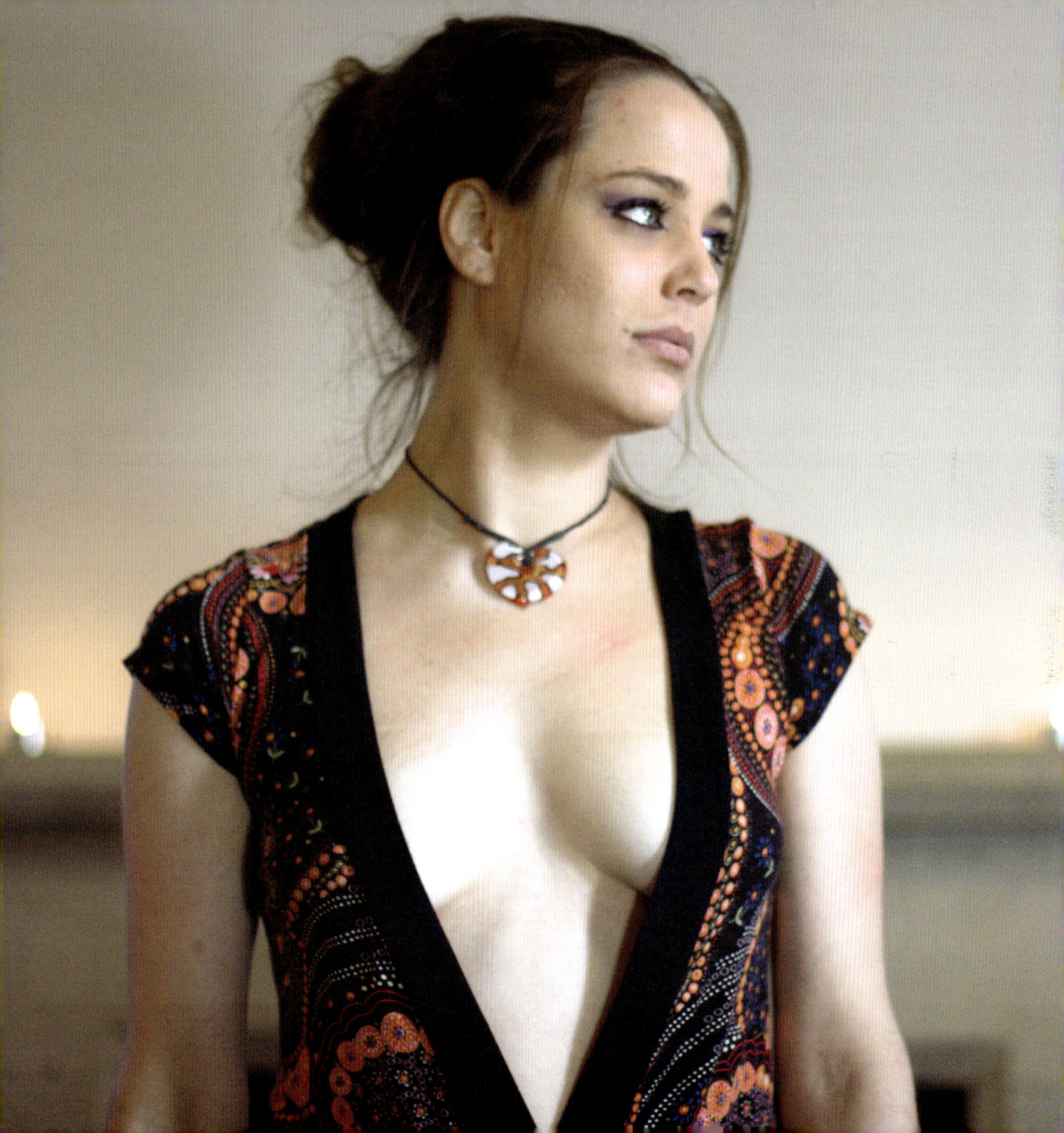

She waits in submission
The young girl
Uncertain what will happen
What will be her punishment?

The rope binds her young breasts
Beauty is released as they are bound
What did she do to deserve THIS?
What did she do to DESERVE this

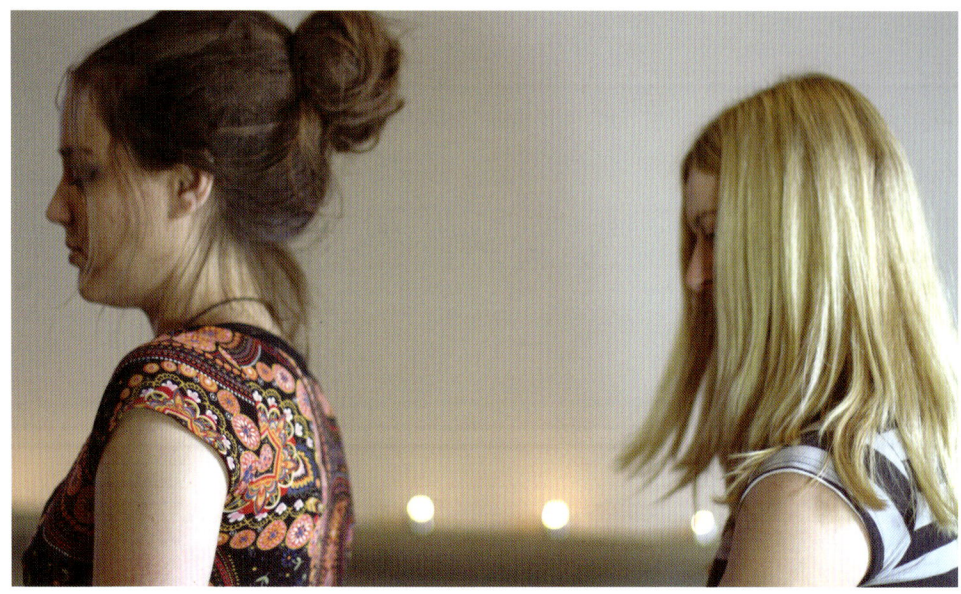

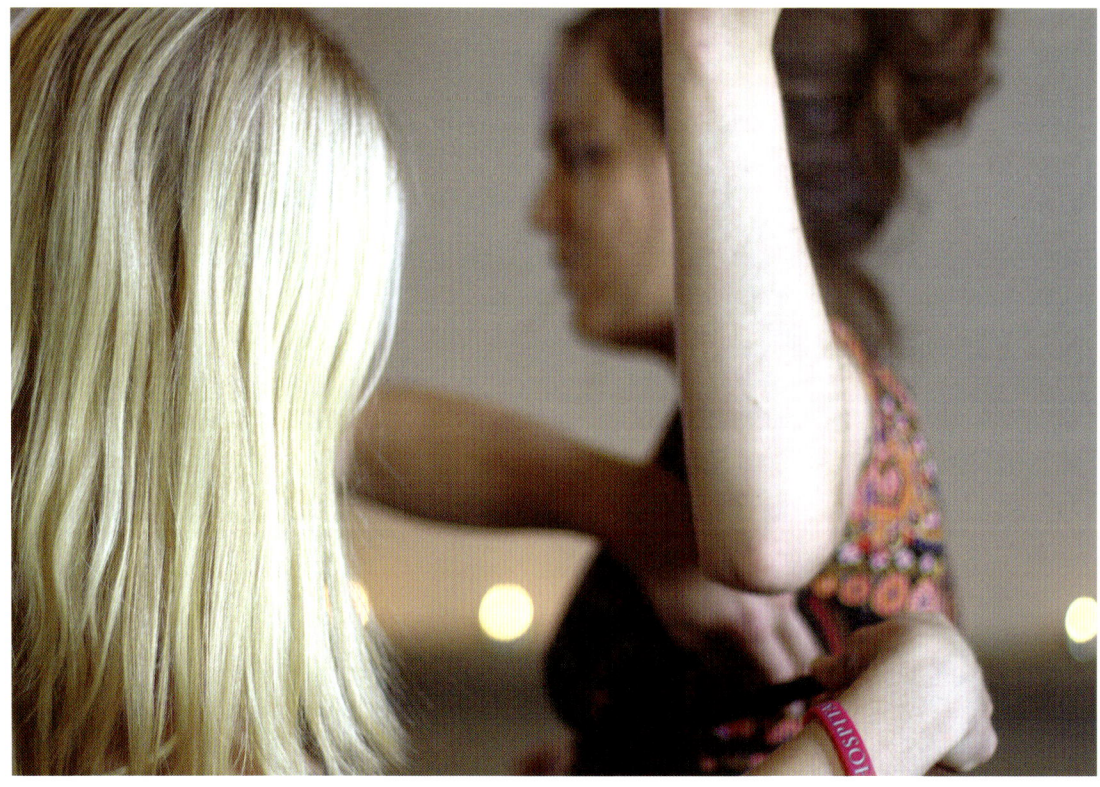

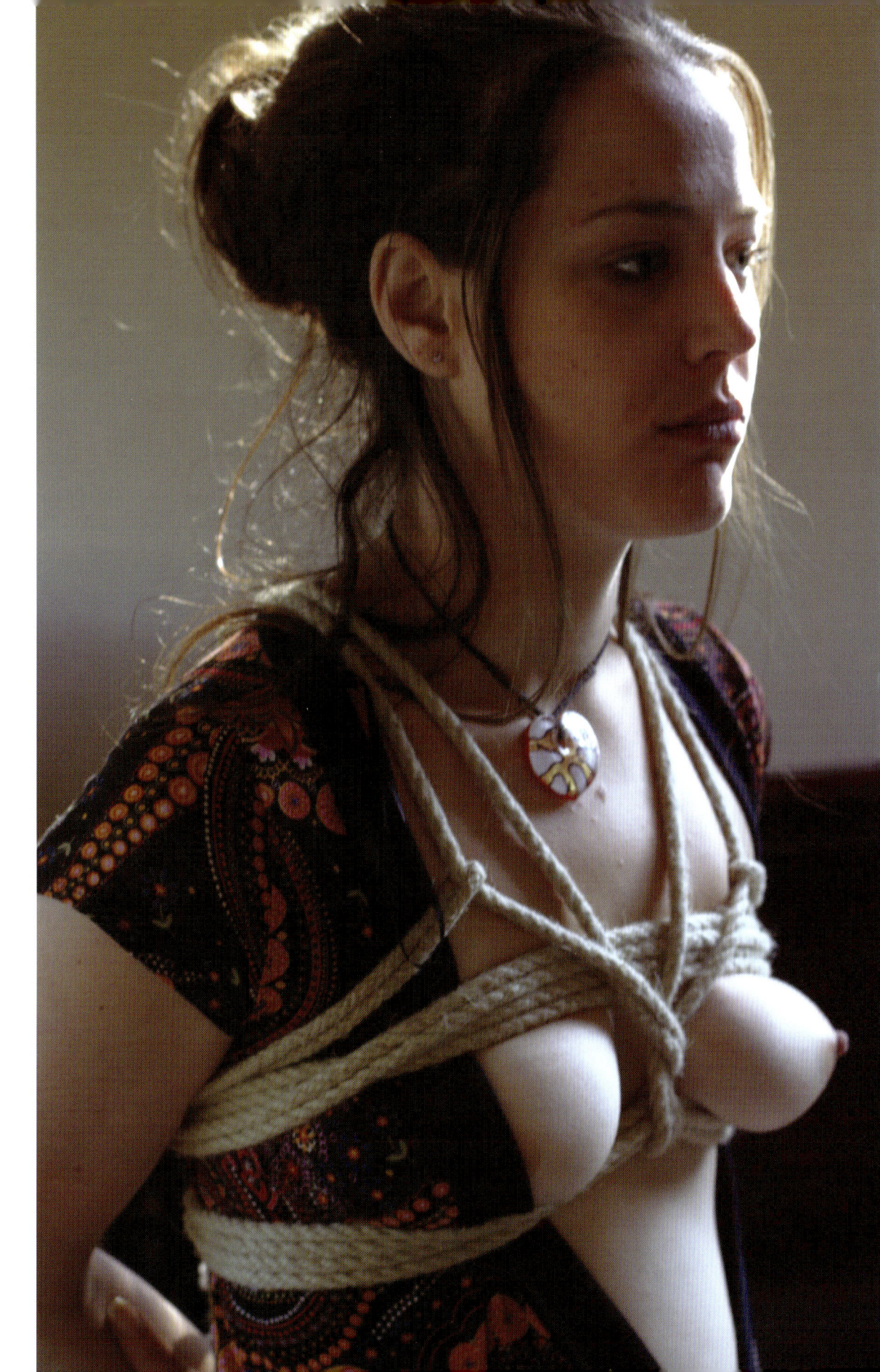

Only ropes clothe her now

But she is confident

No submission here

There is freedom in acceptance

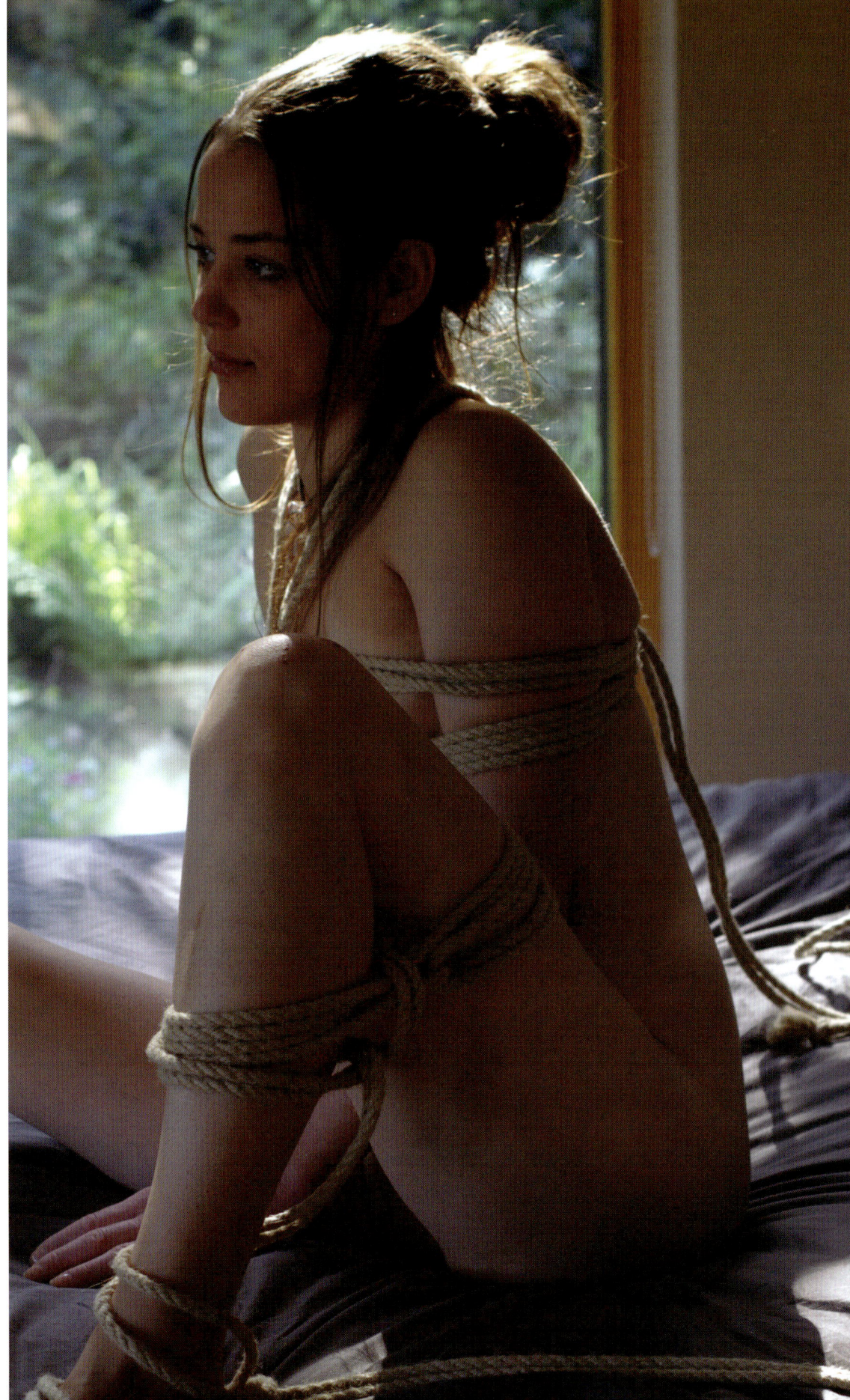

So far the trial is easy

No discomfort

No pain

Just uncertainty

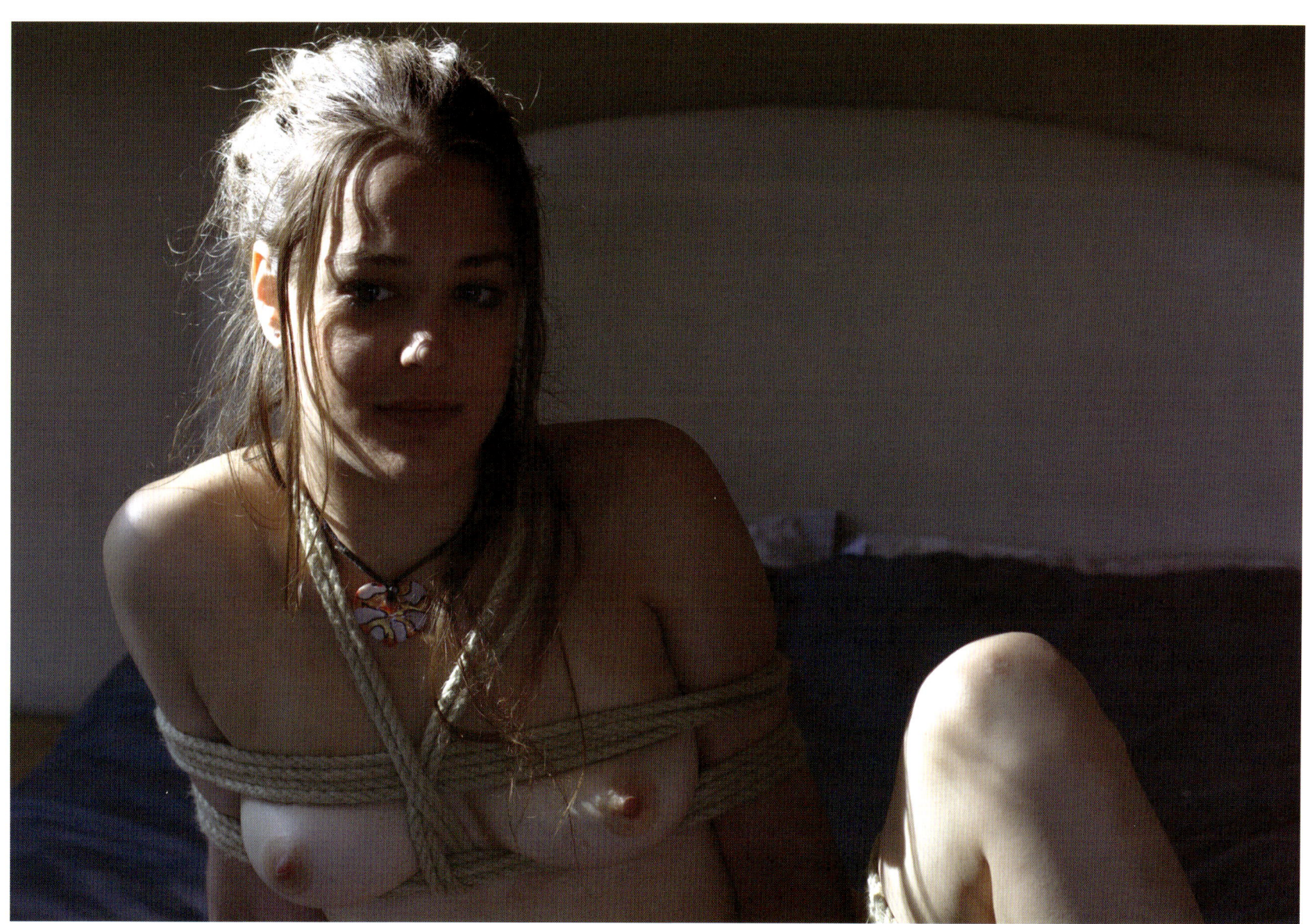

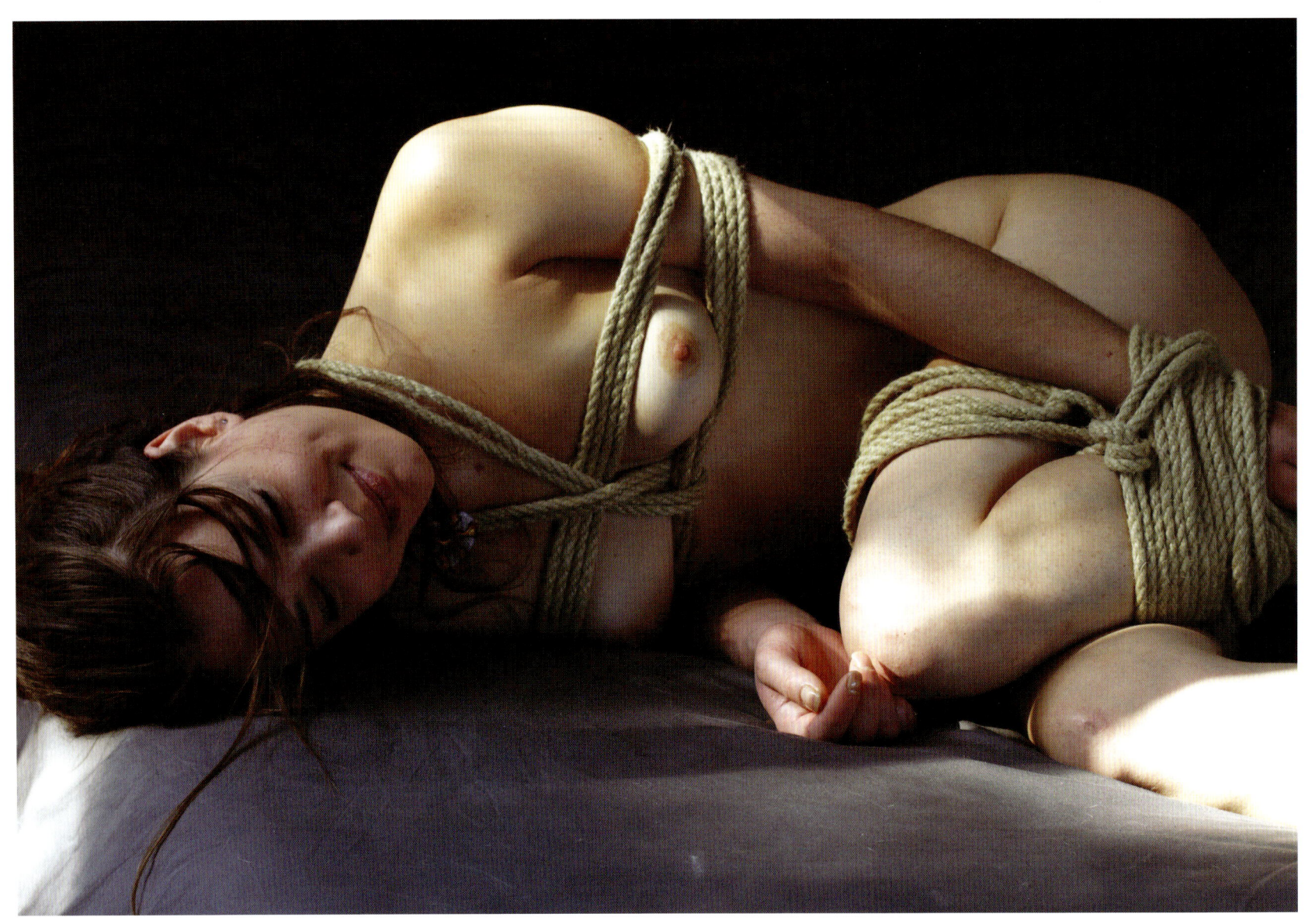

She is being prepared

Played with

Lulled into a false sense of security

Awaiting her sentence

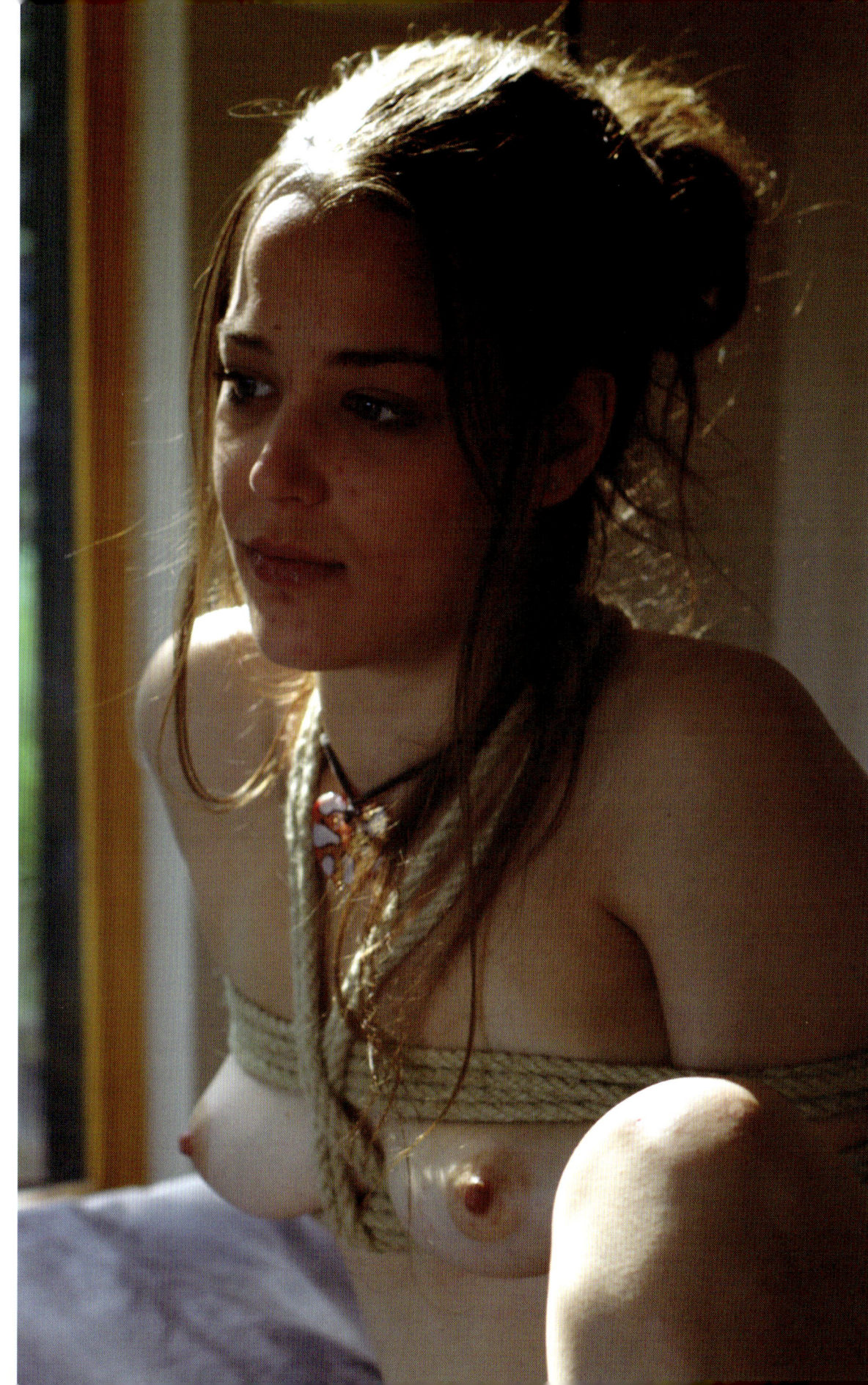

She will be hung

She will not stand on the earth

The ropes will do their job

Keeping her safe and also in pain

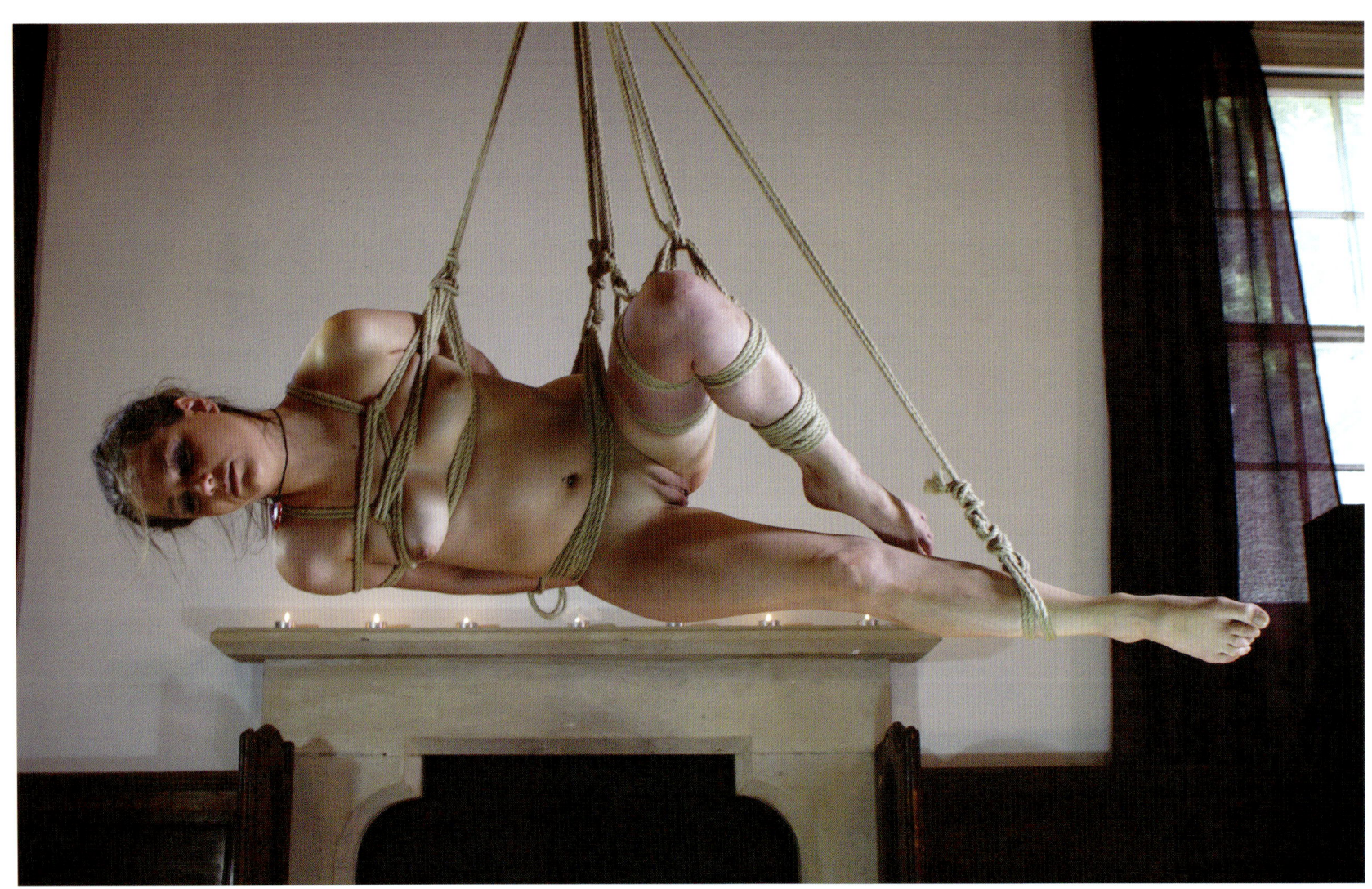

She forms an alliance

With her bondage

She submits to her captor

She strikes a deal

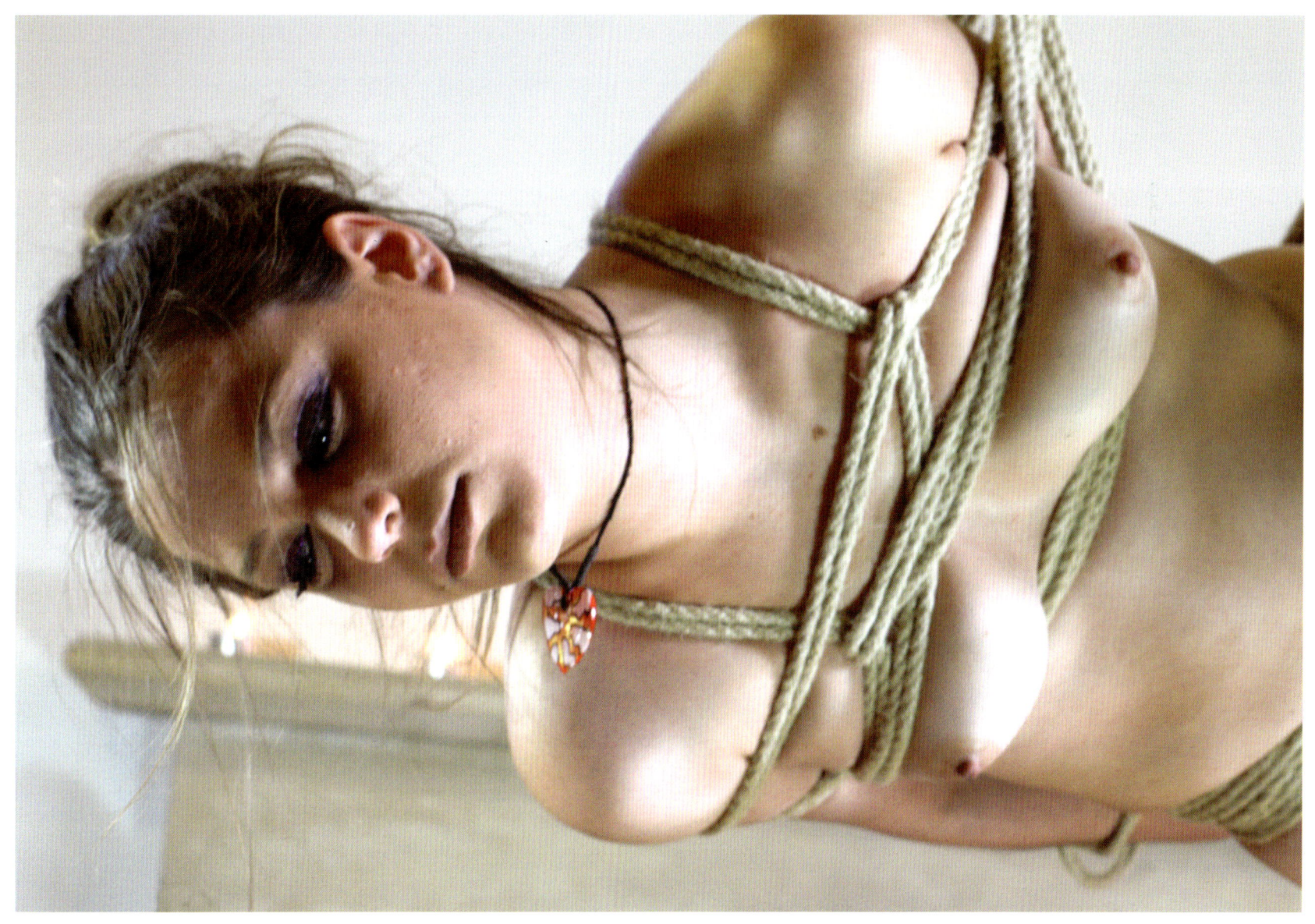

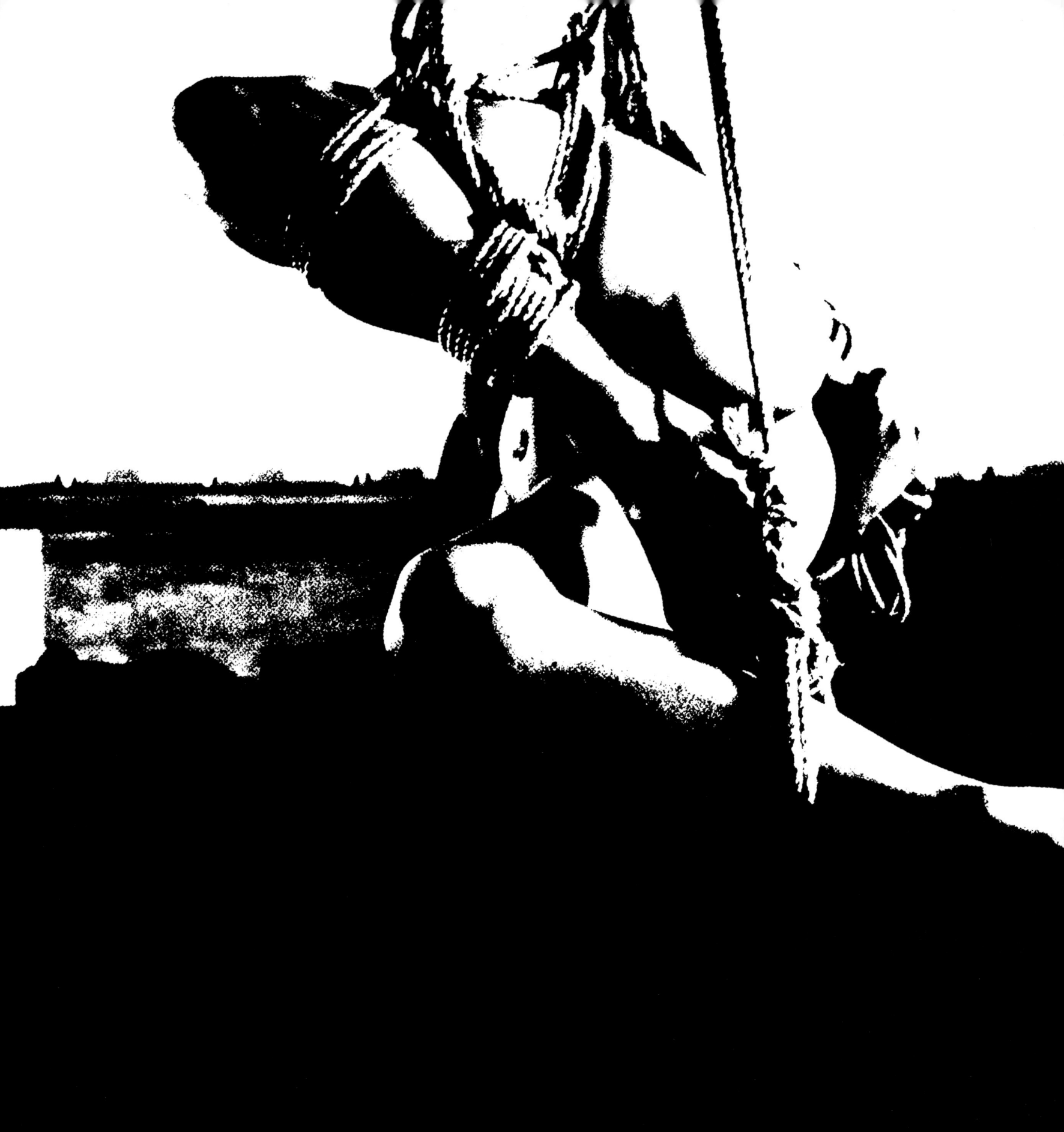

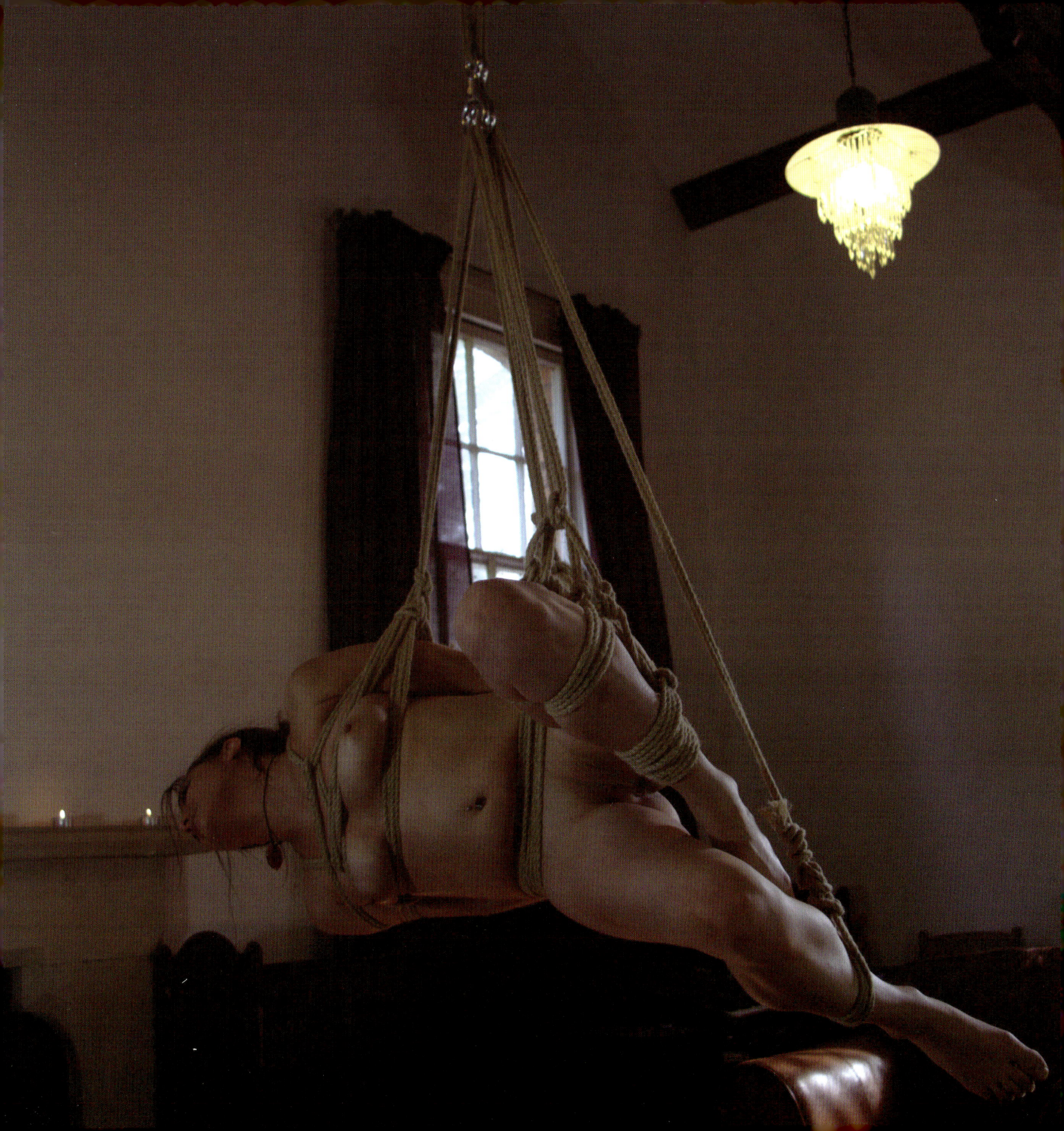

Although her sentence

Is to be hung

She discovers

That she will be hung until she is alive

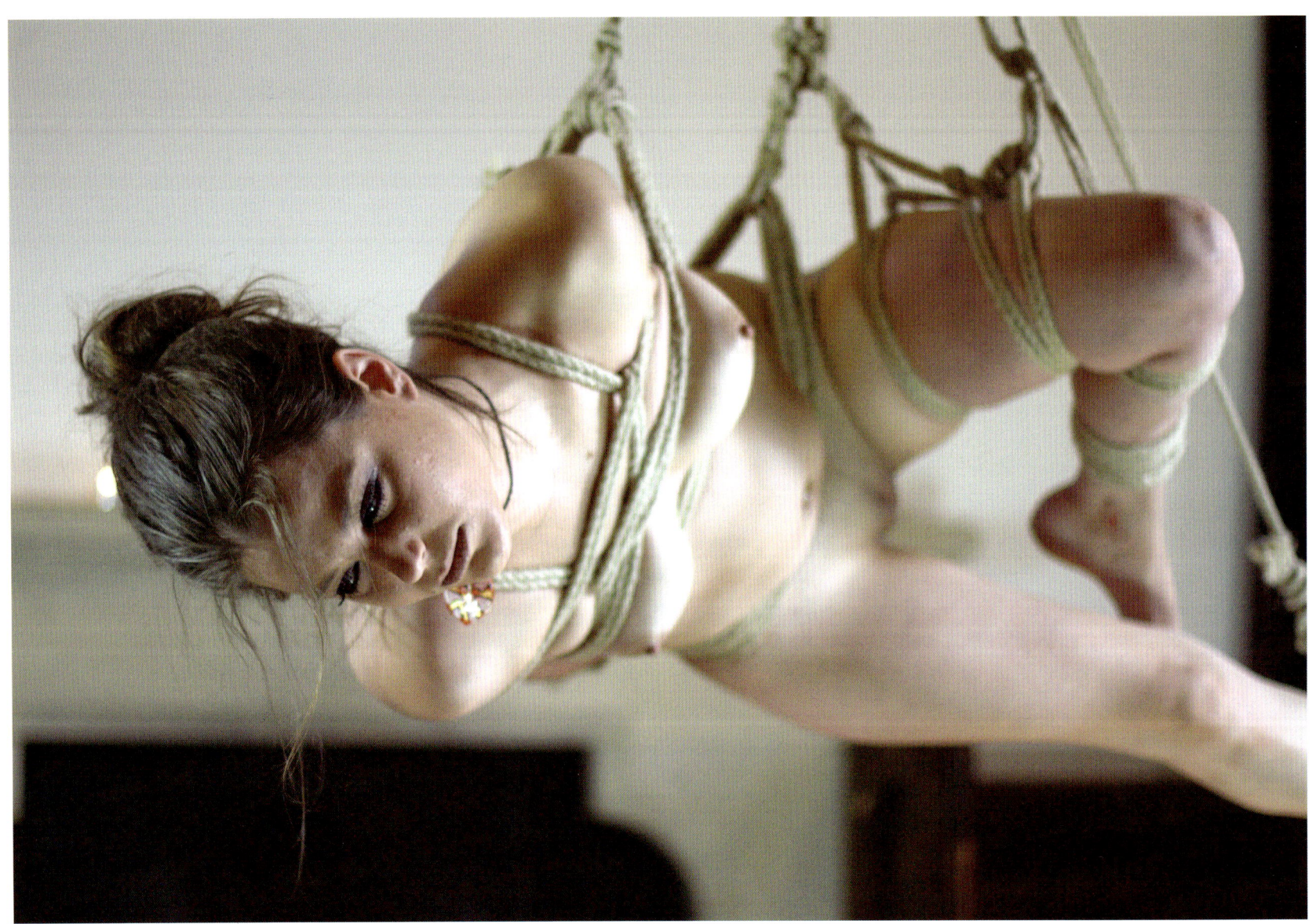

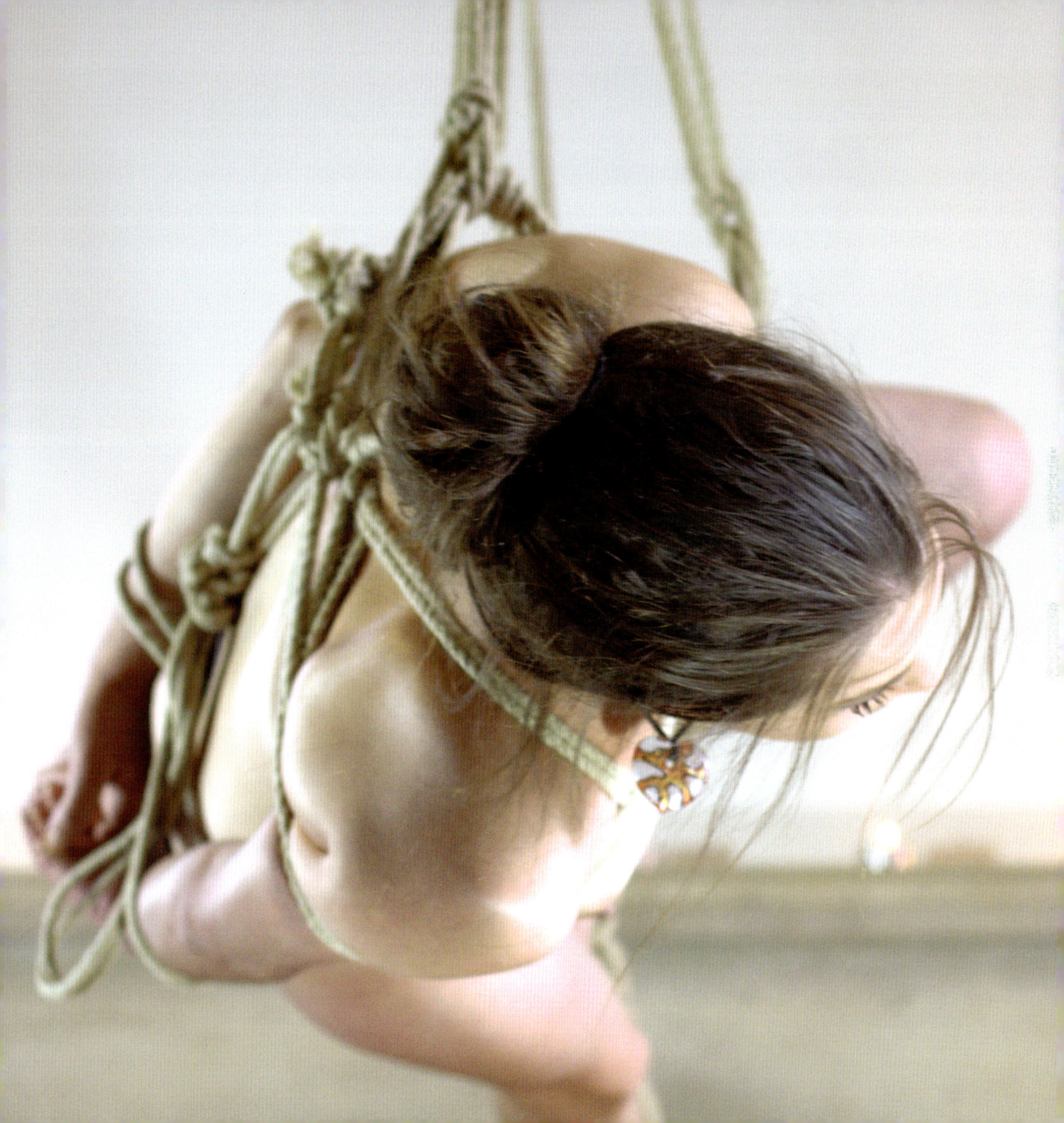

Chapter 8

Miumi-U meets Adé-dì Kàn

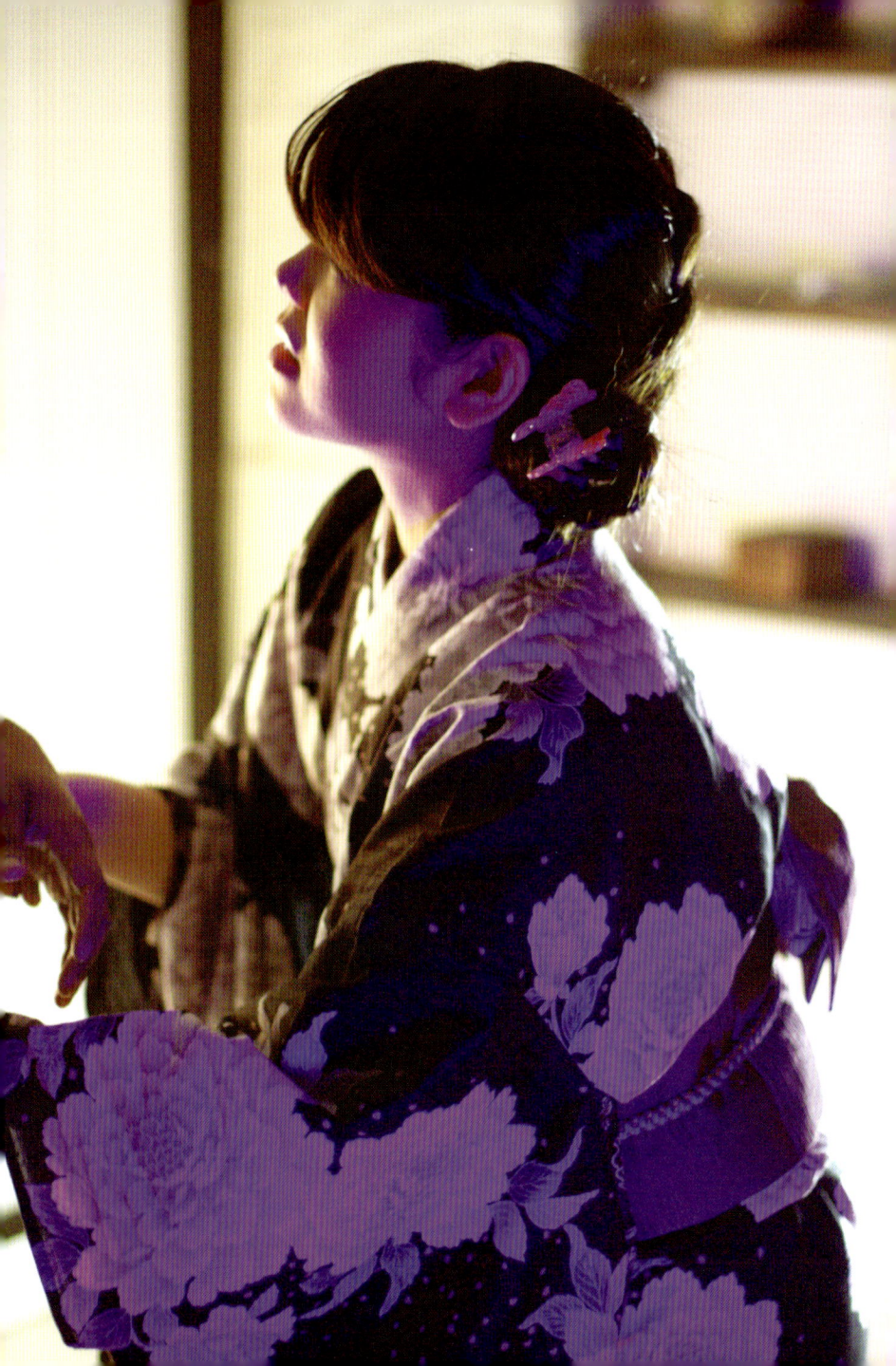

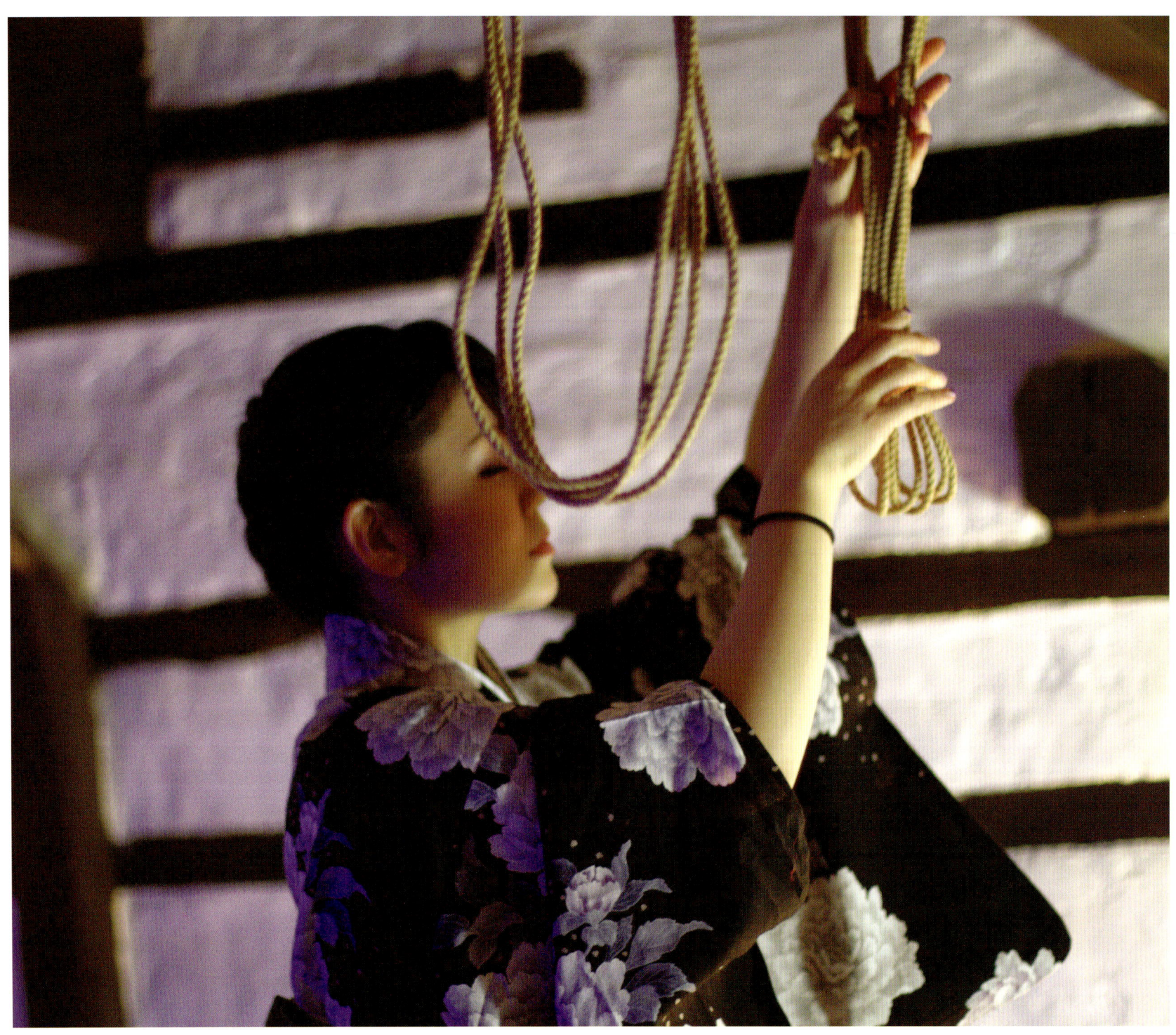

My first thought when I heard about Shibari was 'I don't think so'. Fast forward to one year later 'I am a sworn addict'

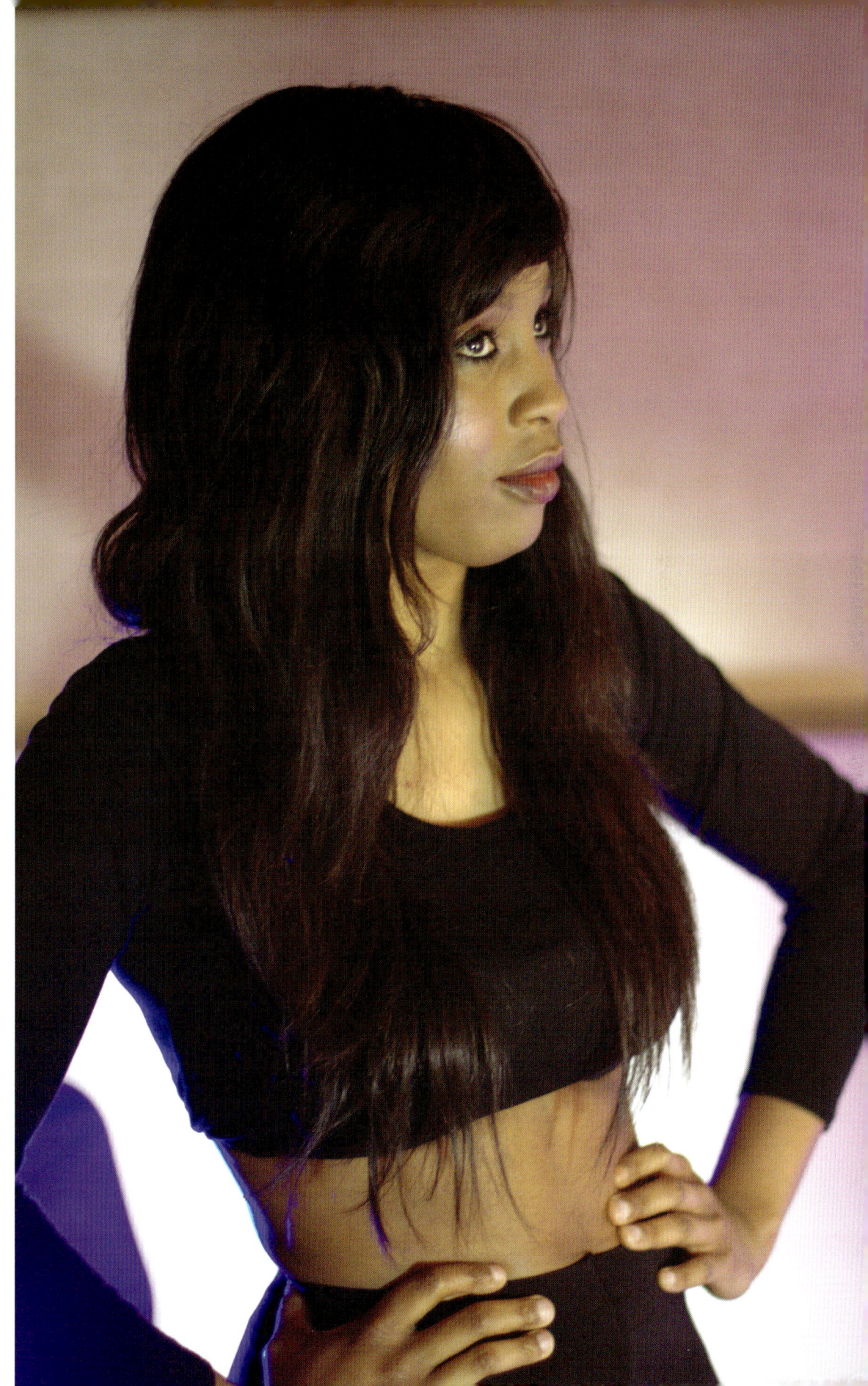

For me it is a form of emotional release...
a release from my thoughts... a release from
life troubles... a release from responsibility...

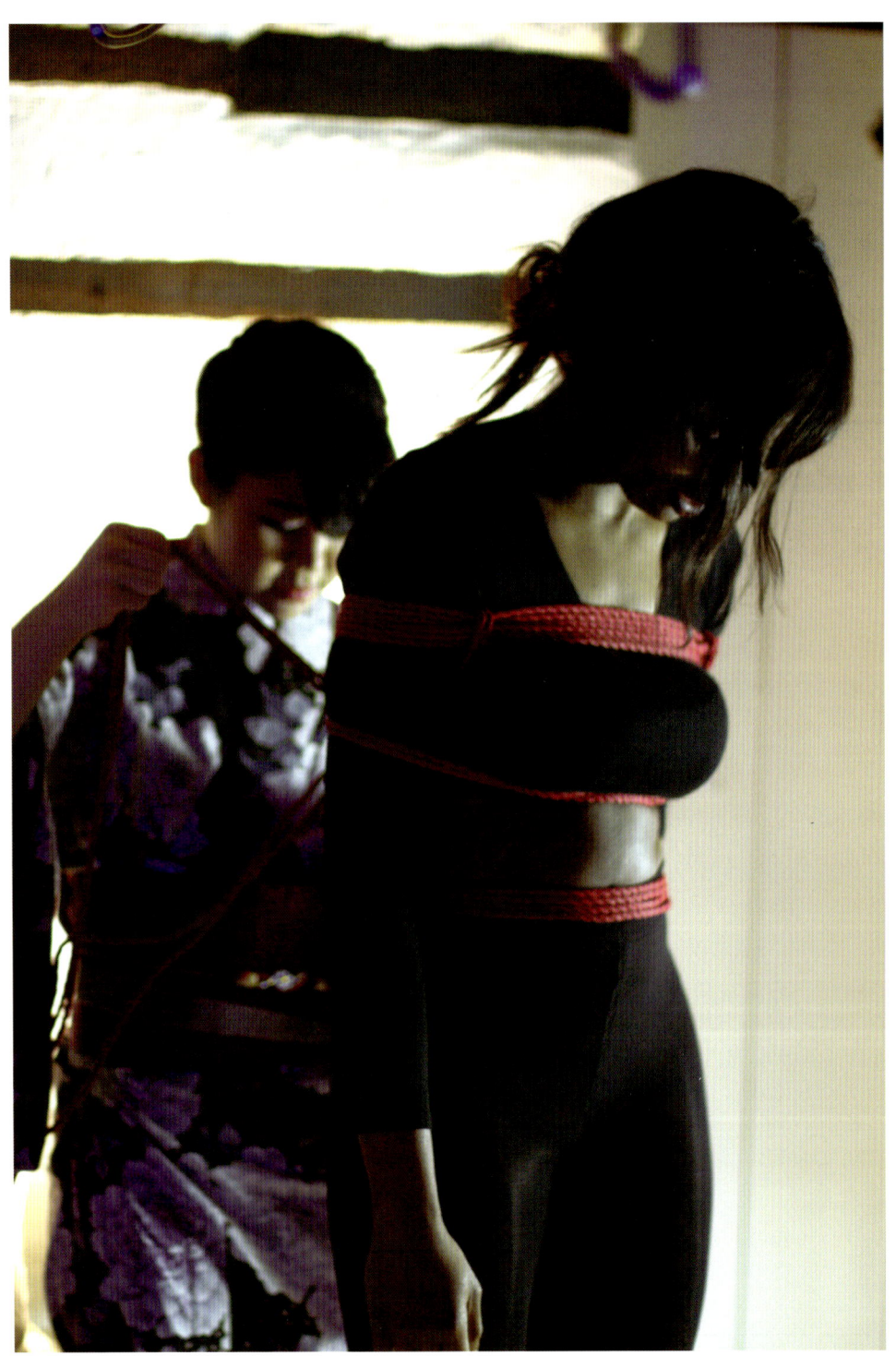

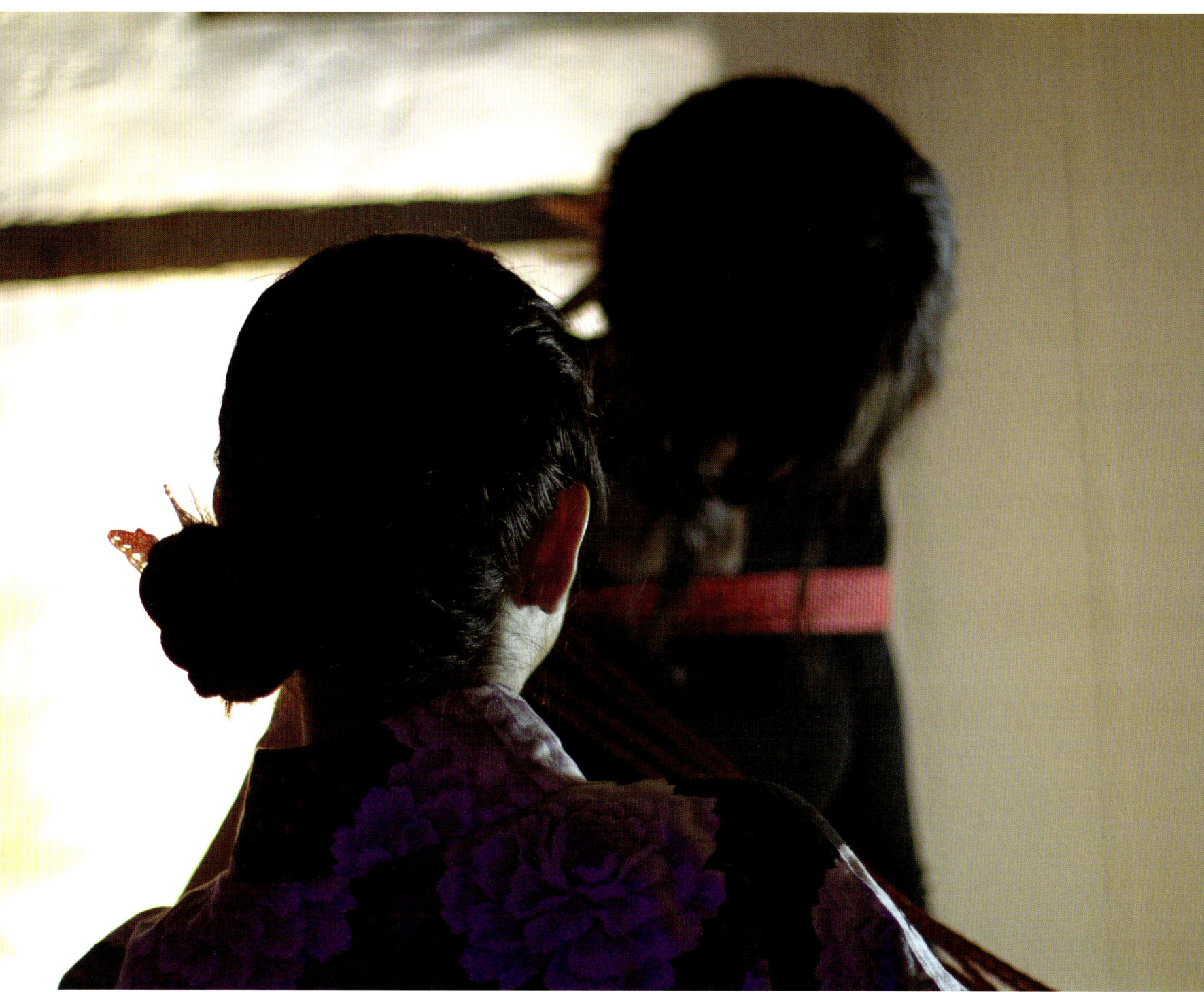

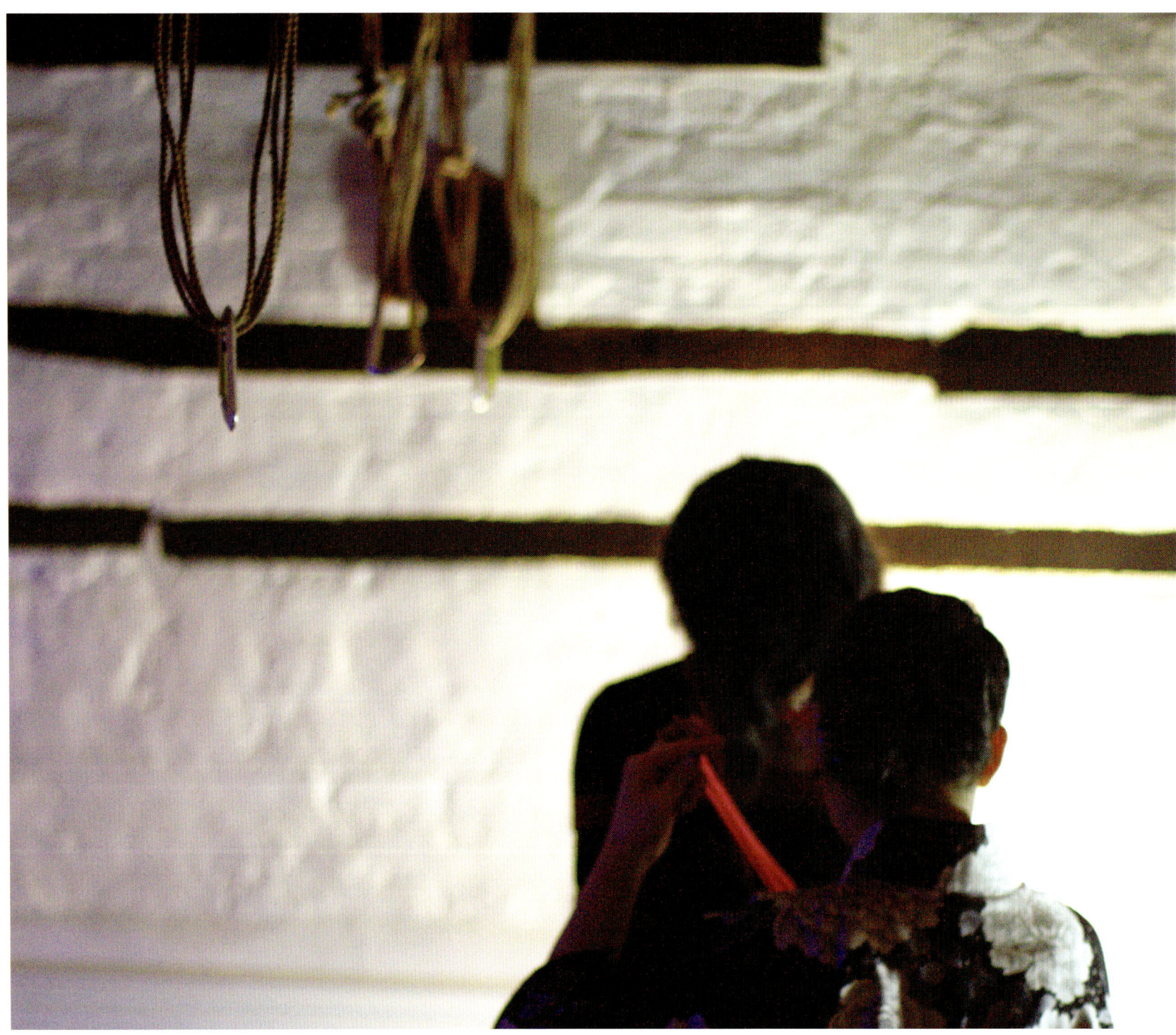

Being suspended in the air with nothing to hold on to but your mind... is a surreal experience... it is indescribable... it is perfect... it is beautiful... it is whole...

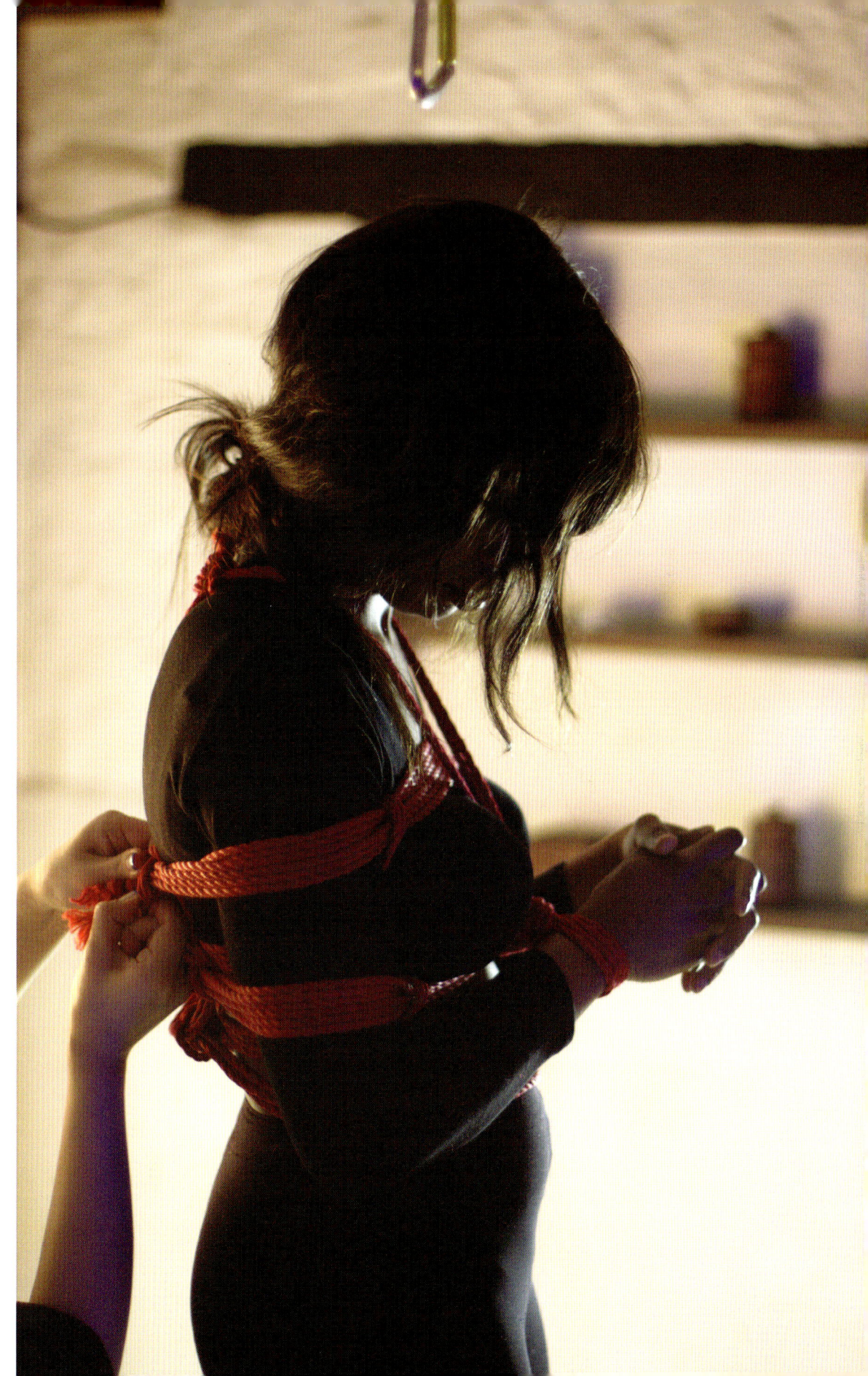

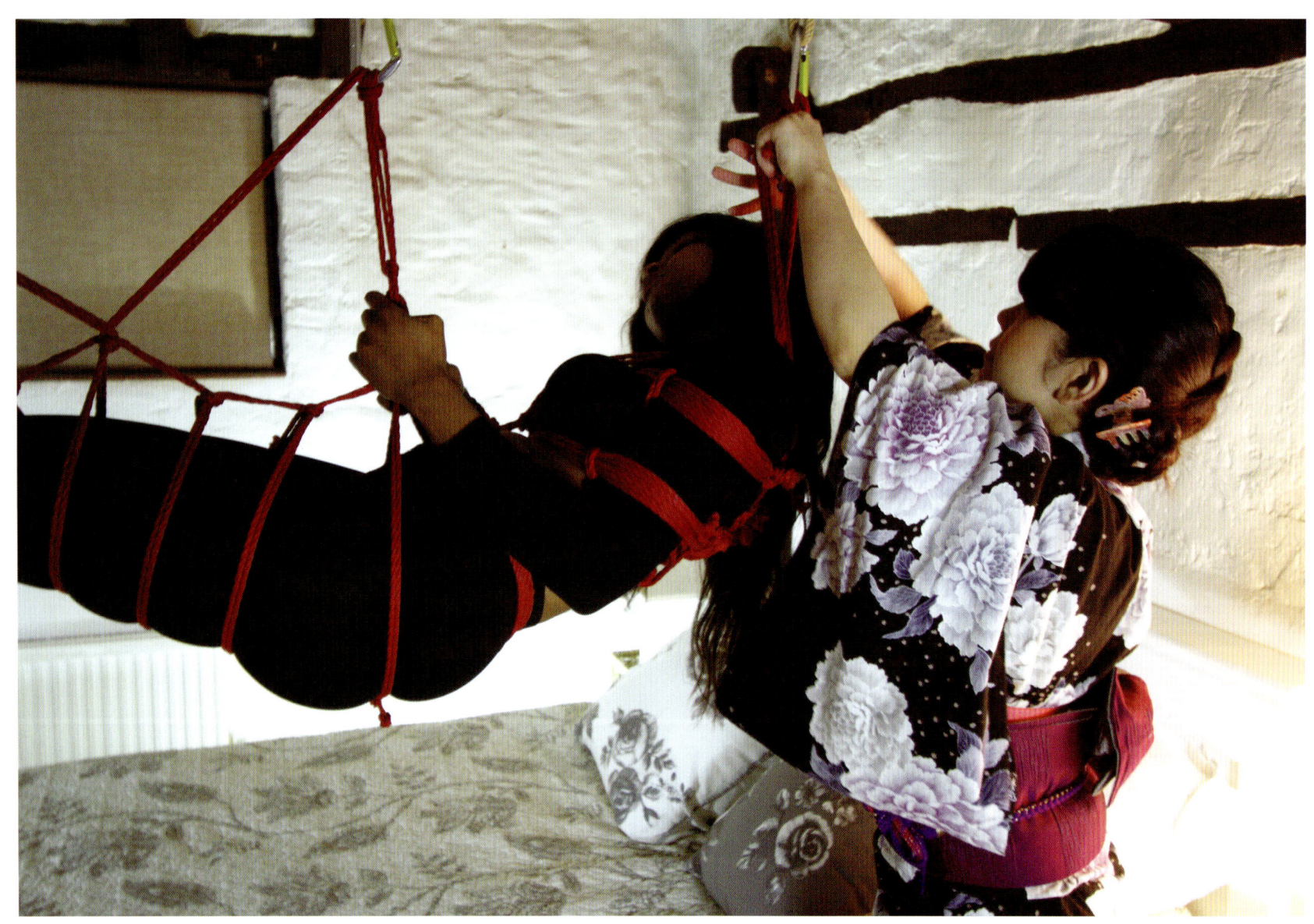

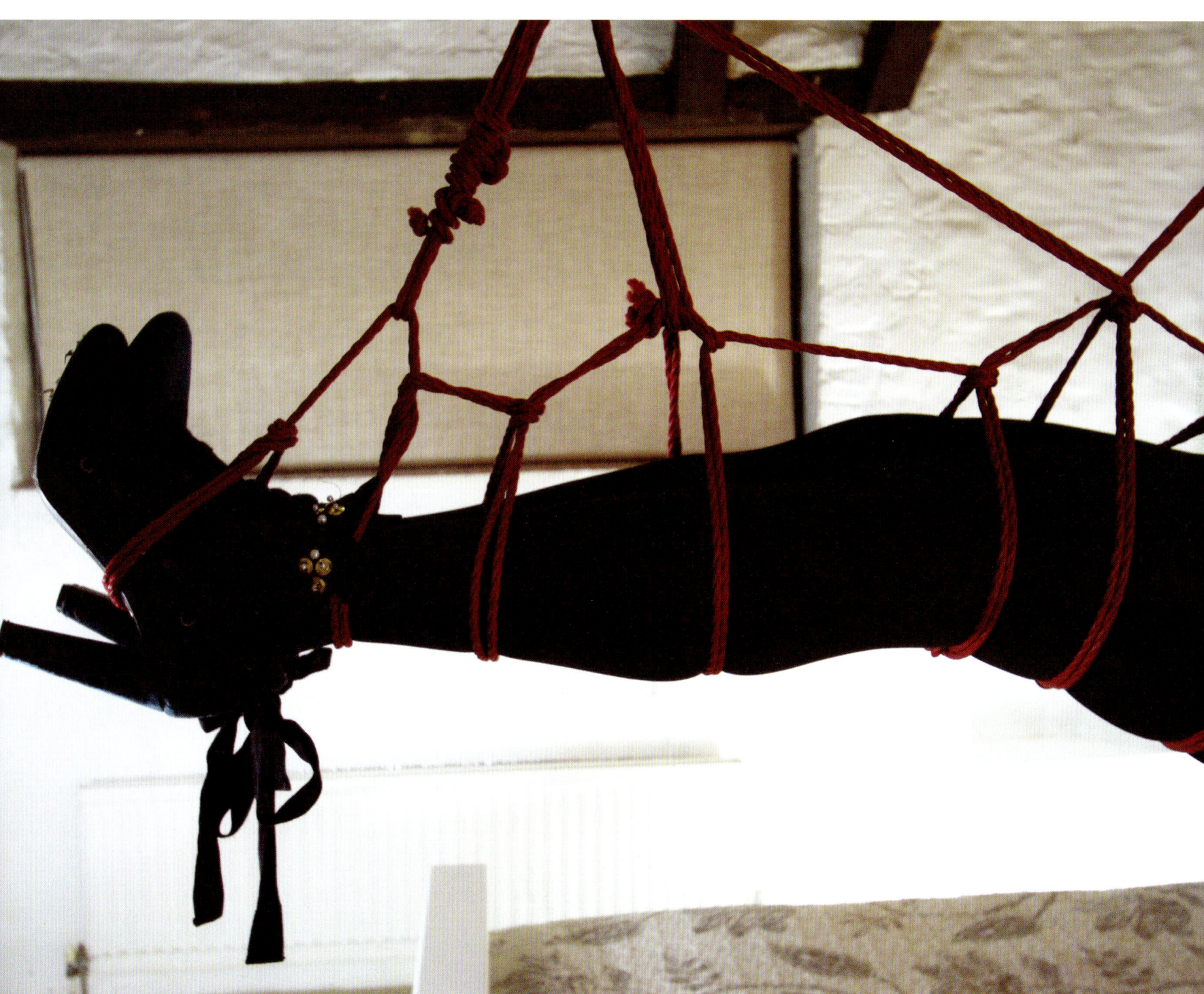

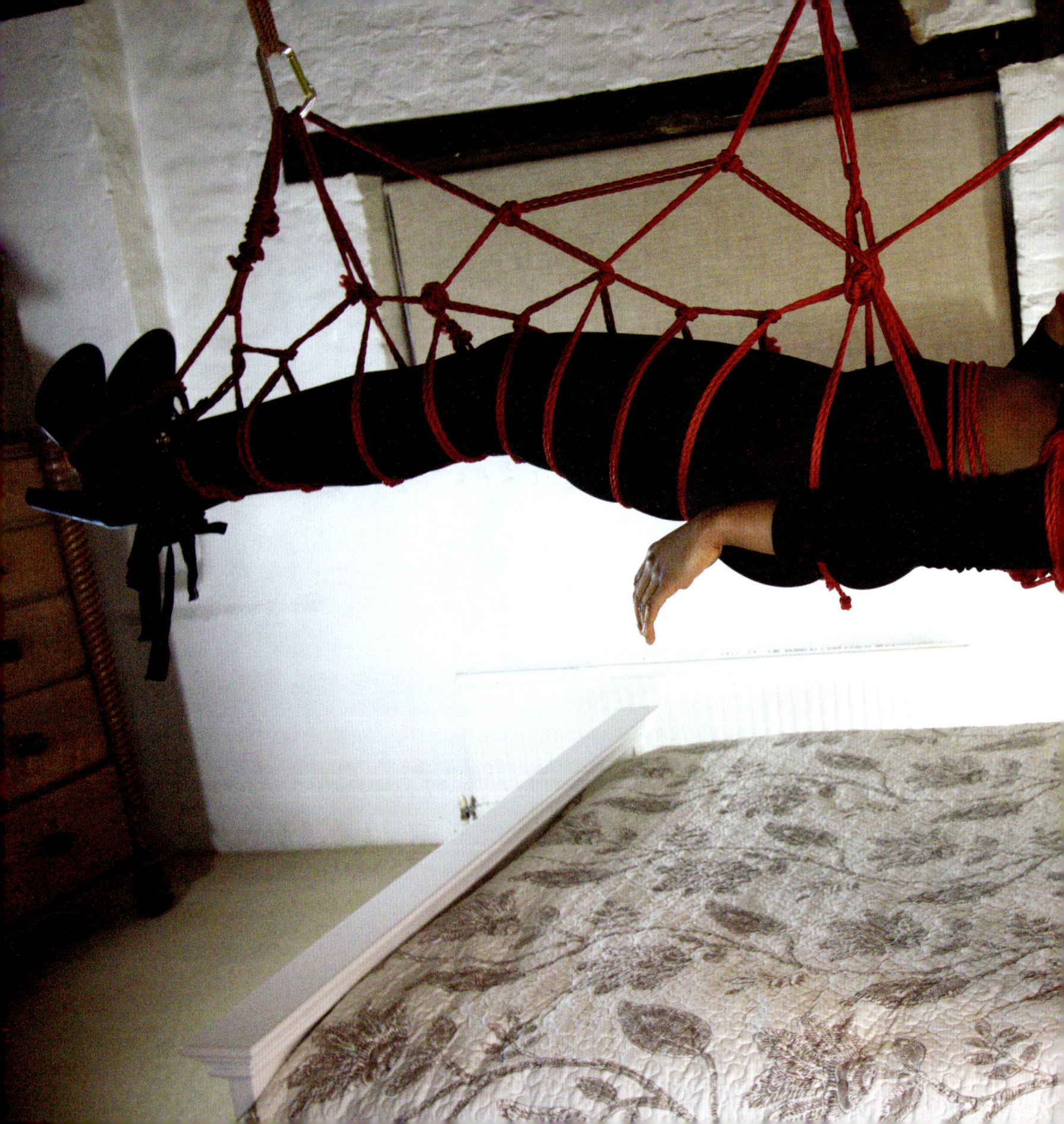

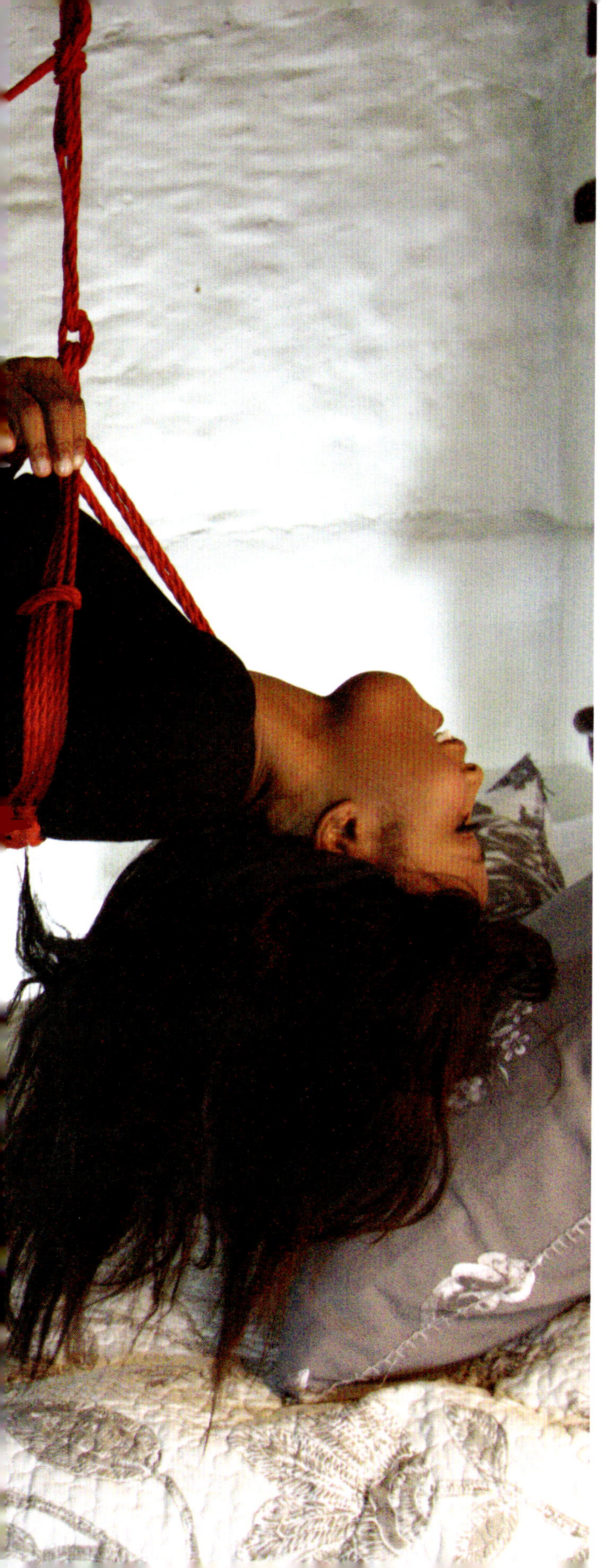

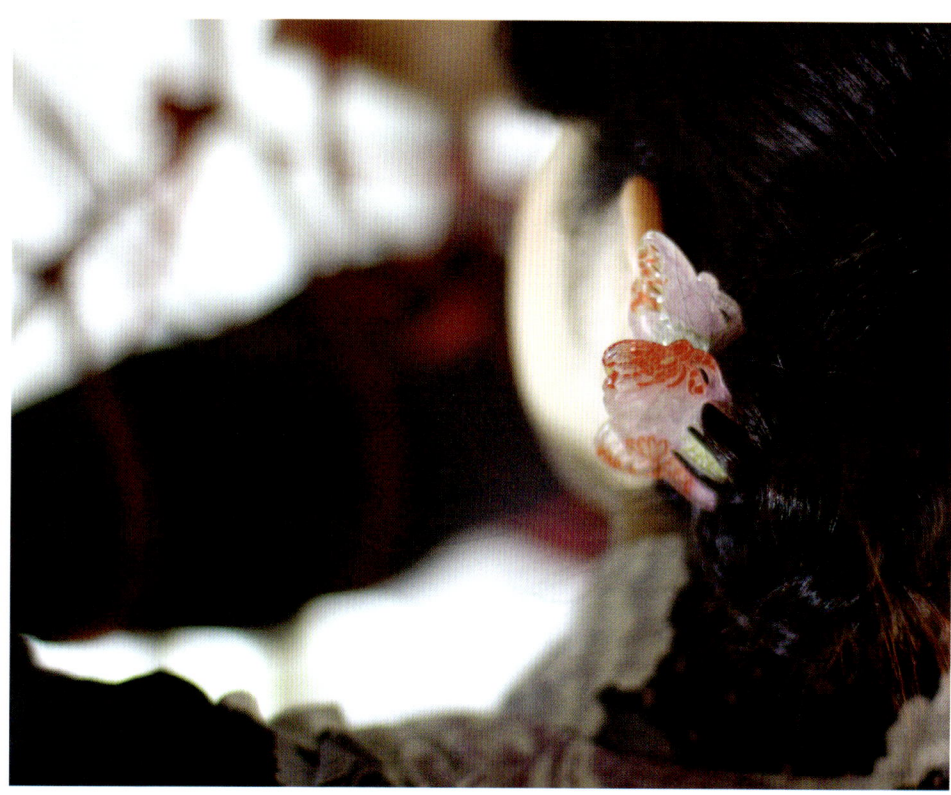

Meeting Miumi-U took the experience to another level...

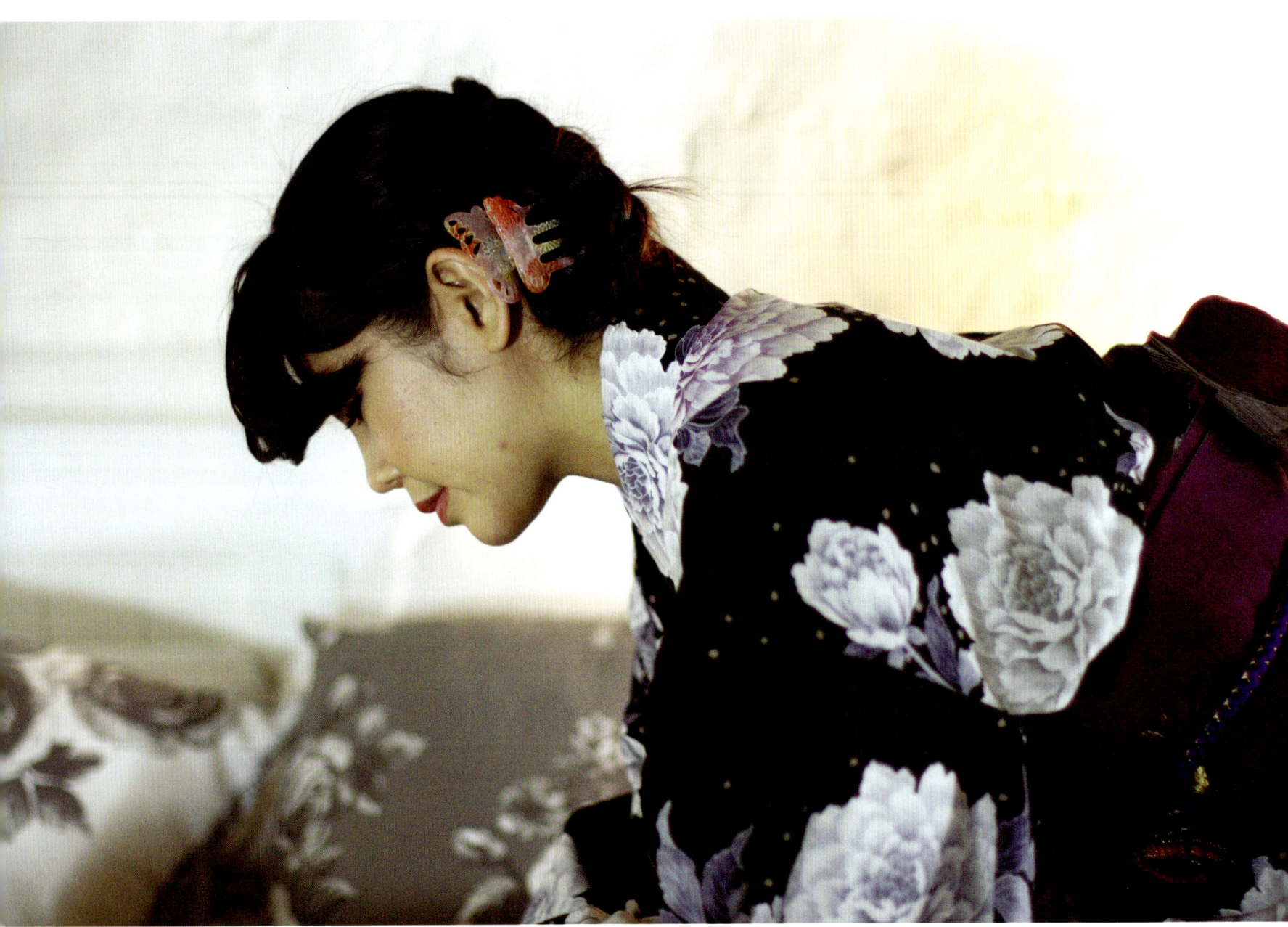

To have a 'delicate flower' tie you up
so gently gives me the feeling that I am
untouchable, I can do anything in the
world... I am whole.... I am beautiful...
I AM WOMAN.

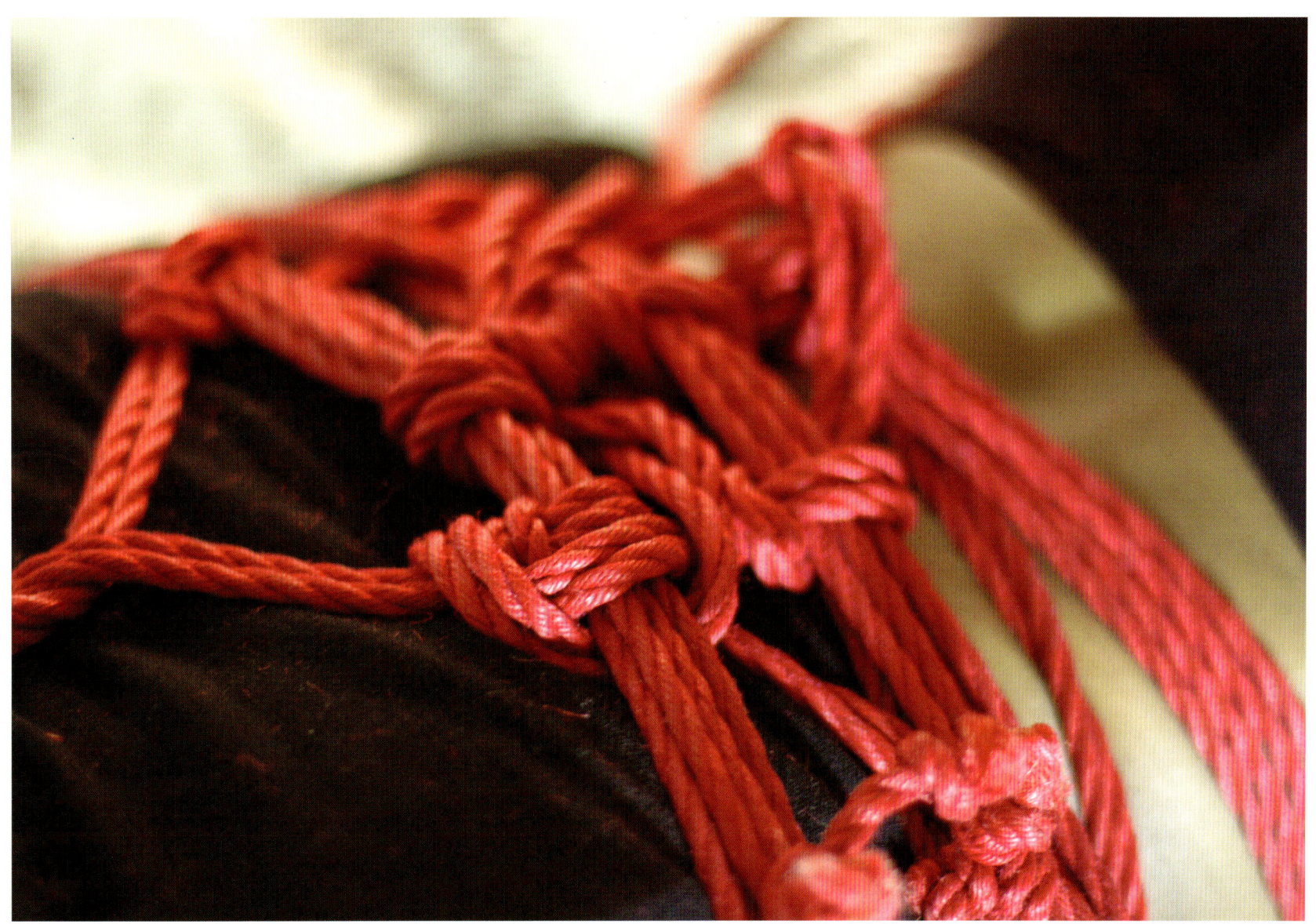

Halcyon

Azure Dragon writes: I am a photographer working in London but originally from the Far East. I started in landscape photography from age of eight. It's very lucky that I had full access to a dark room and printing facility so that I could take photos and print them by myself. This gave me a lot of detailed understanding about photography from early age. Over time I became more interested in portrait, art nude and emotions of people. This partially led me to go down to the path of photographing Japanese shibari.

The discovery of Japanese kinbaku is purely by chance for me. The strong emotion and magical bond between the rope master and the person who is tied deeply impressed me. The rope is the intermediator between the sides, it is very individual, personal and carries the message from the master's mind. There are certainly extreme aspects of Janpanese kinbaku, and I like to use strong light and shadow contrast to express these feelings, to tell the story of what an observer may witness. It took me a while to understood the relationship and the love between the master and the person being tied. Suspension demands more from the rope master and model, but when it is in the right form, they are beautiful, balanced and carry strong emotions. I have been working on a kinbaku project since 2010 and more of my work can also been seen on Fine Art America.

Photography: Azure Dragon

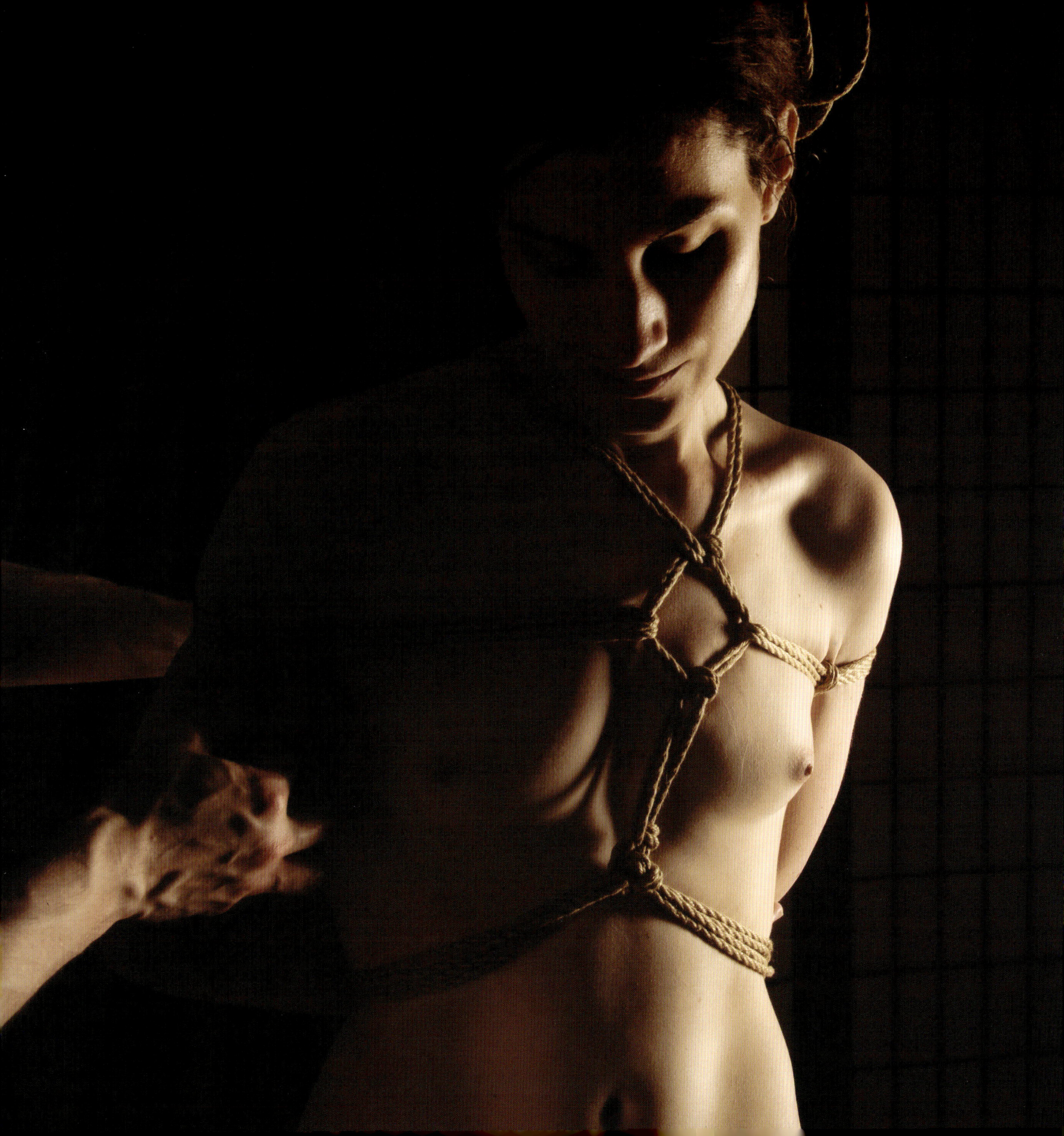

Halcyon - Her personal story

There is something wild about rope, almost primitive, a very tactile form of contact. It can be like water, a gentle, soothing caress. It flows over and around the body, slowly but surely twisting and restricting, ensnaring the body and the mind. Or it can be violent and forceful, like standing on a stormy cliff with the elements raging, swept up in the chaotic energy.

To me one of the main appeals of rope is rooted in the exchange of power that takes place, the feeling of being carried away. There is a very intimate connection with the rope and the person manipulating it, with the rope acting as a mental binding too. The ropes act like a sort of second skin, or a protective cocoon, biting into the skin but holding you securely. Being tied paradoxically brings a feeling of freedom, especially in suspensions where it feels like you're flying or giddy. To me it's a very personal moment, almost contemplative, where the outside world ceases to exist.

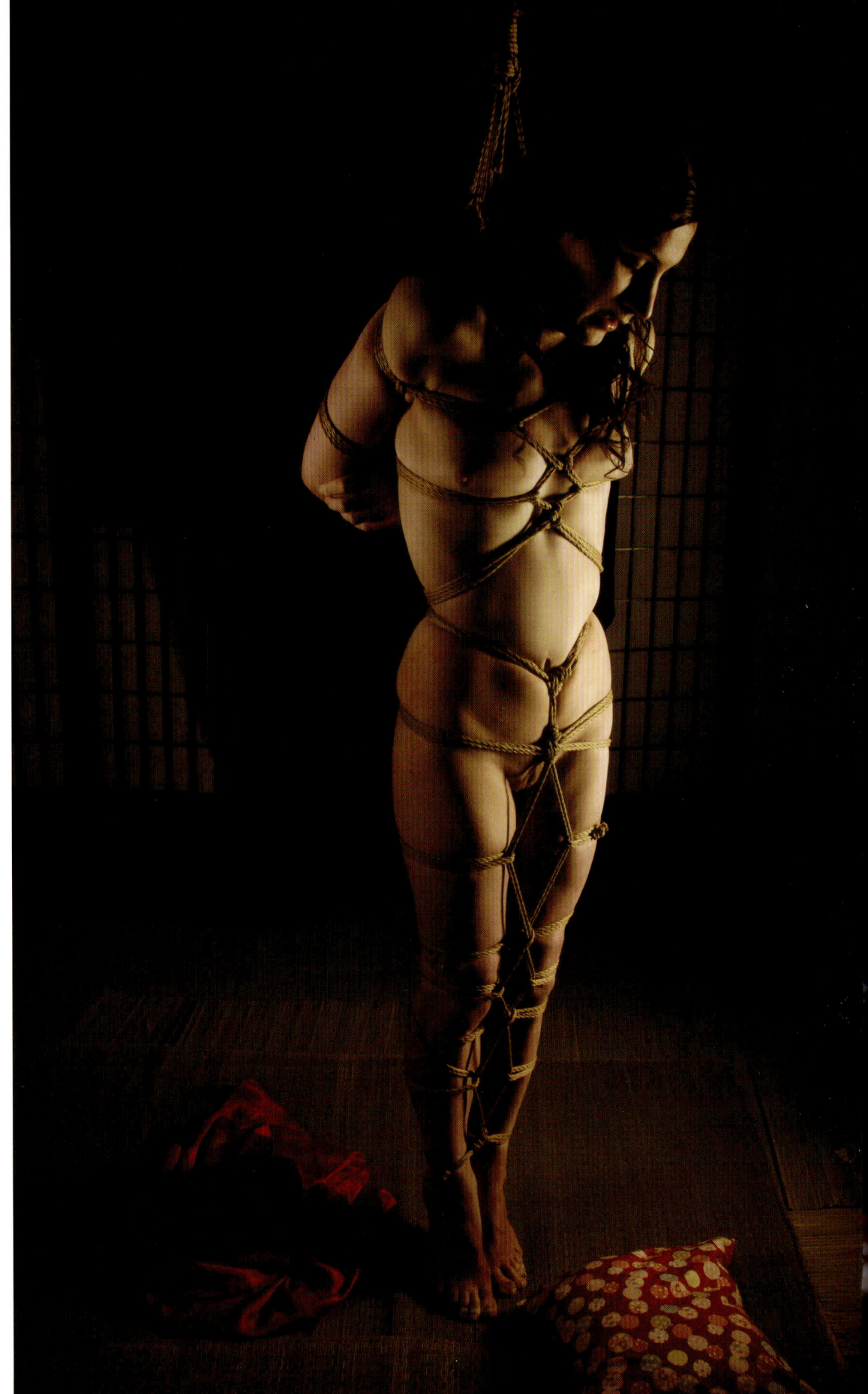

Pain is another major element for me as well, and I'm drawn towards seeking difficult positions that put a stress on the body and the mind. It's a thrill seeking the challenge to see how far your body can be pushed, while taking care still to be safe and suffer no permanent harm. It is not (quite) torture as practised historically, but rope suspensions or predicament bondage can be rather strenuous and put the mind in a meditative state, as the body processes the pain that radiates through the ropes.

Receiving pain while tied is a very different experience compared to being free: it is more of a state of helplessness where all sensations feel more raw, and harder to filter away as the body is denied any form of escaping. Rope does not have to be painful, and it can be more playful as well, or teasing. I must confess that I'm primarily a masochist, and so I tend to mix other forms of SM play with rope, but there is no single truth. Rope is a journey and it's always changing based on the impressions you seek to leave.

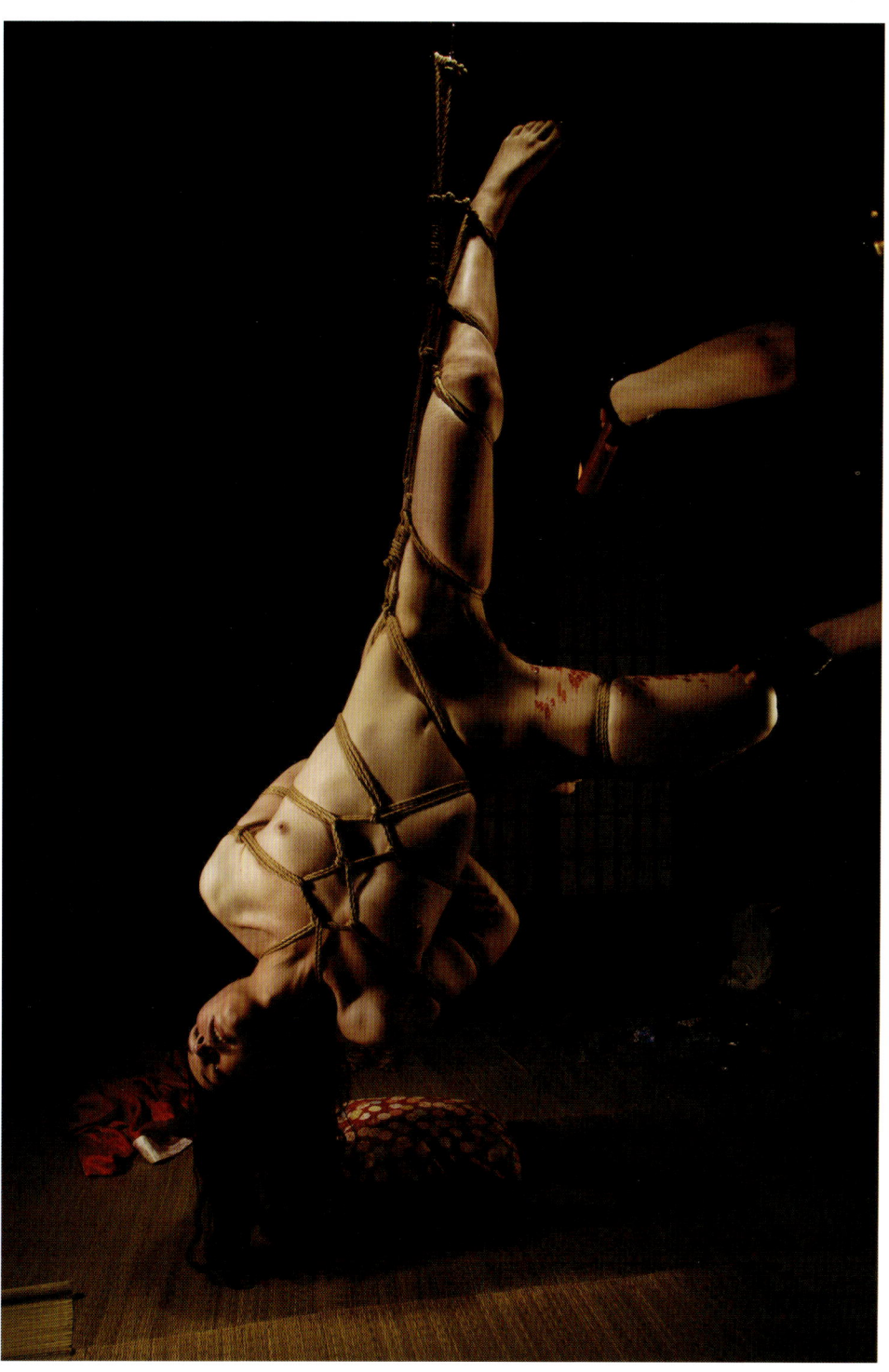

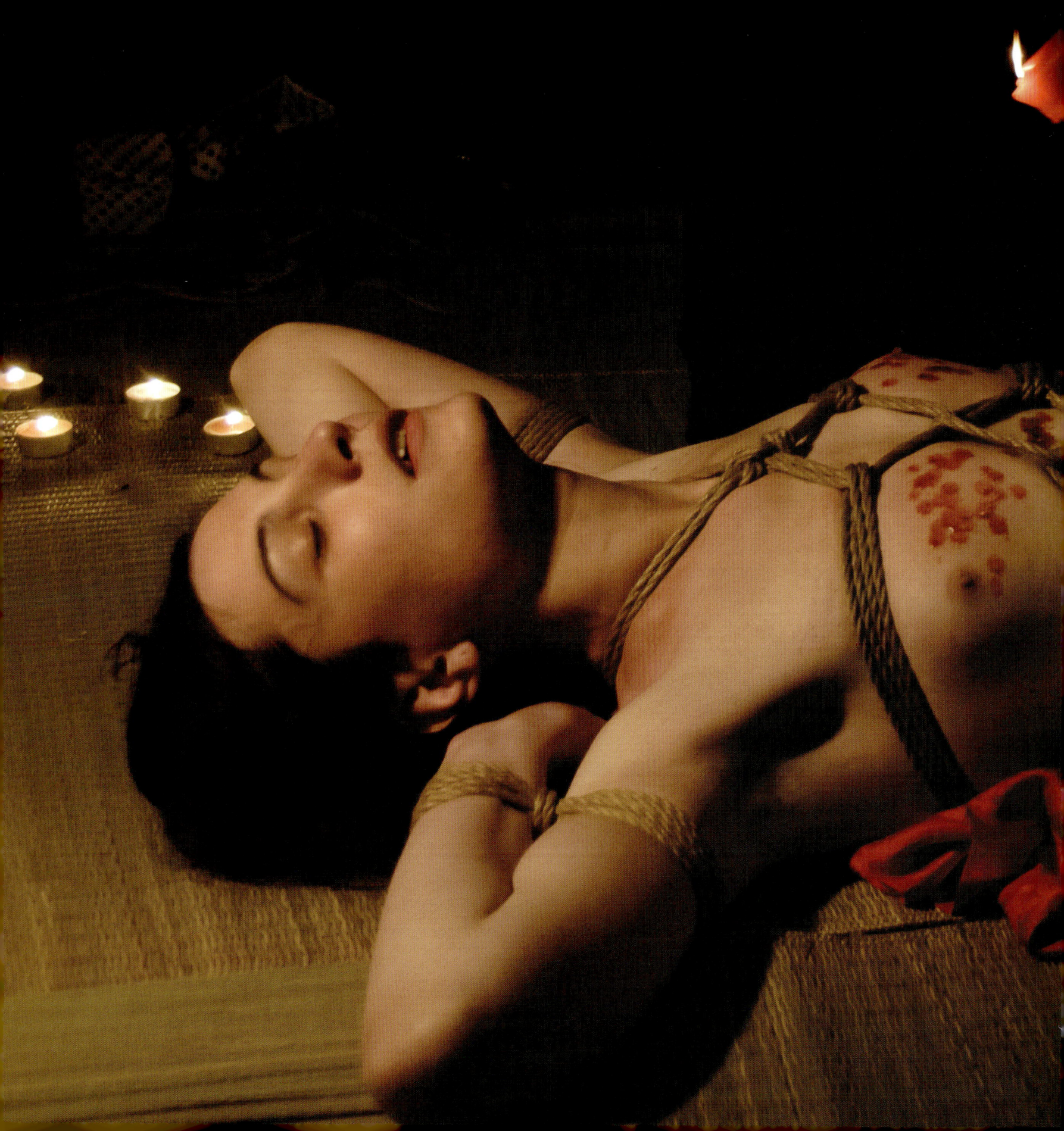

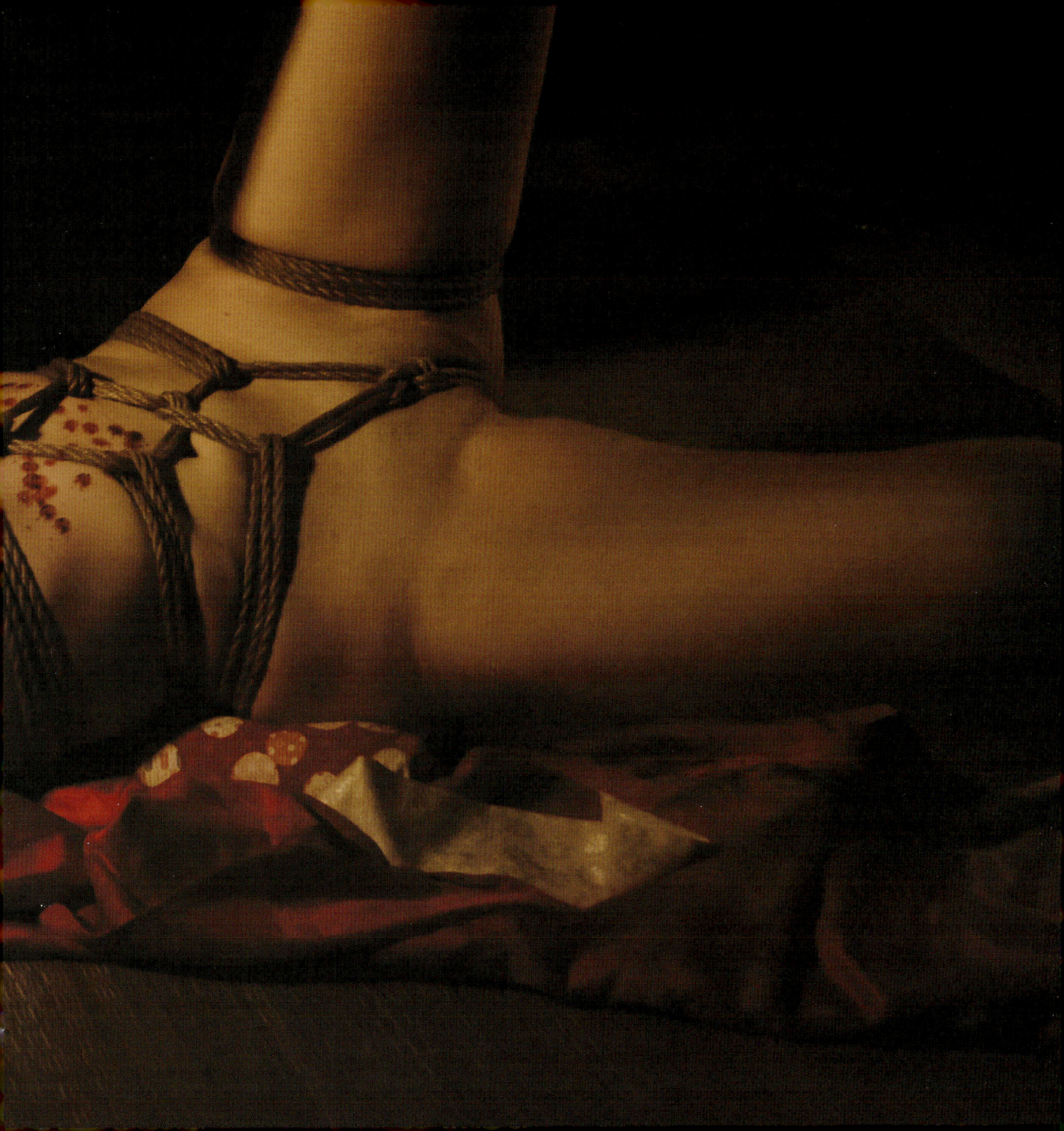

Nawashi Murakawa

Although his name is Japanese, he is without a doubt 100% British. Born in 1947, with almost twenty years Kinbaku experience, and over 1,000 performances and events under his belt, Nawashi Murakawa is regarded as the genuine delegate, and the first pioneer of the European Kinbaku scene.

His forty years as an illustrator have also guided him to a life of total artistic devotion, and in his latter years, a complete and spiritual commitment to Japanese culture, art, theatre, traditional music and religion.

Now in its fifth year, he is the founder, and Artistic Director of the London Festival of the Art of Japanese Rope Bondage, and although now considered as a grandee and semi-retired, is constantly developing his inner awareness of 'kokoru' (Japanese feeling) through his theatre company, 'Kinbaku Geki-jho' and other ventures, with the aim of furthering his beliefs in the ancient culture of Japan in order to disseminate them to those interested, mainly via his Kinbaku performances, and 'Salon of Kinbaku' Japanese bondage Life Drawing Classes, which he has created in recent years all over the UK. Europe and Japan.

His themes are always emotionally driven. The last major performance at the Festival was entitled *Yoshiwara*, and featured three kimono clad models. It told the story of the lost and lonely country girl trapped within the big city and the closed world of the *Edo* courtesan. Her life in a gilded cage, beautiful, desired, but brittle... a perfect vehicle for the emotional projection of guilt, shame and tragedy.

His newest project is the development of a funded *Japanese Arts Foundation*, the intention of which is to elevate the status of *Kinbaku* in association with other significant Japanese theatrical art forms such as *Kabuki, Noh, Seppuku, Bunraku, Jomon* and the traditional storytelling of the *Benchii*.

London 2013

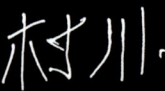

Photography: Nawashi Murakawa

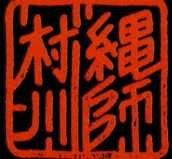

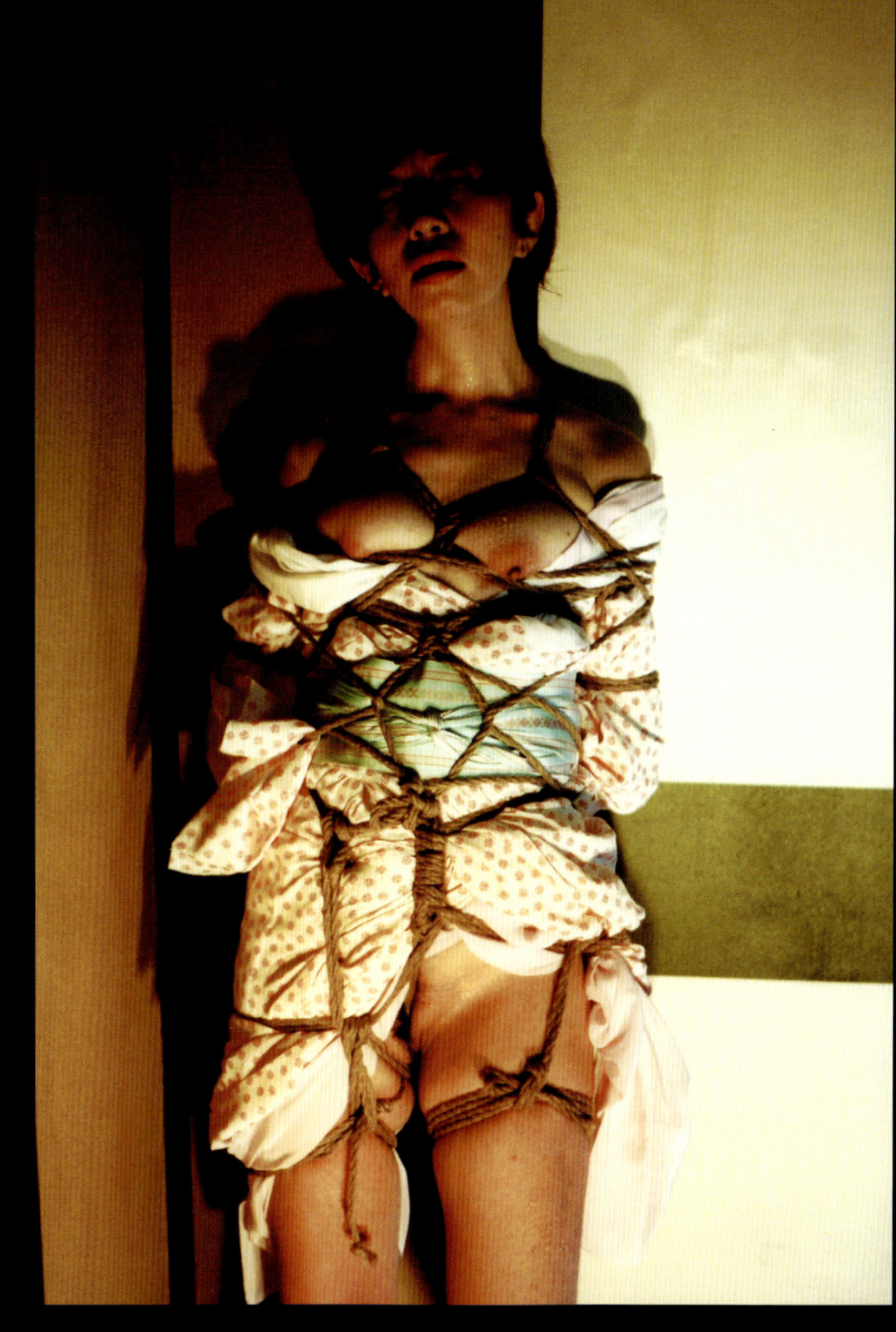

Communication beween Mr Murakawa's rope and my skin by Tsubaki Kanda (SM writer)

For a long time I have regarded myself as a good communicator. The people around me must have thought so, too.

The first encounter with Mr. Murakawa was in the autumn of 2000 when I had just started my career as a writer (at a farewell dinner held in his honour at a traditional restaurant in Shibuya, Tokyo).

When I was a Kinbaku model, (Kinbaku and rope bondage were being discussed around the table) I hated being asked about my personal feelings of being tied by rope. Someone always asks me what it feels like, which for me is hard to explain, and annoys me and that really made me introvert (uncommunicative person). Sometimes there were interviews after video-shoot. Always I felt I have made disasters in them. Especially after a successful video shoots, the language network in my brain was totally messed up' and no coherent words came out of me.

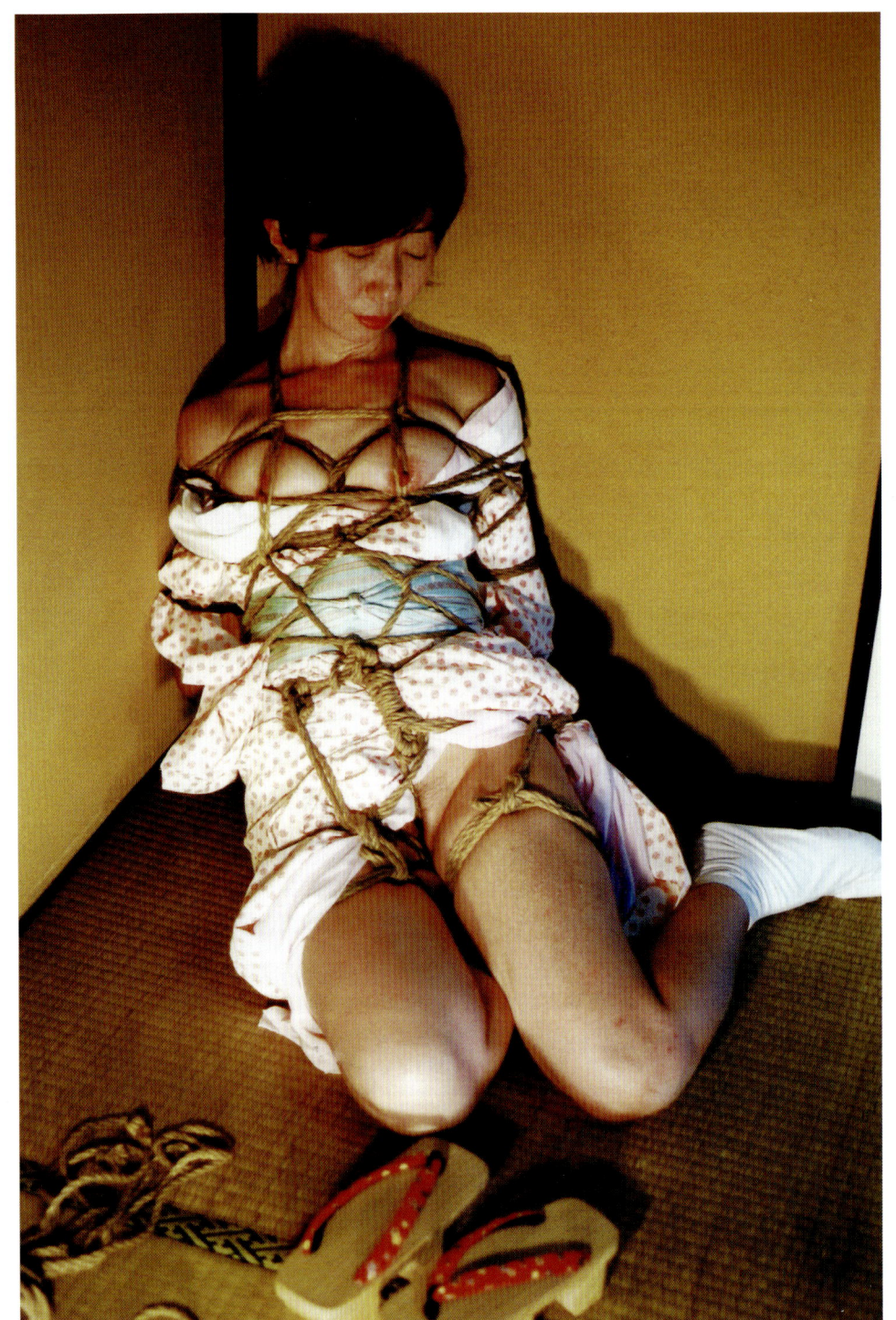

村川さんの縄とわたしの皮膚とが対話をすること

神田つばき

（SM・エロ専門ライター）

わたしは少し前までじぶんのことを、喋ることの得意な
人間だと思いこんでいた。周りの人間もそう思っていた
かも知れない。ジョン＝村川氏にお目にかかったのは、
言葉を操ることを生業とするライターになったばかりの
秋のことだった。

緊縛モデルの仕事をしていた頃、縄に包まれているとき
に感想を聞かれることが、とても苦痛だと思うようにな
った。そこからわたしの『喋るのキライ病』が発病した
のだ。ビデオの撮影などでも、映像の最後にインタビュ
ーが入ることがあるのだが、ことごとく失敗した。いい
映像が撮れたときにかぎって、わたしの頭脳の中では文
字のコードセットが壊れて、口から出てくる言葉が文字
化けを起こして支離滅裂になるのだった。

『支配と奴隷』プレイをしないわたしは、テキストによ
るSMを楽しむタイプではないのだろう。わたしの場合
は肉体がMだけれども、精神はMではなく淫乱かつ母性
そのものの女なだけだと思う。（そんな女はM女の風上
にもおけない、と非難する人もあるかも知れないが、わ
たしは自分に嘘をつけませんので悪しからず。）

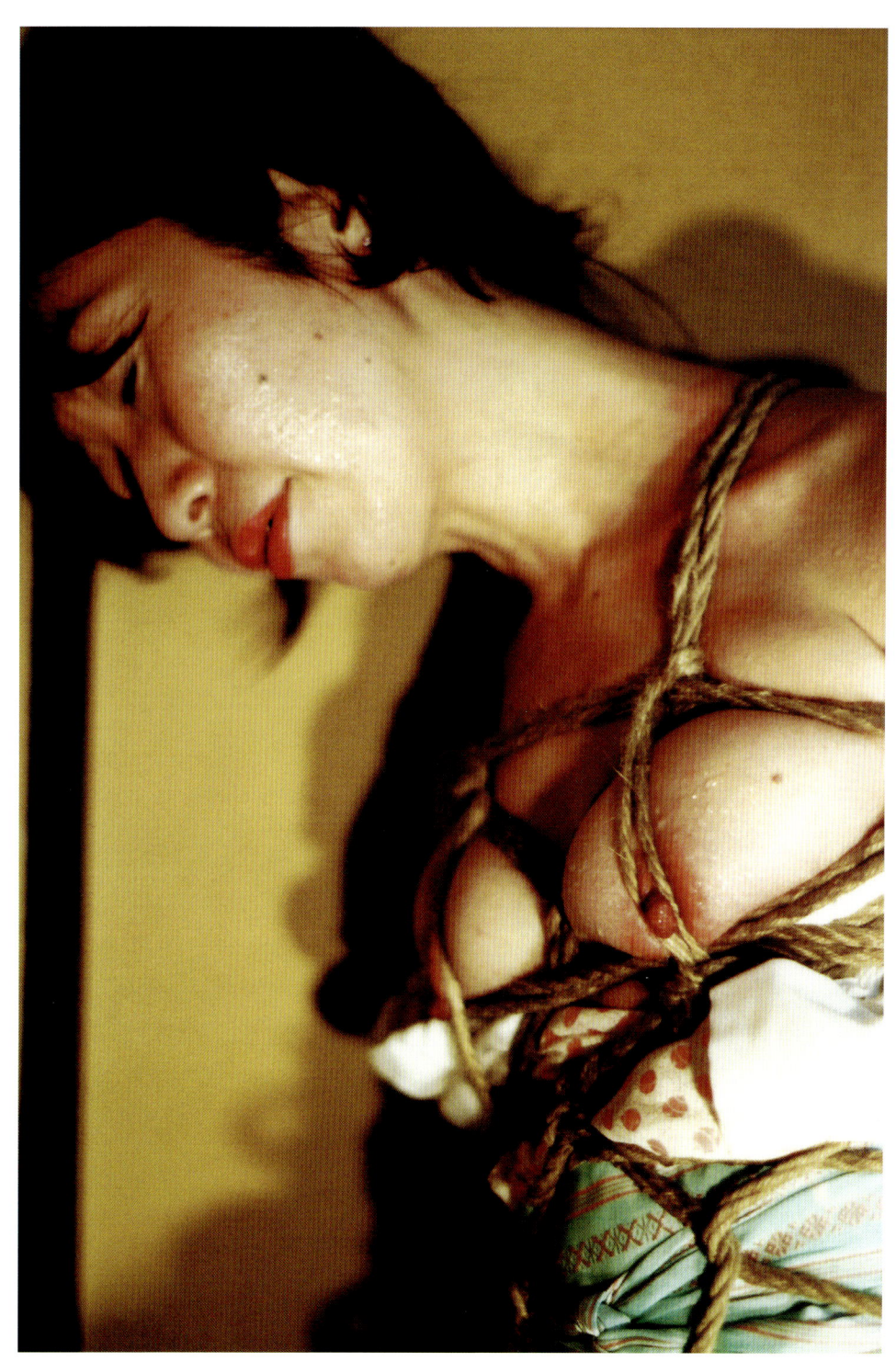

Perhaps because I do not play "master and slave", I am not the type to play S & M in the textual context. I am physically masochistic but mentally, I regard myself as a lustful and maternal woman. (There may be those who criticize a woman being a slave girl but I cannot pretend to be something I am not).

When I met Mr. Murakawa he was calmly eating a fish. I made my mind up to be tied up just by observing him. Without being introduced, I asked him directly …
"I want to be tied by you. Where and when can I do this?" It was decided the location would be at his Ryokan (traditional style Japanese hotel room) at a small hotel nearby. All he asked, was for me to bring traditional kimono, or yukata, and accessories.

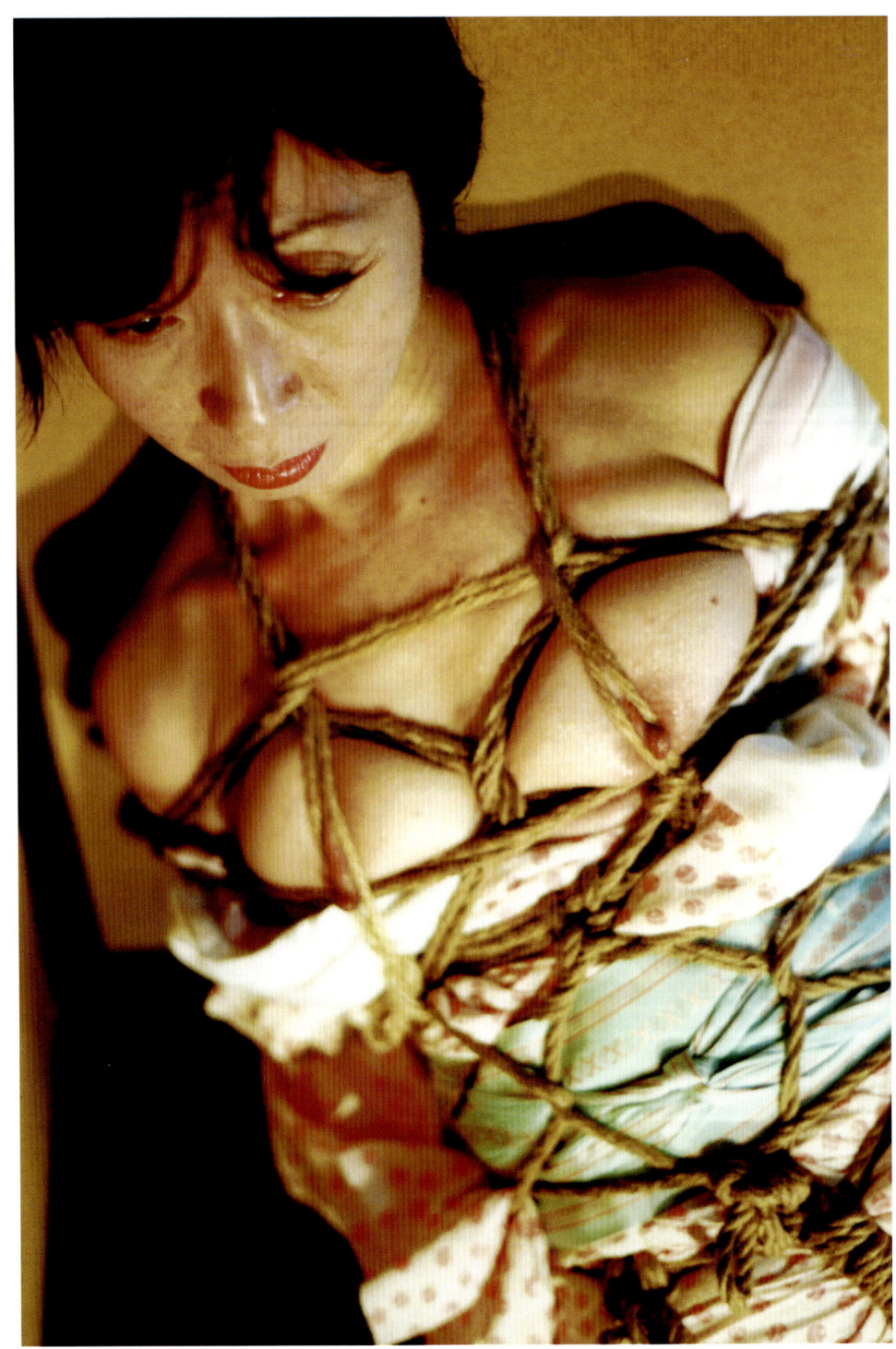

村上氏にお目にかかったとき、静かにお魚などを召し上がっているのを、だまって拝見していて、（そうだ、この人に縛ってもらおう）と心が決まってしまった。ロクにご挨拶もなしに、わたしは村上氏に向かって、

「縛っていただきたいのですが、いつ、どちらに伺えばよろしいですか？」

と、唐突にお願いをした。それが雨の夜の福田屋旅館での撮影になって実現した。

はたして、わたしの信じたとおり、村川氏は言葉にたよらずに縛って写してくださった。

それはわたしの英語力の拙さが、言葉によるコミュニケーションを不可能にしたせいじゃない。言葉は道具だとわたしは思っているので、喋りすぎる人が苦手だ。力に自信がないとき、誰でも饒舌になりがちだ。

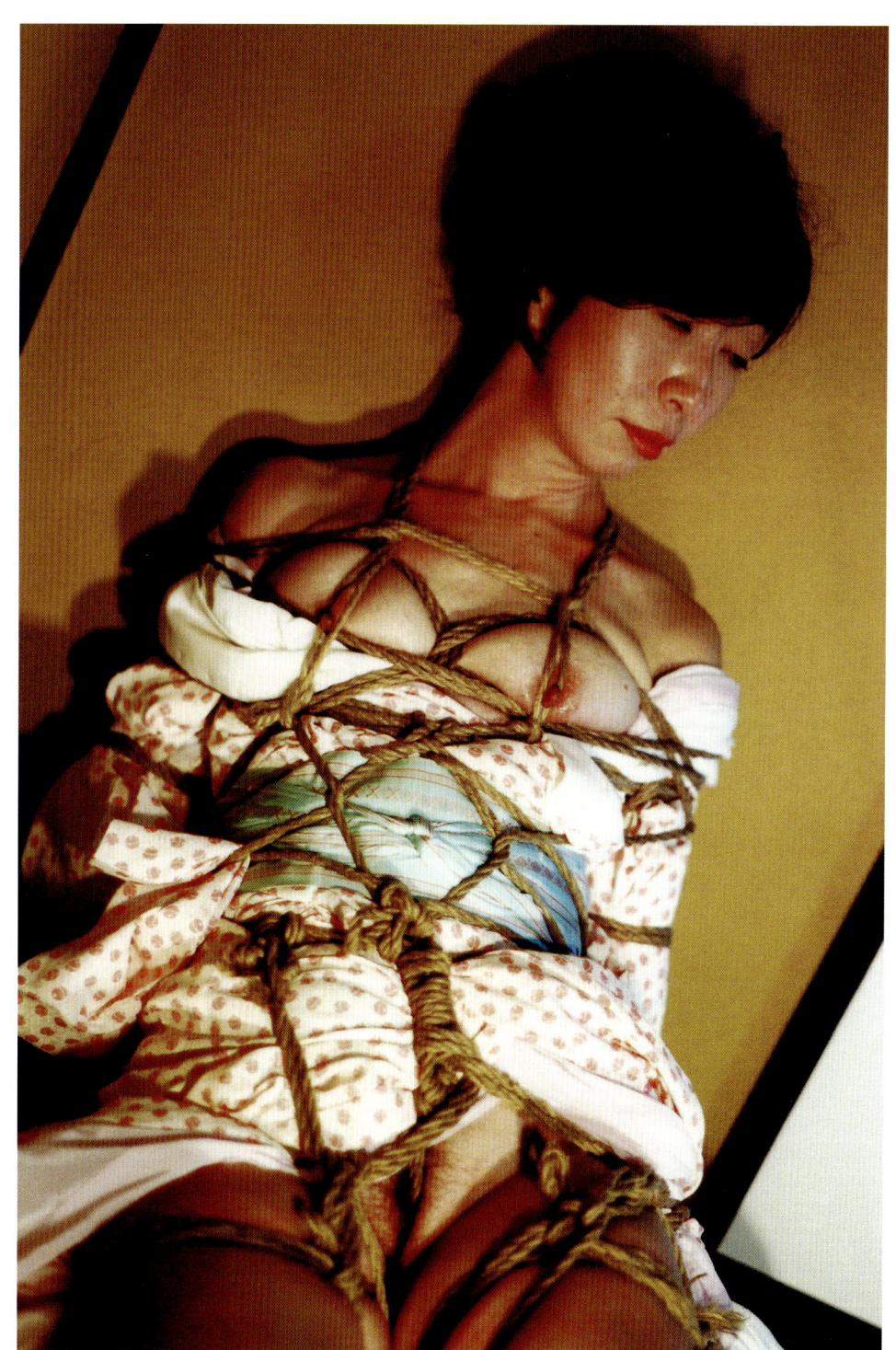

133

It was a rainy night. As I thought,
Mr. Murakawa tied and photographed
me without any need for words. Not
because my English was poor and there
was a language barrier between us, but
words were superfluous as we understood
each other. As I regard words as just a
tool, and nothing more, I cannot get on
well with those who talk too much. I
believe that the lack of confidence often
makes people talkative

As I expected, he used his nawa to
communicate with my body. It was
incredible! The experience was also
extraordinarily comfortable for me.
As if a printed dress would be, reduced
to silk threads, the patterns and wrinkles
on my skin disappeared and my body
was disintegrated to mere silk-threads
which had just been spun by a silkworm.
It was like the warmly forgiveness of God
and could never be expressed by words
such as liberty or freedom. Disintegrated
body of mine dispersed.

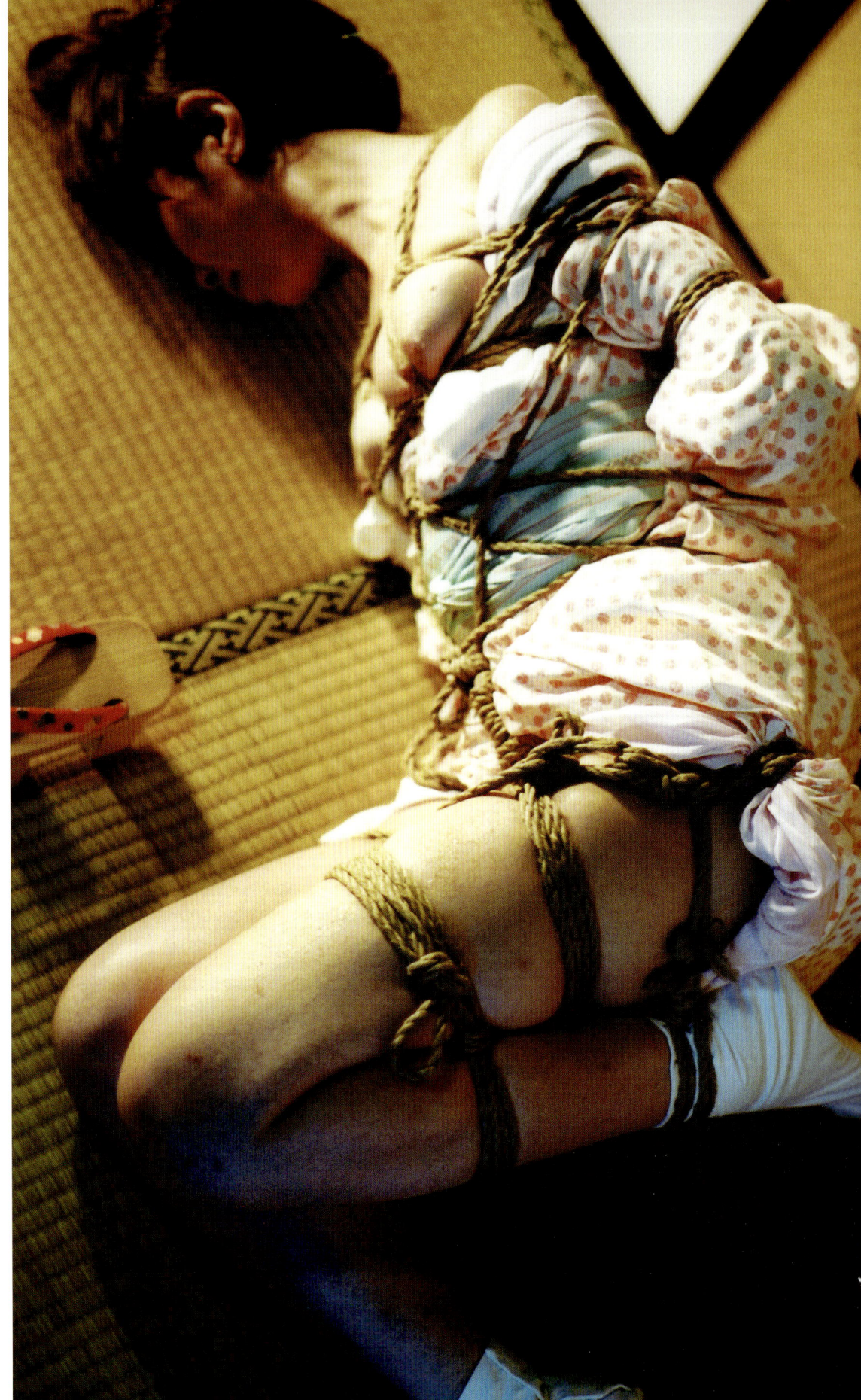

村川さんはテキストではなく、縄を使ってわたしの皮膚
とで対話をしてくださるだろう、と期待したのだ。それ
はわたしにとって、ちょっと現実にはあり得ないくらい
安楽な時間だった。体中の皮膚にプリントされた柄も織
り目もなくなって、わたしの肉体はバラバラにほどけ
て、お蚕さんが吐き出したばかりの絹糸に還元してしま
った。自由とか解放とかの言葉では言いつくせない、神
による赦しのような温かさ。どこまでも緩く解けてひろ
がっていく、わ・た・し。

りを連想するわたしは、かなりテキストに毒されている
のだろう。村川氏の写真をはじめて見たとき、『ナマハ
ゲちっくでプリミティブ』なのが新鮮で、アッと声をあ
げてしまった。

日本人のわたしが忘れているものを、その匂いと温度を
村川氏は知っているようだった。

現実のわたしはかなり痩せているのだが、村川氏の写真
の中ではぽってりとして見える。

長襦袢からのぞくうなじは、幼い頃におんぶしてくれた
田舎のお姉さんの首筋の匂いがしそうだ。乳臭くて日な
た臭い、お米とお豆とお魚で育った日本人独特の濃厚な
体臭を感じる。

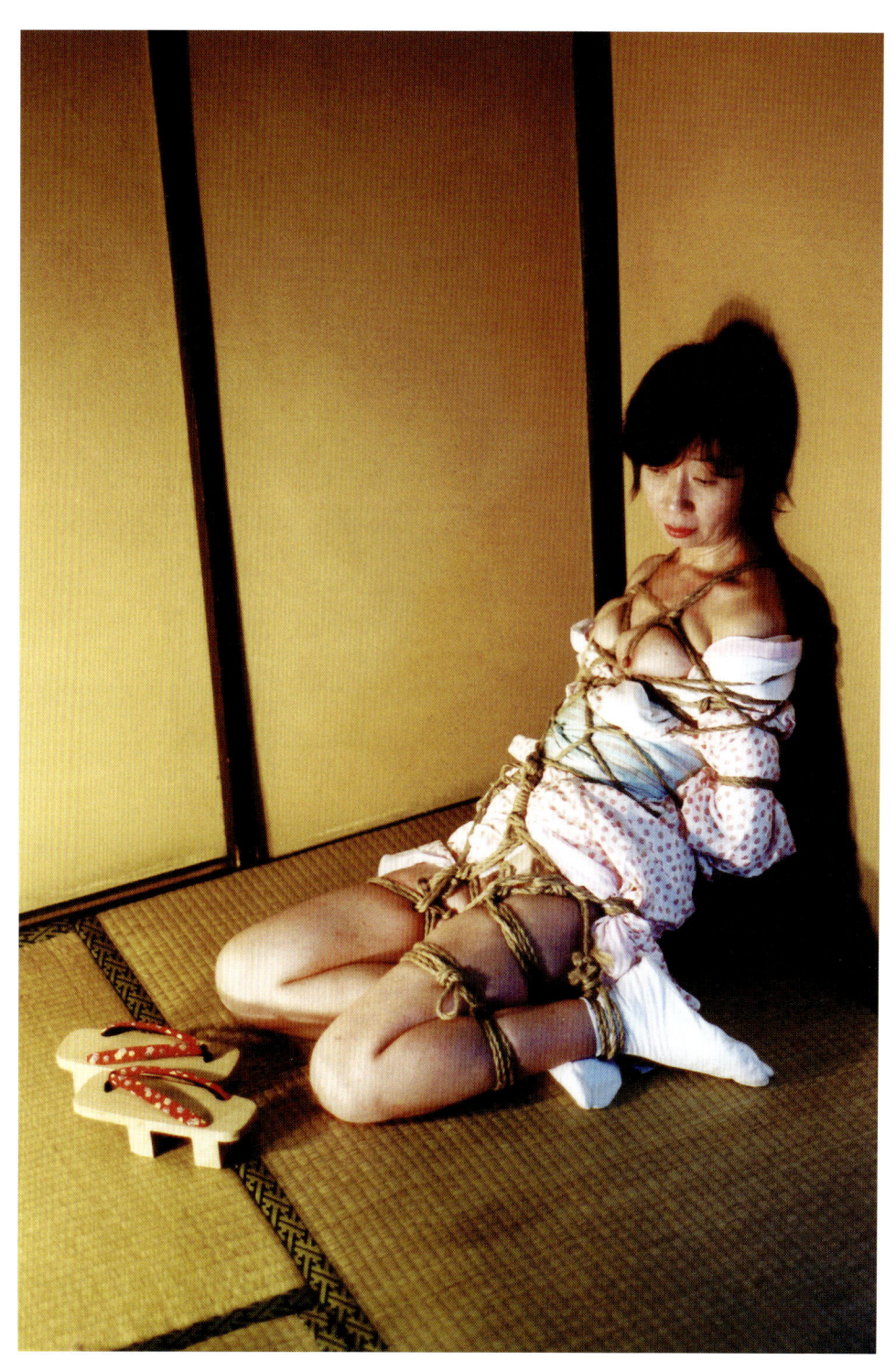

I was too naive to associate 'Noh' (an ancient and noble form of masked drama) and 'Kabuki' (an old and popular style of drama entertainment) with the Japanese tradition, and 'Seiu Ito' (a famous 18th century artist, poet and writer who explored his creativity and spirituality through traditional feeling and rope bondage) with 'Kinbaku'.

I was very surprised at the 'freshness' of Mr Murakawa's photographic works. He seemed to know the senses and atmosphere of Japan, which we Japanese have already forgotten. His camera and intuition exposed the temperature and smell of all of my changing bodily senses. (As the kinbaku session progressed, numerous candid photographs captured all the tiny special moments that are usually never seen in the general SM press, or understood by it. The usual fully lit, all in focus style of the pin-up bondage magazine forgotten, in the artistic pursuit of real feeling).

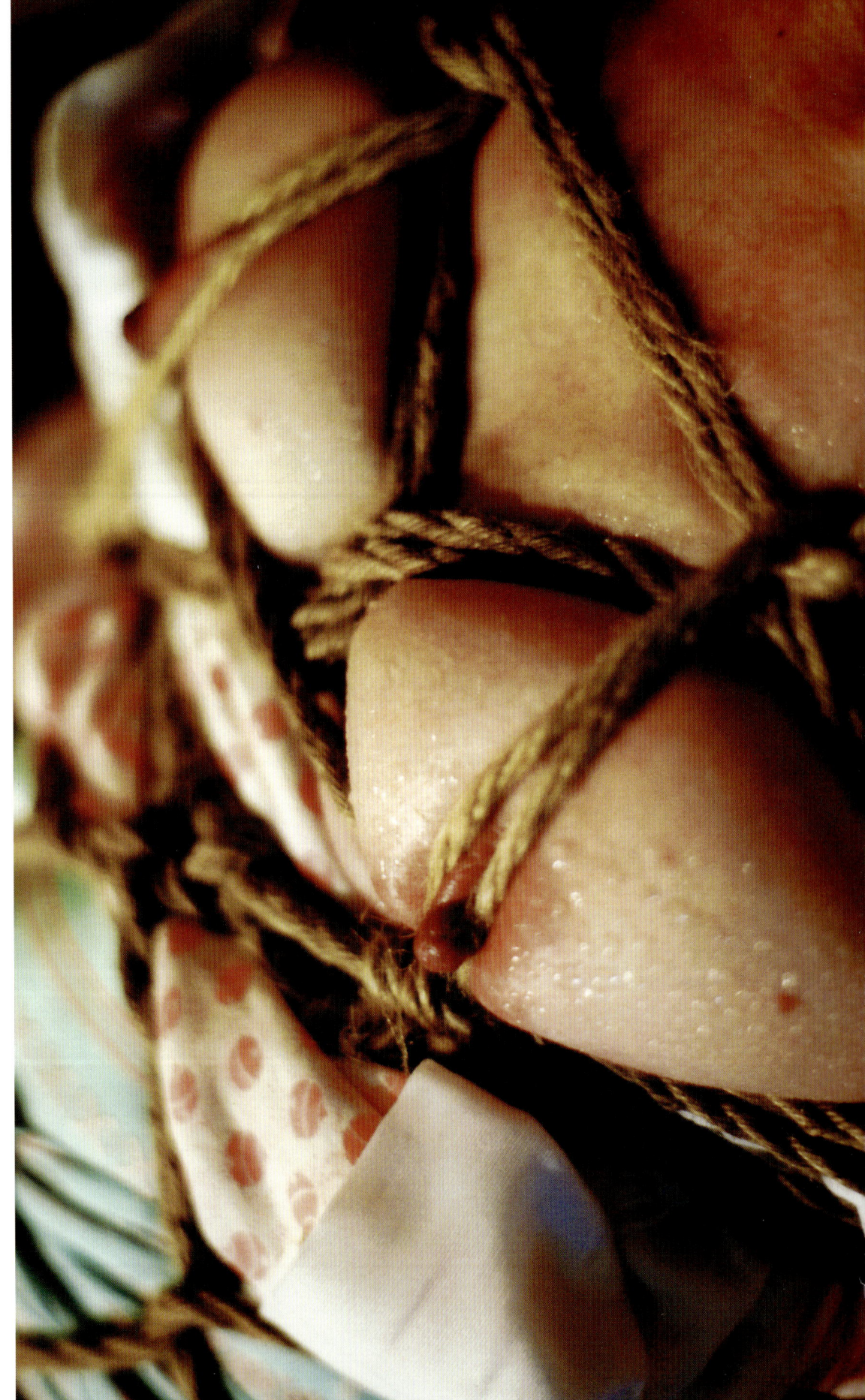

村川氏に縛ってもらって以降、わたしは言葉にこだわることをやめた。ライターでありながら、言葉を操ろうとしなくなった。皮膚で感じたことを、目で見たことを、崩さないように腐らせないように、そうっと言葉に置き換える作業だけに専念するようになった。それが進歩なのか退歩なのかわからないが、自分の中で肉体と精神が一枚になるのは、このうえもない快楽なのである。

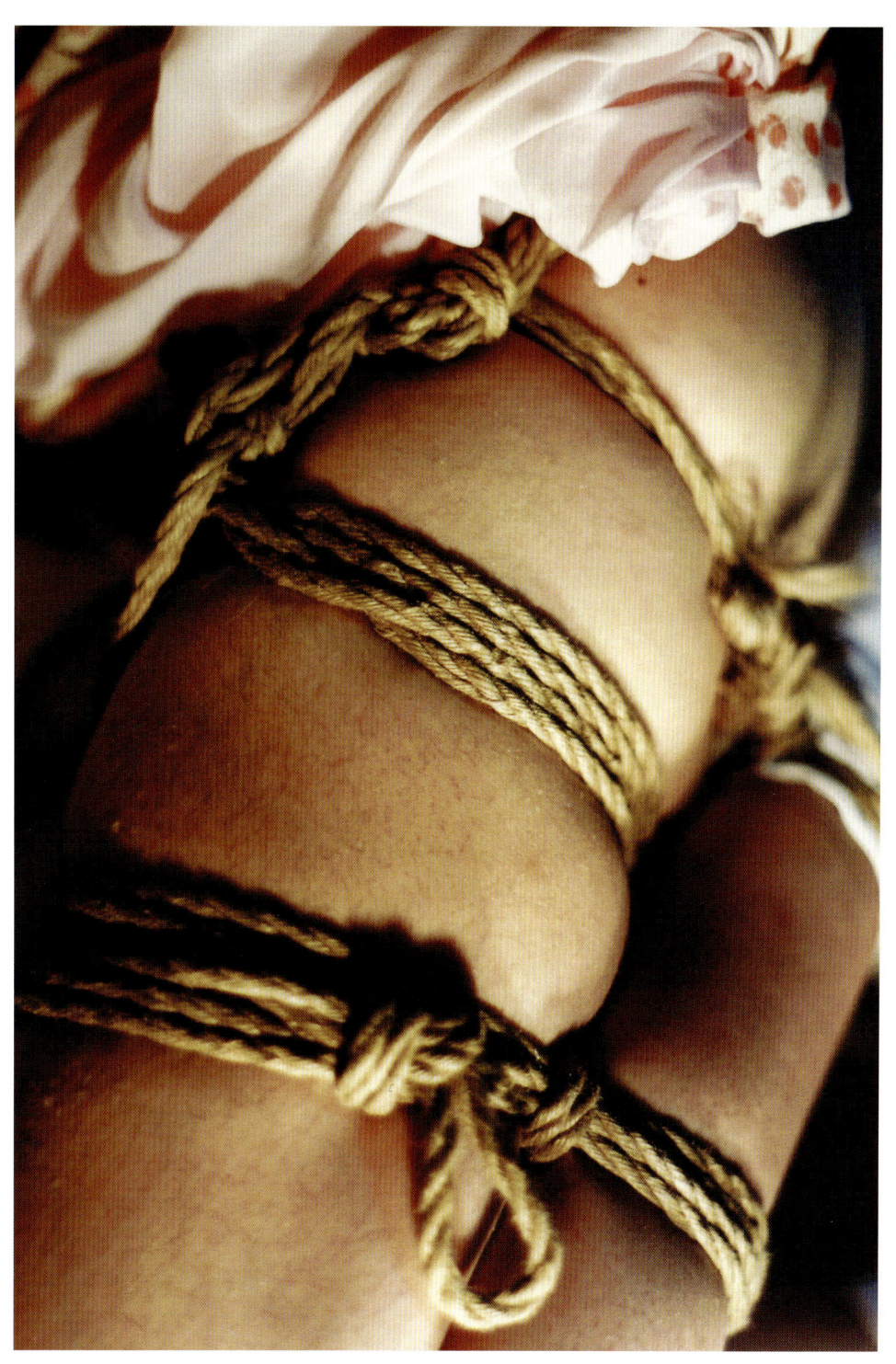

I am actually quite thin, but somehow Mr Murakawa's images have made me look 'chubby'. These pictures especially take me back to a time when I was an infant visiting 'Inaka'. (The countryside, the birth place of mother, father or grandparents home).

As I breathe in, I can smell the back of my sisters neck. She carried me often on her back, 'piggyback' style. In a traditional country style rope and cloth sling called a 'onbu himo'. I recall being tightly bound by this cloth and nawa, my body to hers. (The sister may not be her real sister, as the Japanese use the word 'sister' for any older girl around who looked after her when she visited Inaka). The scruff of her neck smelt milky. The hot summer sunshine liberating and decaying the strong body odour that comes from eating a diet of rice, fish and beans, as we walked forever through the humid fields, in not a breath of wind.

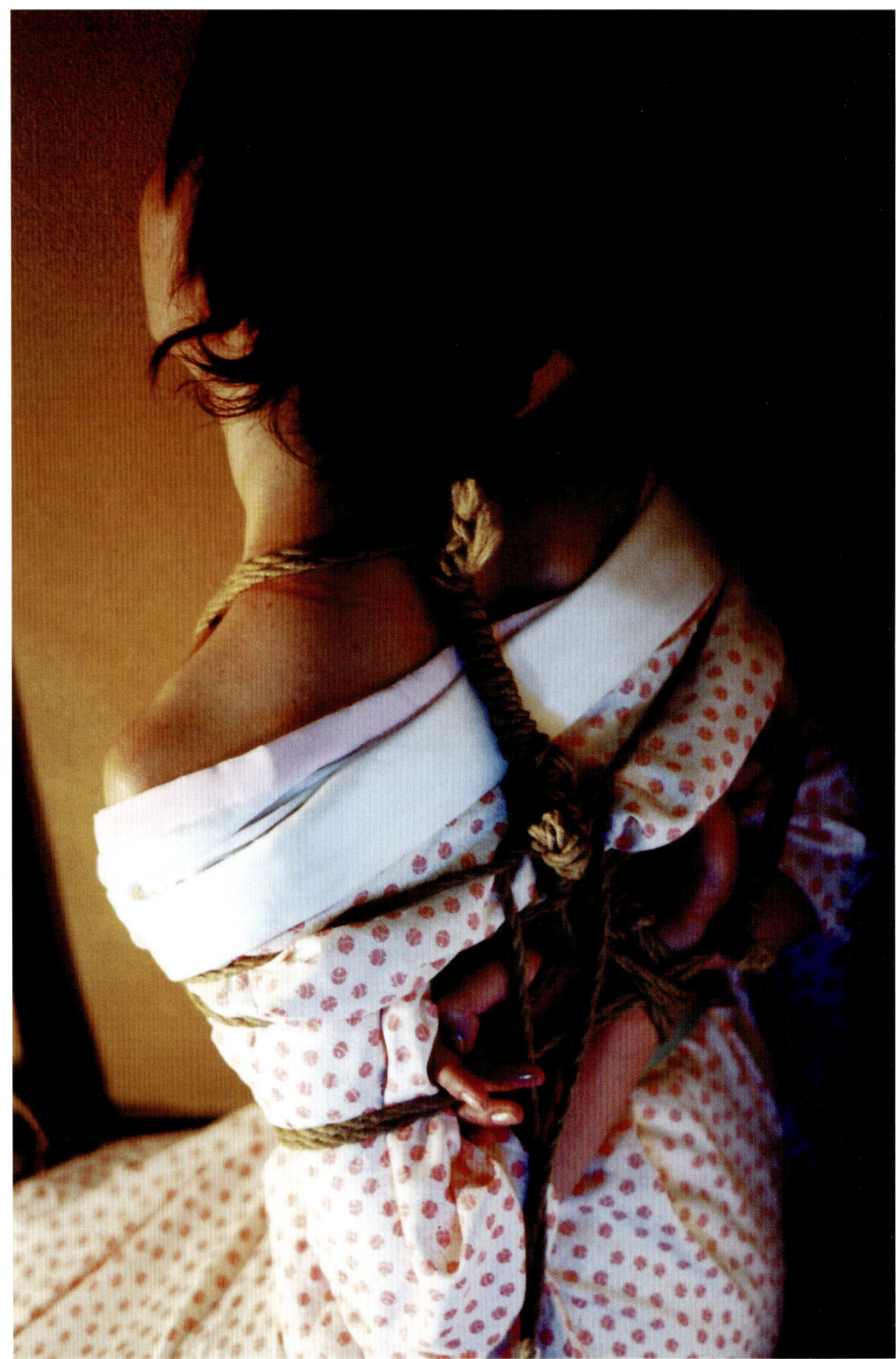

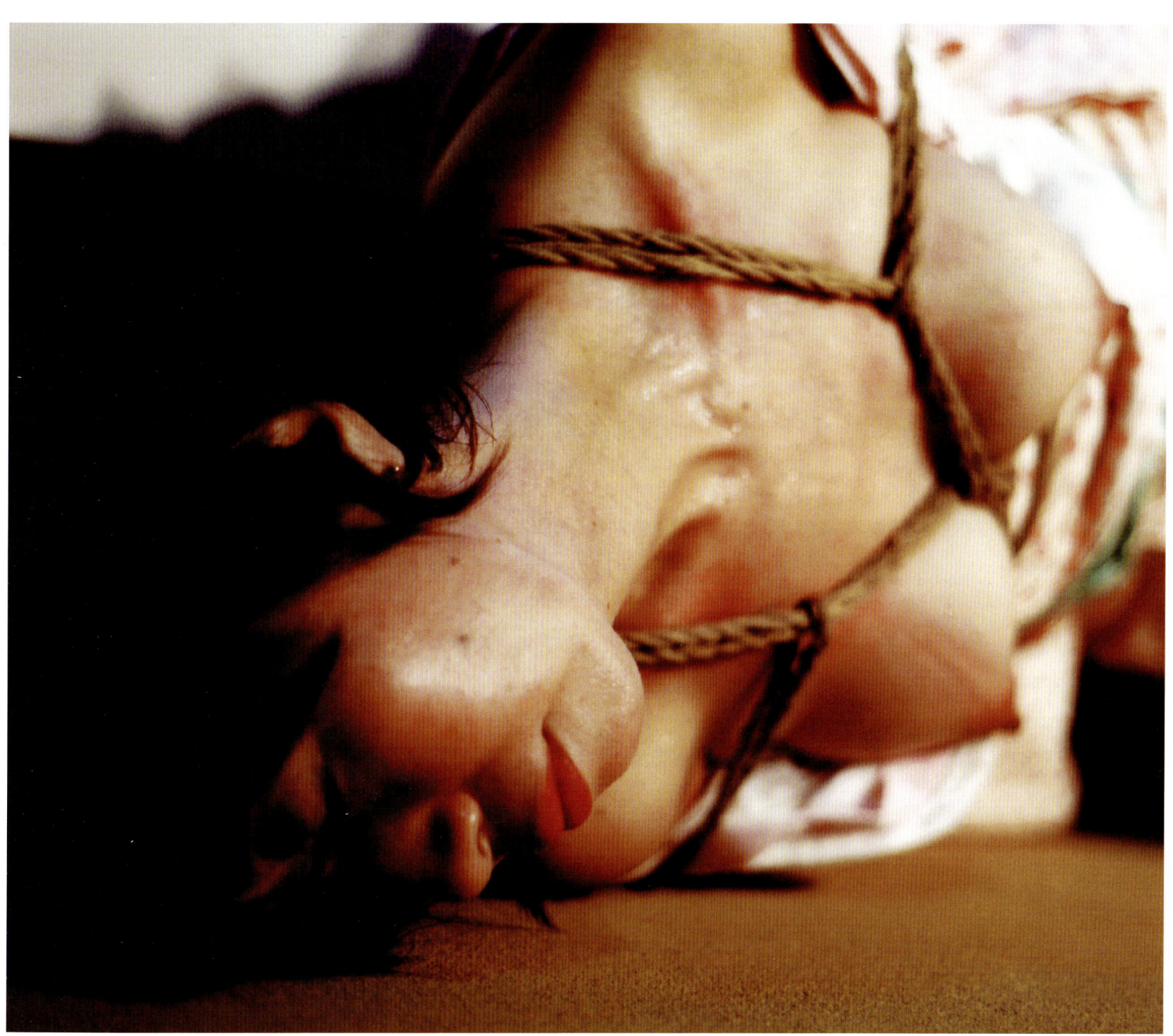

The back of a woman's neck above her kimono and beneath her 'raised hairstyle', emphasises a typical Japanese erotic feeling or 'posture', which many gaijin (non-Japanese) may find hard to comprehend set against their own social/sexual conventions. It is also a polite and deferred way to compliment Mr Murakawa for his understanding of traditional Japan by the warmth and smell expressed in his work.

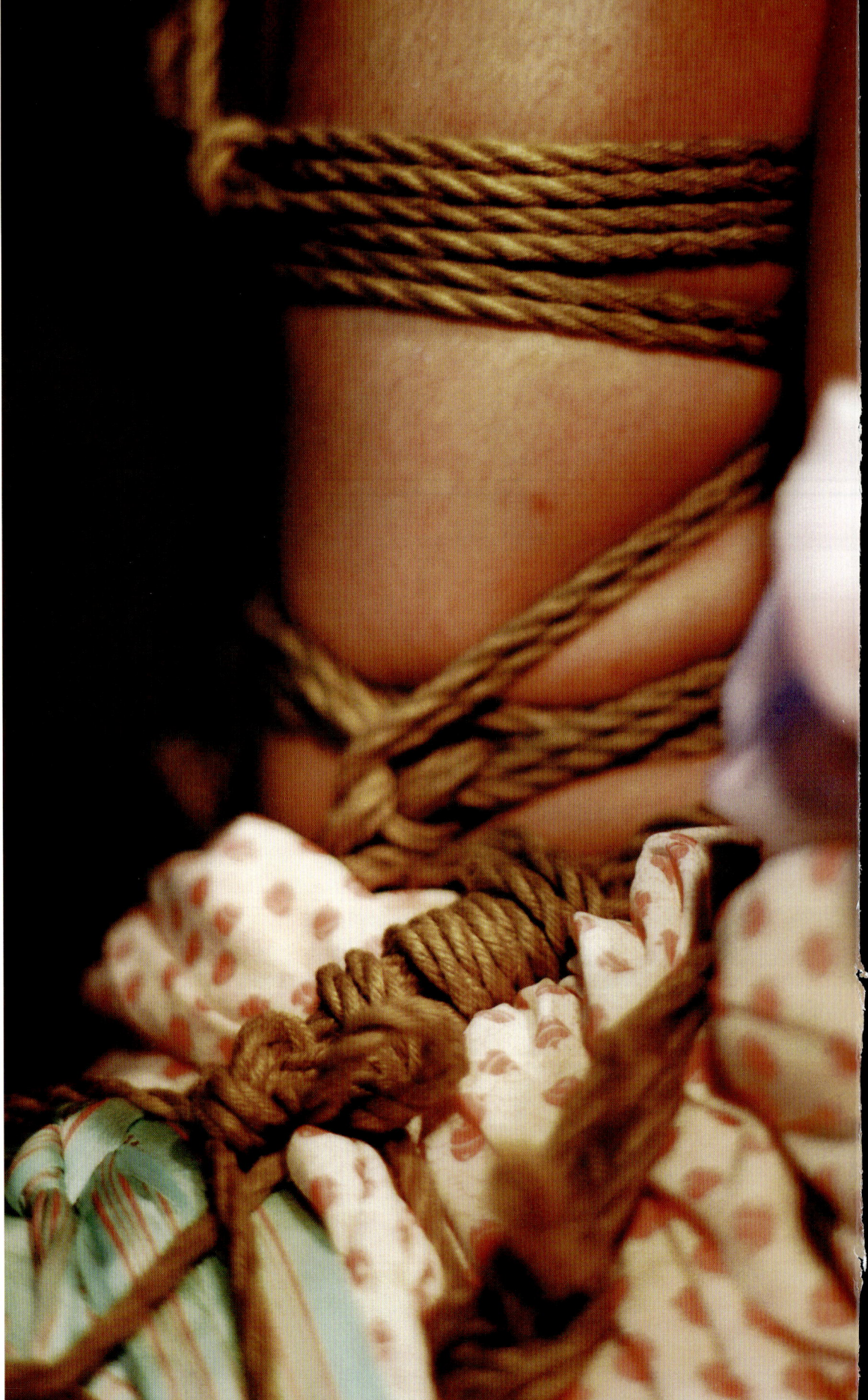

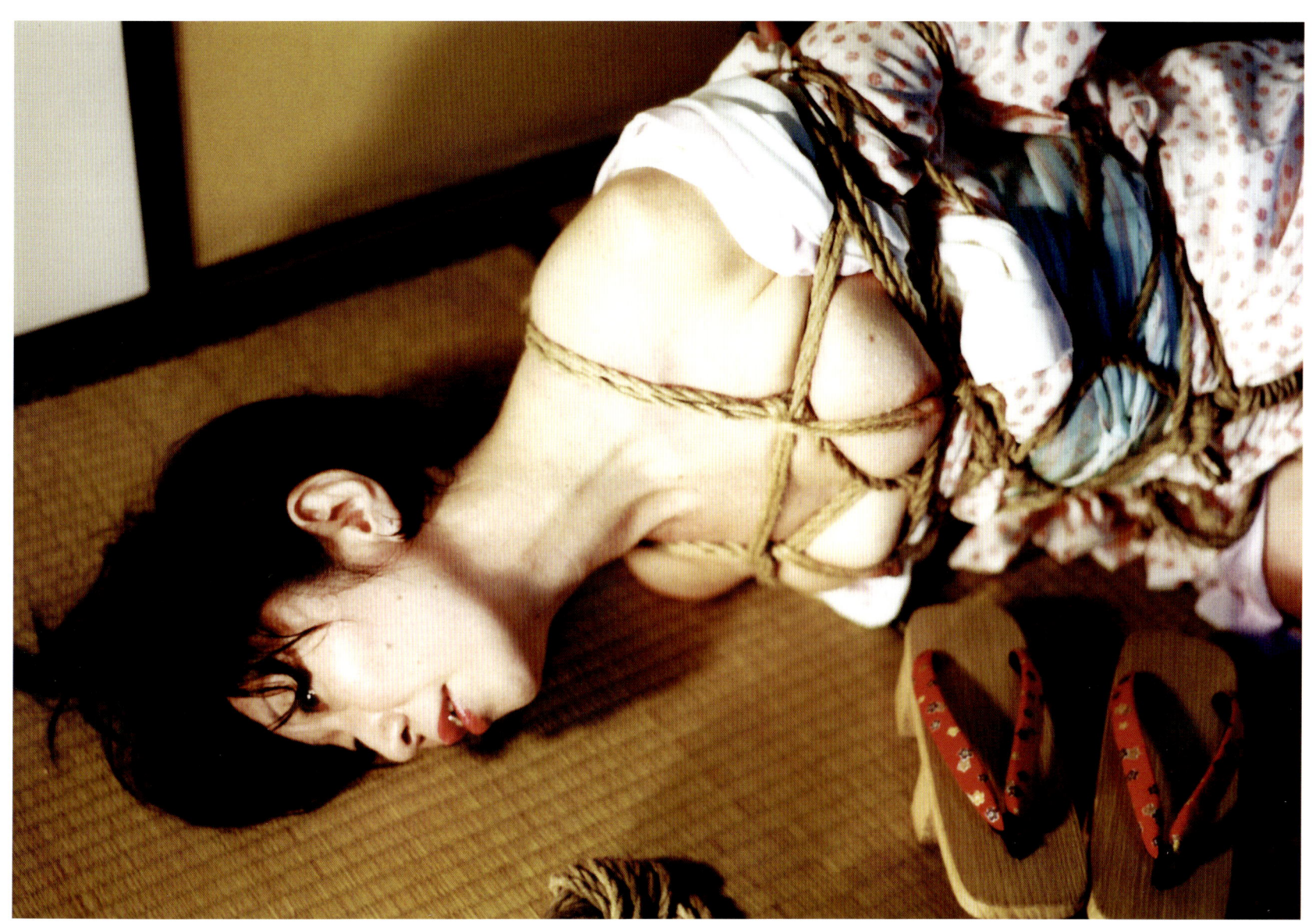

After I had been tied by Mr Murakawa,
I stopped being so particular about my
words. Trying to get them right and so on.
As a writer even though I should, I stopped
manipulating words, and decided to
concentrate properly on my inner senses.
I went carefully, without decay and without
corruption. I don't yet know if this
abundance of words is progress or
regression for me, but it certainly is a
pleasure to have my body and soul
integrated and diffused within myself.

Laying down on the ground, in a haze of
euphoria, eyes still glazed. She smells and
caresses the untied ropes, running her
fingers through them as they lay cast-off all
around her. She looks up at Mr. Murakawa,
who is quietly sitting nearby, and says ...

"I want to do kinbaku everyday .... Everyday!
"She sighs, happy and transported. Still
breathing lightly.

Tsubaki Kanda
Tokyo, Japan
28th April 2001

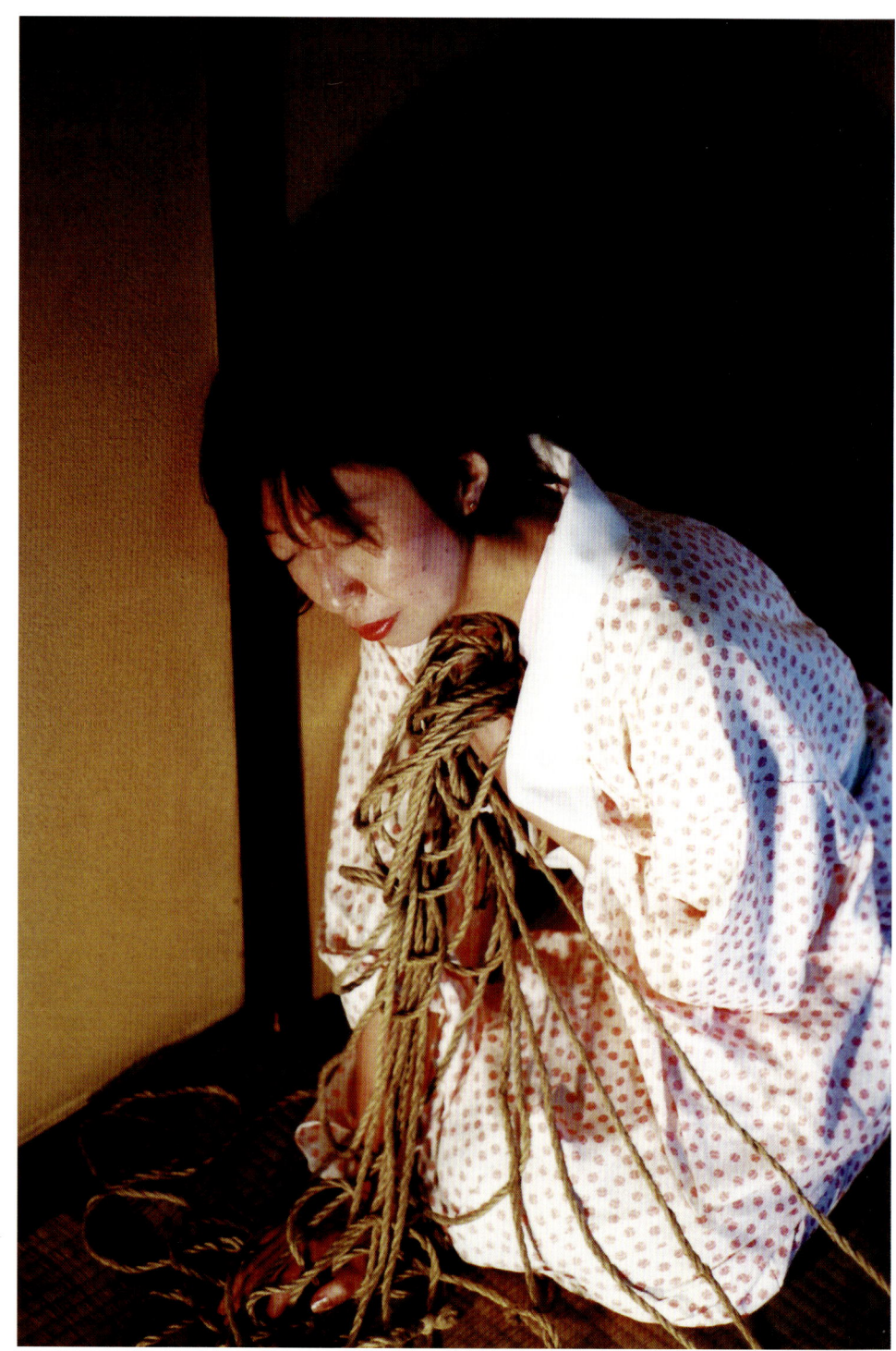

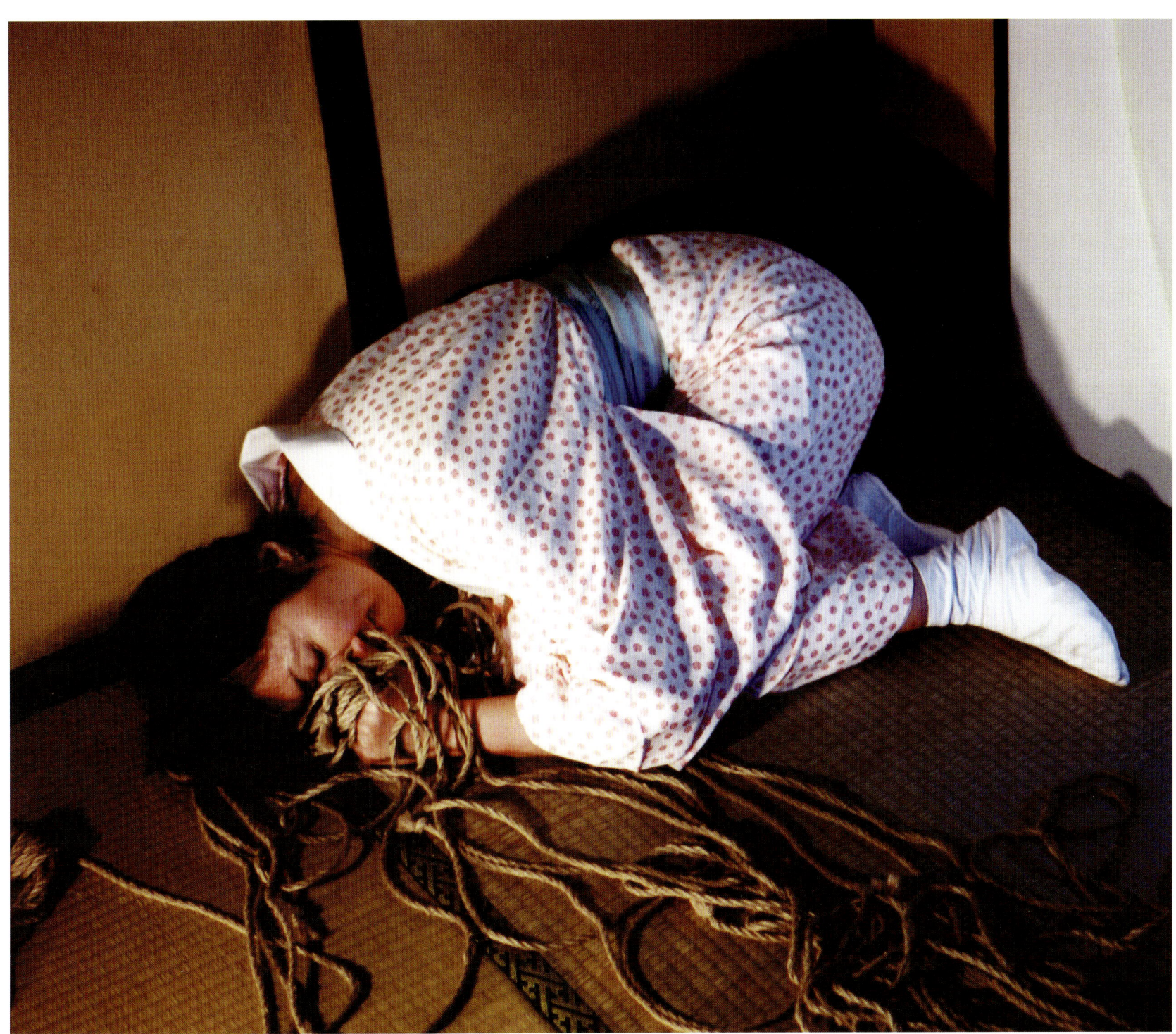

143

Further information

This book owes its existence to many people from around the world. It is their passion, expertise, and lifestyle that enables us to present a broad view of Kinbaku as it is practised in different countries. In particular, we have appreciated the written accounts from models, photographers and rope experts who give a deep insight into the practice of rope bondage.

Further information about Kahboom can be found on:
www.kahboom.com
Any enquiries to Kahboom should be sent to:
office@kahboom.com

Acknowledgements & Credits

Front cover
Photographer: Kahboom
Model: Amy Latina

Chapter 1
Photographer: Tho4ns
http://tho4ns.com/
aj@tho4ns.com

Chapter 2
Photographer: Vlada
Model: Falco
Ropework: Vlada
Text: Vlada
www.shabash.nu

Chapter 3
Photographer: Kahboom
Model: Sam Mori
Ropework: Kahboom
Assistant: Snowy Law
Text: Steve Walker/Kahboom

Chapter 4
Photographer: エロ王子 (Ero o-ji)
Model: 香緒 (Kao)
Ropework: みうみ ゆう (Miumi-U)
Special thanks to 一縄会 (Ichinawa-Kai) and also to 輝 (Teru)

Chapter 5
Photographer: Chi
Model: Lily LeFleur and others
www.rue99.com
photog@rue99.com

Chapter 6
Photograpaher: Kahboom
Model: Sam Mori
Ropework: Miumi-U
Assistant: Snowy Law
Make-up: Karen Sundelowitz
Text: Kahboom

Chapter 7
Photographer: Kahboom
Model: Elissa
Ropework: Kahboom
Assistant: Snowy Law
Make-up: Karen Sundelowitz
Text: Kahboom

Chapter 8
Photogrpaher: Kahboom
Model: Adé-dì Kàn
Ropework: Miumi-U
Assistant: Snowy Law
Make-up: Karen Sundelowitz
Text: Adé-dì Kàn

Chapter 9
Photographer: Azure Dragon
Model: Halcyon
Text: Halcyon
http://fineartamerica.com/profiles/azure-dragon.html

Chapter 10
Photographer: Nawashi Murakawa
Model: Tsubaki Kanda
Ropework: Nawashi Murakawa

Graphics and book preparation: designphd
www.designphd.co.uk